SEX IS NOT SIMPLE

STEPHEN B. LEVINE, M.D.

Ohio Psychology Publishing Company
400 E. Town Street
Suite 020
Columbus, Ohio 43215
614-224-3288

Published by Ohio Psychology Publishing Company
131 North High Street, Suite 300, Columbus, Ohio 43215

Printed and bound in the United States of America.

Library of Congress Cataloging-in-Publication Data
Levine, Stephen B., 1942—Sex Is Not Simple Bibliography: p. Includes index. 1. Sex. 2. Psychosexual disorders. I. Title.
ISBN 0-910707-12-X

Library of Congress Catalogue Card Number 88-25306
First Printing, 1989

CONTENTS

PREFACE

Shortly after finishing my formal training in psychiatry in 1973, I became fascinated with the new field of sex therapy. I was particularly interested in its promise of faster, more effective treatments for common sexual problems than those offered by traditional psychiatry. I quickly discovered however, that although many fine teachers and seventy years of psychiatric writings had been available to guide my learning about the art of psychotherapy, few teachers and books were available to help me become a competent sex therapist. Most of my learning in human sexuality has come directly from helping people with sexual problems.

I became known in the Cleveland area as a therapist and teacher of human sexuality. I was aware, however, that many mental health professionals, though outwardly encouraging and respectful, felt there was something fraudulent about my therapeutic efforts. They were concerned that these new therapies might encourage sexual behavior between therapists and patients. Even when it became clear that specialists in sexual problems have a profound commitment to protect patients from this danger, uneasiness about sex doctors lingered among many colleagues.

I was always fortunate to have several antidotes for these subtle toxins. The most powerful one came from the men and women, individuals and couples, whom I treated. When patients and I failed, as frequently happened, we usually stopped only after we agreed that further progress could not be made at this time in their lives. Another antidote came from the fact that some of my "failures" referred their friends, saying what we had done together had been immensely helpful.

I was also able to continue, skepticism notwithstanding, because medical students, physicians, and young mental health professionals were responding positively to my lectures, seminars, and writings. I became especially convinced about the need for adult sex education as a result of my lectures to people who were not health professionals. It usually was easy to talk seriously and explicitly about sex with these audiences. We laughed about our illusions and regretted our missed opportunities during some wonderfully personal question-and-answer periods. After each of these public meetings, several people would invariably come up to me and say, "Thank you."

In spite of my experiences, I did not seriously consider writing a book until one day after talking on television about physical illness and sex, the host said to me, "By the way, what is the name of your book?" I said, "I don't have a book," and he replied, "Well, you should!" I began to think about it.

Getting from that point to this has been arduous at times. This book would not have been conceived were it not for the early academic support I received from my department chairman, L. Douglas Lenkoski; the years of editing of my earlier professional writings that Barbara Juknialis undertook; the skillful protection that my secretary, Phyllis Polsky, provided; and the intellectual stimulation, kindness and energy of my many colleagues in sexuality at University Hospitals of Cleveland—especially Stanley Althof, Candace Risen, and Louisa Turner.

The transformation of my manuscript from a quasi-professional text to readable work occurred because of the efforts of two remarkable, gifted people. The first, Tobin Simon, from the Proprioceptive Writing Center in Portland, Maine, helped me hear my writing, define my audience, and speak from a more authentic, personal voice. His unselfish patience enabled me to glimpse the art of writing. I now know what it means to be with a great teacher. The second, editor Sanna Longden of Evanston, Illinois, brought simplicity to at least a thousand awkward passages. Her ability to enhance my writing and clarify my ideas never ceased to amaze me. I am grateful to her for her taste, frankness, humor, and respect. I cannot imagine an editor bringing more to the task than Sanna brought to *Sex Is Not Simple*.

Finally, it should become obvious that my deepest gratitude is reserved for my patients, who were courageous enough to trust me with their emotional privacies. They have always been my most consistent and respected teachers. Perhaps they will now be able to feel an added pleasure from thinking that their struggles may have helped others.

1

OUR PRIVATE SEXUAL SELVES

Ginny:	Doctor, you may find this hard to believe, but we never talk about sex.
Jerry:	That's right, we've been married twenty-one years, we're each other's best friends, and we talk about everything else, but not about that.
Doctor:	You mean you haven't talked about sex since the impotence began?
Ginny:	Not from the beginning, even when we were having a good time.
Doctor:	What's the explanation?
Jerry:	I don't know. Neither of us heard it discussed in our families. Our friends only joke about it. We've never talked about it to our kids.

Doctor: When things were fine sexually, didn't you comment on the lovemaking that just happened or say what you would like to try some other time?

Ginny: I've certainly read about and envied such conversations, but, for me, these things are too private to talk about. I know it's stupid to feel that way. We are educated people and we love each other, but I never could tell Jerry what I like and what I don't. He doesn't say anything like that to me, either.

Doctor: Well, was it difficult to decide to make an appointment about the problem?

Jerry: We didn't talk about it—our family doctor decided we ought to seek help for us.

Doctor: I don't understand.

Ginny: I had a very sore throat and went to see our family doctor. Somehow I told him about our sex problem and that it was getting worse. Thankfully, he called Jerry then and there, and told him to phone your office immediately. Jerry did, and here we are.

Doctor: Well, I'm glad you're finally here.

If we assume that sex is a simple matter—one that involves only instinct, power, or technique—we may often be disappointed and angry. If we assume, on the other hand, that human sexuality is very complex, then we can gradually come to understand the principles that govern sexual behavior and use them for our own benefit.

However, we might find it difficult to view sexuality as complex. Our minds lull us into thinking that many of our sexual needs and feelings are straightforward. For example, the need for privacy, one of the most basic psychological characteristics of human sexual behavior, seems to require no explanation. But there is a great deal to this subject. The privacy which envelops and protects our sexual selves is composed of many interacting, hidden layers. Under the right circumstances, the outer layers may give way, but the deepest layers never yield.

The innermost layer is formed by our need to keep sexual secrets from ourselves. No matter how well we may think we know ourselves, we cannot fully grasp the source and meaning of all of our sexual impulses, curiosities, and wishes. These secrets are too unnerving to see and understand, except in bits and pieces.

Privacy from others, another impenetrable layer, surrounds the secrets-from-ourselves layer. No matter how close we may be to a partner, there is always something about our own sexuality that is known only to us. No human being—even the most intimate of lovers or trusted of therapists—gains a complete view of the sexual thoughts, feelings, and behaviors of another. Our need for sexual privacy is so strong that the presence of the inner two layers is rarely acknowledged.

A third layer is formed when two people share sexual behavior. What happens between them automatically becomes private without any discussion to keep it so. It is the third layer that is usually referred to when sex is said to be a private matter. We usually do not like to have this layer intruded upon. "I'll give you a perfect example of why I dislike my brother so. I told him how much I liked Beth, how special she is. I told him we found the same things funny and felt so comfortable together, and then he said, 'Did you get much?' " Some parts of this layer, however, may be surrendered to very good listeners or to professionals who can help with medical, sexual, relationship, or emotional problems.

A fourth layer is cultural and is formed by unwritten social rules for how we are allowed to discuss sexual concerns. These rules tend to be suppressive—heaven forbid that someone admits he or she has a sexual problem!—and find expression in politeness and appropriateness: "We don't talk about that!" "That" can refer to all matters from the genitals, menstruation, abortion, and intercourse to penis size, living together, and so on. The basic social principles seem to be that sex can be joked about—"Did you hear about the sign on the whore house door? Closed, beat it!" or talked about vaguely—"You should never touch yourself down there!" or discussed as an intellectual issue that has nothing to do with anyone we know—"Of course, adolescent masturbation is a perfectly normal developmental stage." With the exception of a few gifted comedians who can use our worry and interest about sexuality to entertain and educate, these social rules usually make the public discussion of sexual matters dishonest, misleading, and tiresome.

Every inquiry into human sexuality has to deal with privacy's multiple layers. Sexual privacy must be acknowledged, respected, and understood in order to see what lies behind its protective shield. One of the themes of this book is that no single person or couple can ever be fully revealed. Privacy is one of the factors that created sexual mystery. Another factor is that we do not understand or discuss the essence, the basic ingredients, of our sexual selves.

Sexuality is like the wind, a force of mysterious natural origins that is known only by its impact on ourselves and others. It can destroy or bring relief, and it is inescapable. We feel it and react to it, often unconsciously, but we seldom fully understand it. The understanding we do achieve comes slowly.

There are four important but rarely asked questions whose answers explain a great deal about our sexual selves:

- What exactly is our sexuality?
- What are the sources of our private sexual interests, behaviors, and capacities?
- What role does sexuality play in our lives?
- What determines our sexual fate over a lifetime?

These questions require thoughtful answers that will be discussed throughout the book. Our sexuality, healthy or problematic, is a characteristic rooted in our individual natures; it is subject to physical and psychological evolution as we age and as our social and emotional environments change.

The intimacy of loving interactions between mother and baby is our earliest sexual expression. Such soothing skin-to-skin experiences, peaceful feeding pleasures, and playful facial games, although mutually sensuous, are usually not considered to be sexual. However, these are actually the child's introduction to bodily pleasure, which is a basic characteristic of sexuality. Throughout her life, the child will face the challenge of becoming comfortable with and knowledgeable about her body and its pleasures. "I'll show you mine if you show me yours." The challenge, which continues throughout adulthood, is inseparable from the maturing process.

Personal experience is one of the main ways to learn about sexuality, but generally it is not enough. Most people are curious about other people's sex lives and privately enjoy hearing about them. Young children are eager to learn what their parents do in the bedroom. One of the reasons grade schoolers want to sleep in their parents' bed is to find out what is going on between them. They often refer to sexual behavior as "doing IT" without having any idea what "IT" is. Teenagers talk about sex a great deal—"You're kidding! He put his mouth there! Yuck!" Curiosity persists into adulthood, although our concepts of politeness limit the exchange of information. It is usually quite difficult to ask friends anything about their sex lives, like "Are you trying to get pregnant?" or "Have you ever used a French tickler?" let alone, "Which is your favorite position?" Privacy frustrates our eagerness to learn about our sexual selves through the experiences of others.

Talking About Sex

Sex education classes and movie love scenes do not come close to satisfying our sexual curiosity. Informal discussion about sex and detailed accounts of sexual experience in fiction are other vital sources of learning about the sexual world beyond our own experience. However, our ability to learn about sex is limited by our inability to talk about it. Although we may avidly enjoy graphic sexual descriptions in books, words fail even the most articulate of us when trying to describe our own sex lives. Winks, leers, nervous laughter, and remarks such as "You know what I mean" take the place of direct statements. Not only are we uncomfortable about revealing a private experience, but we are also unable to find words that capture our feelings and actions during sex. And the psychological aspects of sex are even more difficult to describe.

This sexual language failure begins in childhood. Toddlers

are taught the correct names for all body parts except the genitals. Little boys believe they have arms, hands, a nose, and a "weewee," "peepee," or "whizzer." Girls may grow up without ever knowing the correct names for their genital parts. "Vagina" is often the name given to their external genitals; "clitoris" is rarely uttered. The only term some young girls hear is "down there."

The inability to apply straightforward names to sexual organs contributes to a sense of mystery about sex—simultaneously bestowing it with importance and shame. This is reinforced when children learn about adult sexual behavior. Not only is this awareness shocking—"My parents don't do that!"—it is usually filled with uncertainties and distortions about what actually goes on.

By late adolescence, two distinct sexual vocabularies are in place: an informal "dirty" dialect used for thinking and talking to friends, and an anatomically correct, frequently mispronounced, and inefficiently recalled language used for more formal occasions. "Doctor, I have a sore on my dick—uh, penis." The overall result is either silence or euphemistic, vague references to sexual behavior. There must be a better way to describe one of life's greatest pleasures than "messing around"! There must be a better means of referring to sexual life than "Did you hear the one about the farmer's daughter who . . . ."

This language problem is part of a larger set of barriers to understanding and being at ease with our own and others' sexuality. Sexual language failure derives from the fourth layer of privacy and filters down to the deeper psychological layers. Language failure serves to keep the inner layers impenetrable: Secrets are better kept from ourselves and others if words do not exist to express them.

Four Sexual Tasks

Society's taboos against learning about our bodies and their sexual capabilities have relaxed considerably in the past several decades. Our sexual lives are free of many negative influences that affected previous generations; i.e., nice women don't enjoy sex. Those of us living in the latter part of the twentieth century have a better chance of developing unhindered by sexual ignorance than our parents and grandparents.

Nonetheless, full sexual development still is difficult to attain. It occupies us from early childhood in struggles that we often dimly understand. In order to acquire and maintain a problem-free sexual life, we must complete four developmental tasks:

- learning about and accepting our sexual selves
- managing sexual experience without fear, victimization, or destructiveness
- understanding where our intense sexual feelings come from
- keeping the pleasure alive

Psychological Intimacy

Psychological intimacy is related to each of these four sexual developmental tasks because it is the most powerful and lasting aphrodisiac. It differs from physical intimacy, which implies shared sexual behavior; it refers instead to psychological closeness without sexual or bodily closeness. This second type of intimacy is the ideal preparation for sexual behavior with a partner. Understanding psychological intimacy may help us keep the pleasure of sexuality intact through most of our lives.

Intimacy begins with ourselves. It is a freedom to accept the entire range of our feelings and to fully experience our conflicts, paradoxes, and dilemmas. At its most basic level, intimacy is the capacity to know what exists in the privacy of our own minds. It is not easy to be comfortable with ourselves in this way; in fact, no one can be self-aware all the time. Not only do we have a secrets-from-ourselves layer to our sexual privacy, but we routinely hide our nonsexual conflicts from ourselves. It follows that those who are extremely uncomfortable about their own feelings have a more difficult time being intimate with other people.

However, being relatively comfortable with ourselves is no guarantee that we will be able to create intimacy with others. This intimacy is brought about by sharing our personal thoughts, feelings, and behaviors with someone who calmly and respectfully accepts them as a privilege, and regards them as confidential. The degree of psychological intimacy we can have with our partners is limited by our personal needs for privacy.

In order to have psychological intimacy, we must first trust that what is said will remain private. We must believe the other person is safe. "Are you kidding? Talk to Tammy about that? The next thing I know I'll be hearing about me all over town!" "I can't discuss it with Sid—he'll rub my nose in it during our next fight."

The initial intimacy between two people prepares the way for further sharing of themselves. The exhilaration of new intimacy continues as long as we keep sharing more about ourselves. Once this process slows to a trickle, distance appears. Many find comfort and safety in that distance, but others begin to feel that they need to reconnect with each other.

Although psychological intimacy should be a pleasure, it can also be frightening. Talking intimately to another makes us worry what we are going to say about ourselves next. "I didn't know what was going to come out of my mouth. It wasn't that I didn't want her to know—I wasn't sure I wanted to know." Also, the first shared privacy may be handled well by the other person, but the one that follows may not be. "I told Ted the whole nine yards about the relationship with my sister. But I still don't think I'll be able to tell him how I feel about my mother. He's so attached to his own mother that I think he'll disapprove of me."

In addition, intimacy can stir up erotic feelings for no apparent reason. "So there we were car-pooling for the fifth day. I was really enjoying talking to this young man, and all of a sudden I started thinking about making love with him. I'm old enough to be his mother—and then some. I thought, 'What's happening to me?' "

Even after we establish intimacy with another person, maintaining it is a day-to-day job. Between our partners' responses to us and our anticipation of these responses, the calm, respectful acceptance of each other often does not last. Some people never learn how to comfortably be with another person. "I can't talk to Wilson; either he only half listens to me or he gets angry at me for what I feel." "Elena asks me to tell her what is going on with me, and when I say what's on my mind, right away she tells me I'm wrong. It's getting hard to talk to her about anything. Lately, it's been only 'pass the margarine' and 'what time will you be home?' "

Once two people sexualize their psychological intimacy, they may use sex to recreate the closeness that previously was only established by psychological intimacy. When men and women feel their sexual lives are too routine, their boredom may not be a failure of sexual technique but the result of relying on sex to reconnect intimately. One effective prescription for better sex is to first spend more time discovering what is currently happening psychologically within each other. Unfortunately, many people can no longer do this on their own.

The following chapters illustrate the struggles of a number of people to achieve and maintain the four sexual developmental tasks. Their struggles, although rarely discussed from the vantage point of these tasks, are certainly not unusual. Others can learn from them so that they, too, may become more comfortable with their private sexual selves.

Toward a Problem-Free Sexual Life

We need to:

- learn about and accept our sexual selves
- manage sexual experience without fear, victimization, and destructiveness
- understand where our intense feelings come from
- keep sexual pleasure alive throughout our lives
- develop the capacity for psychological intimacy

2

LOSING SEXUAL FEAR

The possibility of physical intimacy with another person for the first time makes us all uneasy, however secure we might appear to be. When this lovemaking actually happens, each partner is nervous. Early lovemaking experiences are a bit like a two-horse race in which the popular favorite, Excitement, runs against Fear. If all goes well, Excitement is the clear winner. In the next running, Fear finishes farther behind and soon is no longer in the race.

For many people, however, Excitement wins by a nose and Fear remains a strong contender in subsequent match ups. In others, Fear may prevail for a while, but gradually Excitement stays in more of the contest until Fear eventually weakens, and drops out. For still other people, Excitement never enters the race.

> "We hated the first few days of our honeymoon. It took us three days to admit to each other that we were not having a good time. Sex was disappointing. We waited because I wanted to and when we finally had intercourse, I was so tense that I didn't enjoy it. We didn't have it the first night because I had a splitting headache and was nauseated from the champagne at the wedding. Jeff didn't seem to mind. The evening after we had intercourse the second time, Jeff joked that he hoped our sex life improved. That seemed to break the ice and we finally admitted sex was a little disappointing. We waited a few days before we tried it again. That was a good decision because we were less nervous. I think we just had to get the first experience over and done with."

Most of us feel similar anxiety or tension at the beginning of each new sexual partnership. There is not as much uneasiness if we have become psychologically intimate, but even this does not fully remove the apprehension. Even after decades of absence, the two-horse race can start all over again.

> Ralph, a fifty-year-old widower: "You would have thought I was a twenty-year-old kid again. I had intercourse with my wife, I don't know, at least a thousand times I guess, but I was worried. Worried how I would perform, worried what she [new woman friend] would think of me, whether I could keep my erection. Silly I know, I've never been impotent but I was just worried. She was wonderful. I was fine. She seemed to like everything. [He laughs] If she didn't, I don't want to know about it!

When some of the sources of fear are revealed in this chapter, it will be clear that sex is not simple. Many important steps must be taken before people can fully enjoy the sexual experience. Without these, the sexual drama is intimidating and crippled by anxiety.

Numerous small-scale studies have suggested that sexual problems and dissatisfactions are widespread. An important study by Dr. Ellen Frank and her colleagues several years ago found that 2 percent of young and middle-aged couples, who

	Women (148)	Men (64)
Sexual Identity Problems		
Gender Identity	3%	6%
Orientation	15%	5%
Intention	11%	9%
Sexual Function Problems		
Limited Desire	16%	14%
Limited Arousal	50%	27%
Premature Ejaculation	—	41%
Inability to Have Orgasm	18%	3%
Pain during Intercourse	21%	2%
No Sexual Problems Whatsoever	25%	26%

*Study by Moshe Schein, M.D., et al, Cleveland, Ohio 1988

Fig. 1 Frequency of Current or Recent Past Sexual Problems among 212 Adults at a Family Doctor's Office

independently said they were happily married, had never attempted intercourse. Another 8 percent of these subjects had sexual contact with their spouses less than monthly. One-fifth of the women and one-third of the men said they were sexually dissatisfied. Research in North America and Europe suggests that these patterns are common: About 40 percent of married men reported in recent surveys think they have premature ejaculation, and 15 to 25 percent are troubled with periodic impotence; about 15 percent of women are unable to have orgasm with a partner, and many more have trouble maintaining a high degree of arousal during lovemaking. In fact, studies involving long-term relationships indicate many men and women do not feel a desire for their partner much of the time.

Additional studies, including one by Dr. Moshe Schein and our group in Cleveland, Ohio, based on questionnaires filled out in a family doctor's office, point to the fact that even those who are usually assumed to be sexually well—the happily married, the physically healthy, young singles—have many sexual problems (figure 1). People who have never married, who are divorced or unhappily married, and who are physically and emotionally ill have even more difficulties. Of course, many people in one or more of these categories may be sexually well, but for others the race between Excitement and Fear continues regardless of marital and health status.

Where Does The Fear Come From?

Fear during physical intimacy has many sources—familial, cultural, and psychological. Susceptibility to these sources of fear varies from one person to another.

There are four categories of fear about sexual intimacy. The first comes from being emotionally unready for intercourse. The second is not being comfortable with the sensual self. The third comes from a lack of trust in ourselves and our partners, and the fourth results from sexual identity struggles.

Emotional Unreadiness

The first experience of intercourse is called loss of virginity. It makes more sense, however, to emphasize that this is not the end of something, but actually an important beginning. Something momentous happens when we take this step. We are aware that powerful emotional forces are unleashed in ourselves and our partners through intercourse. These forces either can cause profound upset or lead to exhilaration and further maturation. The trick is to discover how to manage sexual behavior so that it results in pleasure and understanding rather than depression, worry, and bewilderment.

> Arlene, twenty-three, recalled that when she first necked at age sixteen, she got so excited that she felt she was losing control and became panicky. She jumped off the hay wagon, leaving her date dumbfounded and herself embarrassed. When she ventured into lovemaking two years later after numerous discussions with her friends about boys, she was able to relax and enjoy her arousal without being afraid of losing control.

Some teenagers try intercourse and then avoid it for several more years because the experience was disappointing or embarrassing and not worth the anxiety it caused—worrying about being caught by their parents, by pregnancy, or by disease. They are not emotionally ready for sex and are mature enough to know it. Many other teenagers, of course, continue to have intercourse whether they are emotionally ready or not.

Inhibition of the Sensual Self

One of the basic developmental steps makes it possible for sex to be pleasurable—we must discover our bodies as legitimate sources of sensual pleasure. Until we learn to accept our sexual potential and allow ourselves to acquire sensual skills, we will continue to be anxious or inhibited (sexual anxiety in disguise). Acceptance usually does not occur with the first physical intimacy. It takes time to cast off the ideas that genital pleasures and sexual behavior are not legitimate.

The acceptance of the sensual self does not automatically take place because a person marries or has a long, loving relationship. It usually evolves gradually during the early years of regular sexual behavior under the supportive conditions of a deepening relationship. Many people do accomplish this developmental task during marriage or before. Some only accomplish it in an extramarital affair. Other individuals, however, grow old without learning to enjoy their bodies.

> "I think Penny helped me immensely. She was so comfortable with her body during lovemaking. She caressed herself along with my caresses. I was not insulted be-

> cause she seemed to be loving all the sensations. I got to thinking about this. I thought I was having good sex in my first marriage, but it was only after being with Penny that I realized I was uptight about my body. I envied Penny's comfort with herself and the pleasure she got from sex. I'm learning. I'm enjoying her caresses a lot more. She is still light-years ahead of me."

Both men and women have to undergo this learning process. The stereotype of the more experienced young man as sexual teacher of his naive partner is both false and dangerous. One of the great pleasures—and difficulties—of early love is to create a relationship in which two nervous people can support each other through their sensual awakenings without pretense. They learn to accept their bodily pleasures through their tentative forays into new and various means of lovemaking. Experienced partners who have already accepted their sensual selves may help inexperienced partners a great deal; however, those who only pretend to be calm may rob sex of its joy. Sexual anxiety, though denied, can be contagious. "When Bob and I make love, I can feel his nervousness—his whole body is stiff and his caresses are wooden. I can't relax under these conditions." Unlike two nervous people who can deal forthrightly with their apprehension, dishonest partners trap themselves. Nervousness during sexual intimacy is not a crime. It just requires acknowledgement and honest discussion so people can learn to enjoy their sexual feelings and sensual selves.

Lack of Trust

Many early sexual experiences are conducted somewhat deceitfully. Each person may hide the major motive for wanting to make love—he, saying, "I like you very much," is thinking, "I'm not going to call her again, so why not?" She, smiling with pleasure, is thinking, "I like sex, he seems nice, maybe this will work out." The personal price of such dishonesty—he, guilty for exploiting her; she, depressed because he does not call—is greater than the physical pleasure derived. After emotionally unsatisfying sexual experiences, men and women may ask themselves, "Why am I here? What am I doing? Am I being honest with my partner? Do I like the me I see in this relationship?" Some of this anxiety can be prevented by answering these questions before having sex.

This is a two-sided issue—some of a person's anxiety is also about the trustworthiness of the partner. People may ask themselves, "What does my partner want? Is it safe to be more honest with this person? Will I get AIDS?"

These questions about self and partner lurk in the shadows of physical intimacy and produce nervousness. Always there at the beginning of a relationship, they may reappear suddenly if something happens to create distrust.

Sexual Identity Struggles

If our sexual identity is well-formed during childhood and we develop in an entirely conventional fashion, we are apt to easily grow comfortable with our role in a sexual relationship. For a woman, conventional means feeling feminine, heterosexual, and wishing to exchange pleasure with a male partner without being or creating a victim. For a man, conventional means feeling masculine and wishing to give and receive pleasure with a woman without victimization. How many people have enough ambivalence about their sexual identities to interfere with their ability to relax and enjoy making love? Perhaps as many as 5 to 20 percent of the population, although such statistics are elusive in these very private matters.

Sexual identity is not simply an either/or matter; many identities cannot be classified as entirely conventional. Even those with conventional sexual identities occasionally experience curiosities, interests, and urges that are unconventional. These are usually too private to be revealed to a partner and may lead to unexplained nervousness about sex.

Sexual identity consists of three major elements—gender identity, orientation, and intention. Each of these elements has separate and important behavioral and psychological dimensions, all of which may cause anxiety during physical intimacy or avoidance of sexual behavior.

Gender identity. Gender identity is a combination of our private sense of where we belong on the masculine-feminine spectrum (psychological) and our public role as masculine or feminine people (behavioral). Such gender role behavior may be shown to others in the way we dress, sit, walk, talk, work, and play.

Without much thought, most of us assume the gender roles appropriate to our biological sex. However, some men hide an unusually strong feminine side; similarly, some women feel their true and preferred inner self is masculine. This difference between gender role performance and such private feelings about oneself—gender sense—may cripple physical and psychological intimacy.

If a man has a strong urge to be the woman during lovemaking and his partner's expectation is for him to be the man, he is in sexual trouble. And if, in the privacy of her thoughts, a woman wants to be the man and is limited by the partner's expectation that she will play a female role, she too will be uncomfortable.

> Leslie came to see me to discuss an intimate matter she felt she could not discuss with any of her friends. Her boyfriend of one year seemed to have little sexual interest in her after their initial weeks together. His only explanation was that he didn't think he had much of a sex drive. To her, however, he seemed more nervous than disinterested. Because he occasionally lost his erection during foreplay, she had wondered if he was really impotent. Then, two months ago, on Halloween night, all of this changed. He dressed up as a vampy woman for a costume party. When they got home, they made love while he was still in his garb. They have been having sex frequently since without any sign of impotence, as long as he "fools around" and puts on her slip or pantyhose again. He refuses to discuss this with her except to say, "Hey! Don't knock it!"

If a partner cannot be found who can pleasurably accommodate the unconventional person's gender identity needs, sexual nervousness may cause avoidance of any lovemaking. Leslie had to understand something most people never even have to consider: Cross-dressing increases sexual desire and arousal for some men who feel they possess a secret feminine self. When I told her it was not easy to change this form of gender identity in a man, she grew more certain that she would eventually end their relationship.

> Lorraine, a homosexual woman, maintained for several months of psychotherapy that she could not understand why she so often avoided sex. Eventually she was able to tell of her recurrent fantasy of becoming a man during lovemaking. It was not just that she thought that she was a man with a penis having intercourse, but that she was losing her female self. Sexual activity made her feel that she did not know who or what she was. Her female partner just thought of her as moody and unpredictable.

Whether as extreme as these examples or not, fears about gender identity are rarely revealed to sexual partners.

Orientation. Our sexual orientation is a combination of thoughts, fantasies, and attractions (psychological) and the kind of people with whom we actually have sexual interactions (behavioral). A child's sexual orientation is usually established by the sixth birthday. By this time, the child's mind responds differently to males and females and thereafter will only acknowledge interest in either the opposite or same sex. If in the future, social situations bring the person together with a sexual partner of the "wrong" sex, Fear may run away from Excitement.

> "No! I don't want to have sex with Anne. I know it is cruel to her. She is my wife, but when I am with her I have to force myself to touch her. I am not interested in her sexually. If you must know the truth, I am scared and I don't know why. Anne is a very nice person. I love her but I don't want to touch her and I don't want to have intercourse with her. When I'm with David, I feel normal, relaxed—I always come."

Learning a person's sexual orientation is not simply a matter of looking for effeminacy in a man or masculinity in a woman. These are gender role characteristics, not signs of orientation. Most homosexual men and women are indistinguishable from heterosexuals in appearance and gender role behaviors. Their homoerotic interests are private matters that are known to a chosen few, and may never be publicly revealed.

Homoerotic individuals also can be anxious during homosexual behavior if they have not accepted their homoerotic orientation. This anxiety often is so intense that it prevents orgasm. The developmental task of accepting one's homoeroticism often requires years. Many homosexual men and women never get there. Heterosexuals do not have to deal with acceptance of their orientation since they are viewed as normal by society.

Intention. The least well-known component of sexual identity is intention. Intention is a combination of thoughts and fantasies about what we want to do with a partner (psychological) and how we actually conduct ourselves in sexual situations. A wide gulf may exist between what we lead our partners to believe we want to do and what we repeatedly imagine during erotic moments. Unconventional intentions are an important source of fear during sexual behavior for only that minority who are unable to enjoy mutual pleasure with an adult. Their private wishes may concern humiliation, punishments, cruelty to others, secretly watching others undress or have sex, making obscene phone calls, shocking others with one's erection, and having sex with a child. They are considered unconventional because their intentions have to do with victimization and their erotic world is preoccupied

	Subjective	Objective
Gender	gender identity	gender role
Orientation	erotic orientation	sexual orientation
Intention	erotic intention	sexual intention

Fig. 2 Three Elements of Sexual Identity

with anger, pain, and a sense of defectiveness. In contrast, people with conventional intentions wish for peaceful mutuality—that is, to have experiences of giving to and receiving physical pleasure from a partner.

Figure 2 summarizes the three basic elements of sexual identity and shows the words used throughout this book in describing either people's psychology or behavior. It may be useful to use this chart for reference in subsequent chapters.

Sexual Function as a Barometer

Desire, arousal, orgasm, and emotional satisfaction are other sexual functions that reflect the health of our bodies, minds, and relationships. Problems in any one of these spheres can quickly reduce the quality of our sexual lives or even halt our sexual behavior. Improvements in our health can raise our level of sexual pleasure.

Sometimes our sexual bodies work well. We begin with desire, stay highly aroused, culminate with an intensely pleasurable orgasm, and when finished feel emotionally and physically satisfied. There is an awesome beauty about mutually satisfying sex. It seems so simple, but it is a complicated process based on an exquisite coordination of the nervous systems of two individuals and their personal and interpersonal needs.

As we have seen, sexual nervousness can interfere with a healthy sensual life. Another source of interference is apathy, also known as avoidance, disinterest, low sexual desire, lack of sex drive, or boredom. Whatever label is used, apathy and nervousness are significant enemies of sexual vitality. Apathy is often the result of nervousness that was never outgrown. It has other sources as well, such as suppressed anger, lack of respect for the partner, preference for another person. Apathy comes easily to sexual relationships. Despite the hoopla sex receives, the truth is that many people's lives quickly deteriorate into limited foreplay, tenuous arousal, unthrilling orgasms, and lack of emotional satisfaction.

If sexual apathy appears in our lives, we should ask the following questions: Is something physically wrong with me?

Am I ignoring something within me that needs attention? Am I angry or disappointed with my partner? The source of most sexual dysfunction can be found in the answers to these questions.

Simple Sex

Before dealing with problems, however, we should savor sexual health. A young couple has been talking together with increasing honesty for several weeks. They each feel an unmistakable pleasure in the other. Trust and caring are growing. They hold hands and kiss—a major event for both, nice but a little scary. Later, they tell each other about ambitions that no one else has heard. Then, a confession is made about a shameful problem in one of their families. Soon they are laughing about it; they realize that they are separate from their families. They pet with mutual excitement—also a major event. Eventually they have intercourse accompanied by a little tension and a lot of giggling. Each knows the other is nervous, but both want to be there. Despite the zippers, hooks, and buttons that would not undo, their brief intercourse is pleasant. They are glad they did it and look forward to next time.

During their lovemaking, there were no fantasies. The awkward reality was better than each had ever experienced during masturbation and daydreams. Being touched was real; it was incomparably superior to touching oneself while thinking about being touched.

Now that is simple sex. Congratulations to both! They are beginning in good fashion. Excitement is way ahead of Fear.

Toward a Problem-Free Sexual Life

In order to minimize fear, anxiety, and apathy during sexual behavior with a partner, we need to:

- feel emotionally ready for genital intimacy
- accept our sensual self by strongly believing that sexual behavior and its pleasures are legitimate for us at this time in our life
- trust our motives for lovemaking and the trustworthiness of our partner
- grow comfortable with each element of our sexual identity—gender identity, orientation, and intention
- learn how to read our desire, arousal, orgasm, and emotional satisfaction as barometers of our physical health, our feelings about ourself, and our attitude toward our partner
- ask ourself when we are disinterested in sex if we are healthy or angry or disappointed with our partner

3

HOW TO BE A GOOD LOVER

Edie:	Bill was great in bed, my best sexual partner ever!
Doctor:	What made him so great?
Edie:	We stayed in bed all day. He loved my body—all of it. He was interested in my pleasure. He wasn't uptight. I felt he was in command. He showed me that I could come with oral sex and come again. He helped me get lost in bed. It was a different world. . . .
Doctor:	You stopped talking.
Edie:	I was just thinking that it wasn't real. I knew I had to go back to Jack. My kids were at home. Jack was falling apart every time he couldn't account for my time. Bill was not a person for

> me to build my life around. He wanted to be in bed all day because he had nothing else to do. I wasn't born yesterday. I was not his only diversion, but I didn't care because he was what I needed and wanted—the opposite of Jack. Jack is nervous, always afraid of losing his erection. He makes *me* nervous. I get so angry at him because he is so passive that I feel in command. I don't feel feminine. You know, that's it—I felt like a woman with Bill!

Bill's sensual manner and avid interest in Edie's pleasure had a profound impact on her arousal. He allowed her to discover her sexual capacities which erased her doubts about her gender identity. With Bill, she found the woman she wanted to be, a woman who enjoyed being transported by a strong man. When Edie referred to Bill as a great lover, she meant that her experiences with him were both exhilarating and deeply reassuring. She did not use the word "great" lightly. For almost a year she could not stop arranging these dreamy afternoons, even though she felt much turmoil over her husband and daughters.

Lovers such as Bill meet profound psychological needs in their partners and their ability to provide deep satisfaction may cause partners to overlook their weaknesses. Those who are not as good lovers, although they still may be appreciated, do not fulfill their partners' psychological needs in the same manner. What, then, makes one a good lover?

Characteristics of Good Lovers

Among four characteristics of good lovers, the most important is being comfortable with their own and their partner's intense bodily sensations. They also understand how the body works, they have a good sense of timing about the sequences of stimulation, and they are able to keep distractions and squabbles out of the bedroom.

Sensual Comfort

Edie's Bill had the central characteristic of good lovers: He consistently behaved in ways that encouraged her to relax and abandon herself to her sensations. Like other good lovers, Bill was comfortable with his body and its intense sensations.

Such sensual comfort protects people from the disappointments with lovemaking that afflict many couples who are anxious about the pleasurable use of their bodies. These disappointments are often the sources of these complaints about lovemaking:

My partner dislikes doing something that I want to do. While this complaint usually refers to oral-genital stimulation, other behaviors are often involved–for example, kissing, breast caressing, genital touching, back rubbing, anal touching, rear-entry intercourse.

My partner establishes preconditions. My partner has to be absolutely clean–that is, fresh from the shower, or insists that I be. The lights must be off. My partner must clean up immediately after orgasm. Sex must be in the proper location–always on the bed. These is no sex when we have overnight guests.

My partner is unexpressive during sex. There are no noises, moans, sighs, groans, grunts, or fireworks. My partner is absolutely quiet. I usually do not even know when orgasm has occurred.

My partner is too predictable. Sex always involves the same sequence of behavior, occurs at the same time of day, and requires the same amount of time.

My partner approaches sex with little intensity. I do not feel wanted, consumed, or ignited by my partner's passion.

My partner is rarely interested when I am. I am a morning person; my partner is a night person.

When these statements are rephrased positively, we can see the effects of comfort with sensuality. Good lovers enjoy different sexual behaviors, have few preconditions, are emotionally expressive during sex, are more spontaneous in what they want to do, are often intensely aroused, and cooperate willingly in their partner's interest in sex.

Avoidance of Interpersonal Tangles

Another important characteristic of good lovers is their ability to avoid, in bed, the terrible interpersonal tangles outside the bedroom that make sensual comfort difficult. They guard against unsupportive attitudes and behavior. When problems arise, they recognize and deal with them, unlike the following man who could not understand what was wrong with his sex life.

Gary: What's so frustrating is that Char can be great in bed! But most of the time she is just there. She is so passive that her beautiful body doesn't even matter to me. She ought to be seeing you, doctor.

Doctor: What is different when she is great?

Gary: I don't know except that she seems to want me and enjoy me. It really turns me on to see her so excited. She kisses me all over my ears and neck. She likes what she is doing. The rest of the time—most of the time—I feel like I have to tell her what to do. And if I have to ask for it, it isn't any good.

Doctor: What do you think makes Char like what she is doing?

Gary: Damned if I know! I'm always the same in bed. I like sex. Hell, it's fun, it's normal. I don't think I have any sex hang ups. I like to do most things—don't get me wrong, I'm not kinky. She says it is because I yell at her. But usually that's yesterday and I've already forgotten about it. She has some big hangups. You know, before she met me she never would allow any oral sex.

Doctor: Tell me about your temper.

Gary thought of himself as a very good lover. He could not see how his angry outbursts inhibited his wife. She frustrated him greatly. Her beauty excited him, but her inhibitions tried his patience. The quality of his experience with her was usually so poor that sex was "great" when he could talk himself into thinking she was enjoying it. Both her actual arousal and her more frequent faking allowed him to feel valued and helped him deny that his aggressive outbursts mattered. "Great" came to mean his destructive harshness was forgiven and he was reassured that his marriage would continue a little longer. The purpose of sex was so frequently to "make up" that it lost its joy.

Gary and Char had predictable, unspontaneous, unresponsive sexual experiences that were pleasant enough but only occasionally satisfying. They were both bored with their sex life but could not admit it. When they finally talked about it, they blamed each other, thus making it very difficult to become good lovers.

Gary and Char each found an explanation for the other's sexual problems. He thought it was the impact of his wife's nervous mother and her strict religious background. She thought her husband's need to prove himself in bed indicated that he had impaired masculinity and might be a latent homosexual. Both believed they were victims in their marriage.

An alternative explanation, one that good lovers intuitively appreciate, did not occur to them: It takes two people to create sexual chaos. They could not see that the faults they saw in the other were true of themselves. Gary accused his wife of cruelty in and out of bed; Char thought her husband faked his sexual interest. It took them many months to see that he was accusing her of cruelty, his worst trait, and that her faking during lovemaking was destructive. When they began to understand that they may have been equally responsible for their unhappy sexual experience, they took an important step to becoming good lovers. There are countless men and women like them.

Tom complained that his wife was a "bad deal." He said he spent a lot of money on her neurotic need to keep up

> with the Joneses, but received little in return. Sex was infrequent, unexpressive, and dutiful. He felt she did not appreciate his hard work and his need to relax after work. He resented her criticism in front of their son and her constant emphasis upon how he was a "jerk and a social dud." He was certain this was *her* problem because his mother-in-law, too, felt her husband was a worthless man who never made her life full. Nowhere in Tom's discussions did he recognize that his own name-calling—"stupid," "worthless," "incompetent," and more—played any role in causing his wife's fearful disrespect and her disinterest in sexual experimentation. Nor would he acknowledge for a long time that the cost of his frequently traded boats, sports cars, and ever-changing wardrobe far exceeded her purchases. When these facts were brought to Tom's attention, he said emphatically that it was his money.

Two women had told Tom prior to marriage that he was a wonderful bed partner so he entered his marriage without worry. When people who could be good lovers get themselves into knotty relationships, they are unable to concentrate on sensations during lovemaking. Instead, they become preoccupied with personal anger and disappointment. Both Gary and Tom, the men described in this section, were potentially fine lovers, but their smothering interpersonal tangles kept them from enjoying their partners.

Knowledge of the Body

Good lovers also seem to know about the body and what to do with it during lovemaking. While they learn this primarily through personal sexual experience, books and films also may teach them along the way. Of course, good lovers existed before sexually explicit books and films were widely available. However, there is perhaps more good lovemaking today than ever before because there is greater access to sexual information and more social acceptance in learning about this fascinating aspect of our lives.

Our culture owes a great deal to William Masters and Virginia Johnson for the current availability of information about sexual life. Their book *Human Sexual Response,* published in 1966, triggered a wave of writings about what people could do to solve sexual problems. This flood of information pointed out how difficult it had been to learn about sexual matters and how little most people knew about the subject. Syndicated columnists such as Ann Landers and Abigail Van Buren have brought much useful information to the general public for more than 30 years. Sex is now discussed almost everywhere. Public libraries offer reference materials on sexuality. Churches program lectures for married couples. Sexual picture books are no longer shamefully hidden under the socks, and the advent of AIDS has increased sex education in the schools.

Education alone, however, is not enough to help everyone deal with the sexual doldrums. Therapists have discovered that teaching technique to people does not make them good lovers. An "A" in anatomy is not required for passionate, fulfilling sex. Such education is more useful to those without serious problems for they are emotionally freer to use this knowledge to enhance their experiences.

Skillful lovers know at least something about the anatomy and stimulation of female and male genitals. Knowing the relative locations of the clitoris, urethra, labia, vagina, and anus, and the importance of the clitoris is a vital step toward becoming a good lover. For example, the only visible part of the clitoris is its small tip which changes in size and sensitivity as arousal intensifies. At the highest level of excitement, the clitoris sometimes retracts deeper into the body and seems to disappear. It can become so sensitive during arousal that touching it causes irritation, rather than further arousal. The clitoris is not a magic button that requires pushing. If clitoral stimulation becomes annoying prior to orgasm, stimulation of the surrounding area may be pleasant. After orgasm, the clitoris may again become hypersensitive; any direct touching may be intolerable for a few moments.

Most orgasmic women rely on direct hand or mouth stimulation from their partners to get close to orgasm prior to intercourse or to have an orgasm. The clitoris is an exquisitely sensitive organ whose sole known function is sexual excitation. A woman should let her partner know that the clitoris is as important to her pleasure as the penis is to his.

Different parts of the vagina vary in sensitivity. Its opening is the most sensitive to touch. Although most women love intercourse, the inner parts of the vagina are relatively insensitive to back and forth movements. However, slight pressure on the side walls of the vagina produces intense sensations that vary according to the location of the pressure. The vagina also can be stimulated by various positions of intercourse, hands, or mechanical objects.

Good lovers should know that erections are not necessary for lovemaking, for ejaculation, or for either partner's orgasm; erections are only necessary for intercourse. This is especially important to understand during the latter part of life when erections are more difficult to attain and maintain. It helps to know that stimulation all along the urethral bulge of the length of the penis where the remains of the foreskin are found in circumcised males is more effective than along the opposite sides, since this is the most sensitive spot on the penis. The tip of the penis is relatively insensitive to stimulation, especially when compared to the pleasure that caressing the scrotum can provide.

Lovemaking is difficult to teach. Making love is more than a matter of genital stimulation; it can sometimes involve the entire bodies of both lovers. Timing is more important to the technique of lovemaking than the various positions for intercourse. The difference between having a wonderful and a mediocre sex life can be the timing of lovemaking sequences.

How can we improve our sex lives? Working as a psychiatrist and sex therapist for many years, I have found some guiding principles, which I have incorporated into what I call the "red screen technique."

The Red Screen Technique

Imagine a representation of the entire body on a screen. When part of the body is ready to respond to a caress or a kiss with increased excitement, the appropriate section of the screen will light up red. Light, medium, and intense shades of red will appear on this hypothetical screen to show how receptive and aroused the body is becoming. Viewing the screen could guide people to the next exact location to be caressed in order to maximize their partners' pleasure. When a body part is unresponsive to stimulation, the screen will remain flesh-colored. Partners could avoid that part until the appropriate area of the screen turns red. Watching the screen, or the next best thing, remembering its lesson, would eliminate stimulation that was too fast or the wrong type, and other problems that keep people out of sync with their partners.

The red screen illustrates the following principles of lovemaking:

- The red sequences are almost never identical during lovemaking. In one episode, for example, the breast area will turn medium-red immediately after lip kissing occurs; the same stimulation may not change the color of the breast area in the next episode.

- The red sequences vary greatly from one person to another. For some women, no amount of stimulation will change the shading of the breast area. For others, this area almost always will show in the red range. Stimulation of the nipples of many men will produce only faint red tinges, but a few men will readily generate intense red.

- Lovemaking can be an adventure. The strategy is to anticipate the red zones. Although there are some clues such as changes in breathing, position, and sounds, partners do not have the screen to guide them. And often, verbal instructions may turn the entire screen back to flesh color. Therefore, the best way to carry out the strategy of the red zones is to become a student of your partner's responses.

- A peak experience in the lovemaking adventure consists of turning the entire screen bright red. For a short time after this occurs, any stimulation to any body part is intensely exciting; orgasm will provide explosive release from excitement.

- Sexual partners often believe they can predict the pattern of red sequences. In a limited sense, they are correct. The predicted pattern often involves a sequence of back touching, lip kissing, breast stimulation, genital stimulation, and intercourse. However, this prediction ignores most of the other body surfaces. The shifting redness of legs, arms, back, buttocks, armpits, and fingers may be neither appreciated nor exploited.
- Many males initially expect to or believe they are expected to provide most of the stimulation. The myth exists that the male screen, except for the genitals, remains largely flesh colored. Not true—they have yet to learn how to use their entire bodies as sources of pleasure.
- Changing psychological and biological factors influence the red sequences. The interaction of these factors makes lovemaking unpredictable. Even when a person thinks that his or her screen will remain hopelessly flesh colored, it may turn bright red within a few minutes of stimulation.

No one can be a good lover all the time because sexual desire varies from episode to episode. Even within an unchanging style of lovemaking, there are variations of the intensity of sexual response to stimulation. In addition, interest in creating and experiencing sensation fluctuates from moment to moment. During portions of lovemaking, a person may only want to receive; at other moments, she or he may be more interested in providing pleasure. Good lovers are sensitive to these changes in themselves and their partners, and use rather than resist them.

The ideal time to learn sensual skills and to discover the metaphor of the red screen is during young adulthood. Unfortunately, at that point many people are only interested in sexual results—that is, intercourse and orgasm. Their sexual bodies are working well and they just want to get the job done. They fail to realize the value of giving and receiving, of sensual preoccupation, and of becoming a student of their partner's responses. As they get older, they may find that it is difficult to change their thinking. When erections become unreliable, their sexual lives may be over because this results-oriented, getting-the-job-done mentality makes it almost impossible to imagine lovemaking without intercourse. This is not just a male mentality. Some women think, "Why bother?" when their partners become impotent.

> Clifford and Thelma had a regular sex life for forty-two years until at age seventy-three, Clifford was placed on medication that interfered with his erection. Even after medication was changed, Clifford remained impotent. Eventually the couple found their way to a therapist who suggested that they make love weekly for one month without attempting intercourse. They were shocked to learn that other people, and especially people at their stage in life, did such things. Both assumed that there was no use to lovemaking if intercourse wasn't possible. They followed the therapist's recommendations and soon discovered a sensual world they had previously missed. His potency returned during the month but intercourse became a less important part of their lovemaking than it ever had been before.

While it is important to understand those traits that increase the likelihood of a wonderful sex life, a steady diet of great sex is probably not possible. Many individuals are good lovers for much of their lives; however, it is hard to find a person who is a great lover during every sexual encounter. There are innumerable barriers to good sex. The ordinary events of life—fatigue, preoccupation with a child, worry about a visit from the in-laws, a car breaking down—interfere with our ability to relax and concentrate on sensations each time we have sex.

It is better not to focus on the characteristics of good lovers each time we have sex. Some people could take this so seriously that their pursuit of sensual skills would eliminate all the fun of sex. The concept of a good lover is part truth, part illusion; it is attainable, yet elusive. It requires both seriousness and playfulness—especially playfulness.

Good lovers, because of comfort with their sensual selves, are able to find giving and receiving pleasure worthwhile, and can allow their partners to know this. Good lovers seek variety in sexual behavior and are not frightened by unexpected intensities that occasionally develop. Good lovers have a knack for preventing interpersonal tangles and respect their partners' sexual limitations. Good lovers intuitively know about the red screen. They are perpetual students of their partners' sexual pleasures. Their respect is felt by their partners and enhances trust and sensual abandonment. However, no one can be a good lover alone. Each person needs to be in sync with another and this makes them both good lovers.

Toward A Problem-Free Sexual Life

To become and remain a good lover, we need to:

- be comfortable with our bodies and their sensations
- know genital anatomy and means of their stimulation
- understand the principles of the red screen technique
- become a student of our partners' responses
- deal supportively on nonsexual matters with our partners

4

THE SEXUAL EQUILIBRIUM

There is a sensitive balance between a person's sexual behavior and his or her partner's responses. This is the "sexual equilibrium." It exists both within and between each partner. Each person brings definable sexual traits to the bedroom—for example, a level of desire, an ease or difficulty of arousal, a means of attaining orgasm. The partner regards these characteristics in some manner and responds to them; this response helps or hinders the person's sexual comfort and abilities.

The sexual equilibrium exists in every intimate relationship. It is the most misunderstood psychological influence in our sexual lives. A healthy sexual equilibrium is crucial to lasting sexual function and pleasure. An unhealthy sexual equilibrium desexualizes relationships, produces infidelity, and often ends relationships. Most people presume that the quality of their sexual relationship is determined by the quality of their nonsexual relationship. This is only partly correct.

> Louis has been a faithful husband in a relatively comfortable marriage for forty years. Until his heart surgery four years ago, his major sexual dissatisfaction was his wife's discomfort with actively providing him sexual pleasures beyond intercourse. He stopped mentioning this disappointment long ago because she became distraught and her passivity did not change. In every other aspect, however, their marriage was more than satisfactory. In his early sixties, the years prior to heart surgery, Louis's sexual drive had become less frequent and insistent.
>
> After the surgery, with his doctor's encouragement, he tried to resume intercourse, even though he was afraid it might be too much for his heart. When he was unable to have an erection during the year after surgery, he told himself and his wife that old age had robbed him of potency. He still wanted to make love to his wife, but rarely tried. She, too, wished to continue their sexual activity, but she did not push him.
>
> In the fourth year of Louis's impotence, Rita, a sixty-two-year-old co-worker, expressed an unmistakable physical interest in him. When his jokes about being an old man—even an impotent old man—did not discourage her, he accepted her invitation to have lunch at her apartment. Lunch quickly led to sex. Although Louis couldn't have much of an erection, Rita remained skeptical of his conviction that he was over the hill and happily stimulated him in ways he had only previously imagined. Within several meetings, he was able to have his first orgasm without an erection since the heart surgery. Both were thrilled. As they continued their relationship, Louis became more relaxed each time. After four months of weekly liaisons, he became potent. In another month, his sudden losses of erection during intercourse disappeared. Louis and his wife, however, remained sexually inactive.

The Balancing Act

Three overlapping psychological systems interact to produce our sexual experiences. The first is our individual psychological selves. The second, sexual equilibrium, is the response to each other's sexual traits. The third is the quality of our nonsexual relationship. Each system influences the others. We can best understand our sexual lives by understanding this interaction. Ideas about sex that focus on only one of these systems are oversimplified. Figure 3 represents these three systems.

Louis was involved in two very different sexual relationships. In his marital equilibrium, his level of sexual desire and his ability to attain and maintain an erection had become limited—he was becoming an "old man." In his new sexual equilibrium with a much less passive, more sensuous partner, he no longer felt that he was over the hill.

The sexual equilibrium is complicated because both people are simultaneously responding to their partners' characteristics. It is a delicately balanced, readily changeable system. Every couple's sexual equilibrium is unique because the sexual traits of each individual are slightly different each time lovemaking occurs and no two people interact in the same manner.

> Louis recalled that his wife's sexual behavior was not always predictable. Most of the time she was "just there," passively waiting for him to do everything. Sometimes she seemed to resist becoming aroused so that no matter what he did, he felt sexually alone and selfish. However, on the rare occasions that she became an active participant, his pleasure and excitement varied accordingly. Louis's wife described her notion of how women were supposed to behave in bed. She had noticed that his interest in her was connected with her own arousal, but her inhibitions generally prevented her from becoming a passionate lover.

When a sexual partnership is formed, each person's sexual characteristics accommodate, influence, and interact with

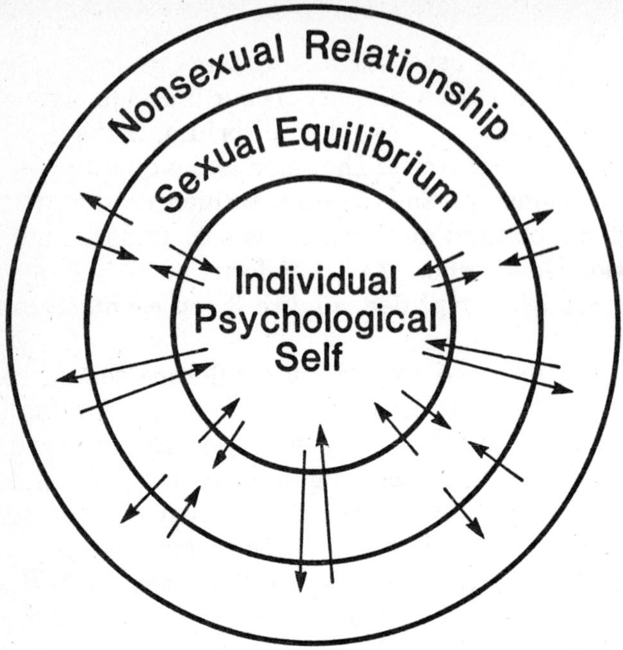

Fig. 3 Three contexts for understanding sexuality.
The influence of the cultural context is not shown here.

those of his partner (figure 4). The product of this interaction is the sexual equilibrium.

The accommodation to each other occurs immediately—partners instantly sense and react to all six sensual elements. Each person's perception of the other's reaction either produces sensual lovemaking or induces painful self-consciousness. The former is the prelude to sexual joy; the latter is an overture to serious problems.

Sexual life is difficult to understand, in part because we do not have the right words. Without this vocabulary, our under-

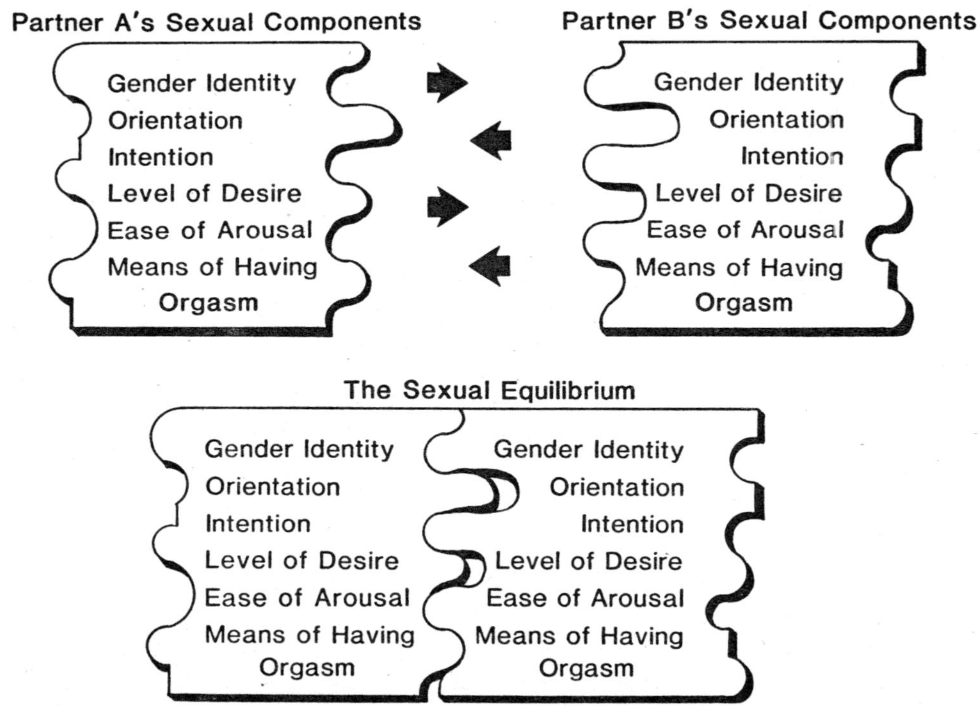

Fig. 4 The origins of the sexual equilibrium.

standing is necessarily incomplete. But to comprehend what happens in the bedroom, we have to know the characteristics of each partner and understand their interactions. For example, many people may have the characteristics of this psychologically healthy young woman:

> By the middle of her teenage years, Sue's sexual identity was well formed. She was entirely conventional or "normal"—both her gender role behavior and her gender identity were comfortably feminine. Her orientation was heteroerotic—that is, males attracted and excited her and she used their images during masturbation. Sue's sexual behavior, which began with necking at age sixteen, was heterosexual. Her mental and behavioral intentions have been peaceful and mutual. She has never been attracted to demeaning behavior with a partner; victimization does not excite her.
>
> During the last five years, Sue has had genital experiences in two relationships. Now twenty-five, she is confident that her sexual functioning is normal. She knows, for example, that she has sexual desire. At least once a week she thinks about having sex and feels genital arousal. When possible, these feelings and thoughts lead to sex with a partner or masturbation. Sue feels that sensuous experiences are an important part of a full life. In her two relationships, she was willing to have sex as long as she was not angry at her partner. She has no guilt about pleasure within a trusting relationship. These three elements of her sexual desire—drive, wish, and motive—have worked together nicely.
>
> Sue was generally quite easily aroused in both relationships. On a few memorable occasions, her entire body became erogenous. She has been orgasmic by hand and oral clitoral stimulation, but she prefers orgasms through intercourse and was regularly orgasmic in the female-on-top position. She has had orgasms in other positions when she or her partner provided simultaneous clitoral stimulation. Her sexual behavior has been emotionally satisfying except when her relationships were ending.

Even though Sue's sexual desire, arousal, orgasm, and emotional satisfaction have developed without problems and she is ready to have a sexually rewarding marriage, there is no guarantee she will attain it: The key is in the sexual equilibrium between herself and the man she plans to marry.

If Sue's husband has reasonably similar component characteristics, her sexual experience within marriage may begin on a fine plane and grow even better. However, if after the courtship, her husband's sexual drive appears only monthly, or his guilt over sexual pleasure leads him to avoid it or to be unable to fully relax, she may be bitterly disappointed. If his quick arousal to orgasm in the vagina frustrates and demoralizes her, she may lose much of her motivation to have sex with him. If he insists on having sex almost daily even when she is unwilling, her wish to please him may become exhausted. She may even find that her former robust sexual drive is dwindling. If he has trouble attaining orgasm, Sue's frustration may cause her to lose all interest in sexual behavior within this equilibrium.

There is no general explanation why some intimate interactions work and some do not. It is not always clear why some people can comfortably tolerate a partner with a low sexual drive, for instance, and others find it a profound insult to their gender identity and self-esteem. The fact is there are great differences in reactions to the way we behave sexually, and these differences play a major role in determining our sexual fate.

This is well illustrated by what is commonly referred to as premature ejaculation. Rapid ejaculation in the vagina is quite common among young men. Some women learn to pace themselves and react to their partner's orgasm with a surge of excitement. This surge leads to the woman's orgasm shortly after the man's. She is pleased to be so powerfully exciting, and her pleasure allows him to relax about how long he lasts in the vagina. Without performance pressures, he may gain more control over his excitement.

Another woman may react to the limited time for intercourse with annoyance and frustration. She feels she is a prisoner of her partner's inadequacy. The man senses this, feels helpless and anxious, and these feelings interfere with his development of ejaculatory control. The same component characteristic, rapid ejaculation in the vagina, can be found in happy as well as miserable sexual relationships.

It is not unusual for a man to believe it is the male's responsibility to "give" an orgasm to his partner. He may even insist that the woman have her orgasm during intercourse as a result of his thrusting. Anything short of this sexual goal he feels is a sign of his inadequacy. His thoughts center on themes such as "My penis is too small," "I'm not a real man—I'm worthless," "She doesn't love me." These powerful ideas may produce major tensions between the fearful man and his partner.

A better-informed man responds realistically to his partner's orgasmic patterns. He acts as though the woman has something to do with her own orgasm. He appreciates that his adequacy as a man is dependent on personal factors other than her orgasmic pattern. He even suspects that rather than "giving" her orgasms, he merely shares in the creation of a sexual equilibrium which facilitates or hinders it.

If a woman agrees with her partner's notion that her orgasmic response is inadequate, the couple will feel trapped by her inferiority as a lover. If she disagrees, tension will exist between them until the issue is discussed and settled. If her disagreement is unexpressed or never settled, the tension that accompanies lovemaking may eventually rob them of emotional satisfaction. When they accept her orgasmic pattern as legitimate, they can begin to get more enjoyment from their sex life.

Changes in the Sexual Equilibrium

Change is part of every long-standing sexual equilibrium as frequency, behavior, and myriad impediments to a healthy sexual life continue to evolve. Healthy equilibriums produce different kinds of experiences from one episode to another. When couples who have been together many years think about their sexual lives as always good, they usually are referring to pleasure. However, what has produced that pleasure has been subtly changing.

Long-time sexual relationships are affected by several influences: day-to-day fluctuations in sexual desire and arousability due to mood, health, and energy; variations in the quality of the nonsexual relationship; and the psychological and biological maturation of each person. There is no escape from these influences.

Sex is not always wonderful, it is not always terrible, it is not always just okay. The motives each partner brings to the bedroom differ somewhat with each experience. Each opportunity generates different degrees of desire, arousal, receptivity, and responsiveness. These subtleties make sexual behavior an adventure. Healthy sexual behavior is not predictable.

Doctor: Can you tell me about your sexual life?

Chuck: What can I say? It's fine, I guess. Everything works okay but sometimes it is better than others. Sometimes we make love, sometimes we just have sex.

Anita: We have two types of sex: a quickie when one of us—usually me—is too tired and the real thing when both of us are in the mood. Both are fun, but I prefer the real thing. Come of think of it, maybe there is a third kind. A couple times a year—usually when we are away from home and the kids, something incredible happens—we really take our time and do things we don't usually do.

Doctor: Like what?

Chuck: We will do everything we can think of: sex on the floor, standing, sitting. We have intercourse several times in an afternoon and exhaust ourselves. Isn't this what vacations are for? Anyway, these things never happen at home.

Why We Make Love When We Do

Why does sexual experience vary so much? For example, why do couples make love on the days and at the times that they do? The answer explains more about the sexual equilibrium and how it is sustained over many years through all its changes.

Three steps must recur so that a couple's sex life will continue. First, one partner must have a motive to make love. Second, the other person must cooperate. Third, the motivation and cooperation must be turned into mutual sexual excitement.

Motives to Make Love

On the surface, a motive to make love appears to be a simple matter, but it is not. Motives for lovemaking are often complicated, deceptive, and hidden from our awareness. Most of the time we just want to make love—we do not want to know why, and we do not always want to know why our partners are interested.

Motivation to make love often peaks when a couple is in the process of falling in love. For this brief period, individuals have trouble keeping their hands off each other. They cannot get enough of the marvelous sexual intimacy which deepens the psychological intimacy already established. People's motives for sexual behavior often decline after a profound loving bond has been established. Having accomplished the developmental task of finding an acceptable person to love who loves back, the couple moves on to other issues.

> I knew the honeymoon couldn't last forever. For the first three months or so, Chris and I made love three or four times a week. It seemed like there was nothing more wonderful, nothing more important. We even found ways to have sex during my period. Then I got busier on my job, Chris started graduate school, and we were making love only on weekends. Actually, I don't mind. I only worried that a young married couple like us ought to be making love more often.

After a couple has formed a relationship, mutual spontaneous passion no longer is the usual cause of lovemaking. Instead, passion is brought about by making love, by experiencing deeper love through nonsexual intimacy, or by repairing disagreements. Emotional distance due to the separateness of individuals' lives inevitably creeps in. One person has less tolerance for emotional distance than the other so he or she wants to make love in order to feel connected again—to reexperience the bond through sexual behavior. Then, feeling reassured, the partner is free again to pursue his or her life. A pattern of closeness followed by distance is subtly set up. Lovemaking temporarily ends the distance.

Sexual drive—that is, the spontaneous appearance of arousal or interest in lovemaking felt in the genitals—can induce the motive to make love in one partner. The frequency of a couple's sexual behavior depends upon each partner's sexual drives. In some couples, the partner with the higher drive determines how often they make love; in others, it is the partner with the lower drive. Couples whose bodies announce at the same time that they are interested are rare, and many partners do not even mention their fleeting arousal.

Sexual arousal and orgasm are pleasurable and most people want to repeat them simply because the experience is fun. This is often complicated, however, by social expectations for lovemaking. Many people harbor a figure in their minds representing the proper number of times to make love: "I think we ought to be doing it at least twice a week." This is their personal standard of normal sexual frequency. When the interval between sex goes beyond this standard, some people may want to make love to be "normal." "My wife often says that we have only made love once this week. Sometimes I think she is counting and wants to have sex not because she is horny, but because she is keeping up with the national average."

Sexual behavior has a marvelous capacity to substitute for words. Many find it easier to express affection and caring through making love than through saying "I love you." A pleasant sexual experience can celebrate the psychological intimacy and deepen the sense of togetherness. Couples use sex as a way of saying "I missed you" after a separation. Without words, sex reaffirms the pleasure of their bond, their oneness.

Sex is also an impressive way of wiping the slate clean of minor annoyances, irritations, and angers. It erases the unpleasantness and lets the partners reaffirm the integrity of their relationship. "We are still a couple!"

Love and closeness are not the only motives for sexual behavior. There is also the need to relieve feelings such as anxiety, worry, insomnia, anger, and disappointment. People may want to have sex because they are tense or having trouble falling asleep. Sex is a powerful distractor from minor everyday pain and stress. "Come on, you're so uptight—let's have a quickie and maybe you'll feel better."

Sexual excitement is an obvious reason for behaving sexually, but where it comes from may not always be apparent. Sometimes sexual drive announces itself through spontaneous genital arousal, sexual fantasies, and distracting attractions to others. Sometimes what passes for drive is the excitement that comes from watching, reading about, overhearing, or imagining the sexual behavior and excitement of others. Such voyeuristic arousal may be kept secret from partners. Partners are even less likely to learn about excitement that arises from lingering eye contact, conversations, flirtations, or unmistakably sensual interactions with others.

> A young man at an important crossroad in his marriage was struggling with the issue of fidelity. He had no complaints about his wife—it was just that there was an attractive colleague with whom he enjoyed working. Lately, the joking flirtations were becoming more serious and he was having erotic fantasies about her. Their business lunches were getting longer and more friendly. His sexual behavior with his wife increased considerably and was accompanied by thoughts of the co-worker. When his wife asked why they were making love so often lately, he told her, "I don't really know, I'm just horny, I guess." He eventually decided not to complicate his life. Others were invited to the working lunches and soon he and his wife were making love twice a week again.

Such diverse motives for lovemaking are in our minds and are often even more private than the intimacy of the sexual equilibrium.

Getting the Partner's Cooperation

The second step to sustaining sexual activity is getting the partner's cooperation. As with motives, this is not as simple as it sounds. First, one person must signal an interest in sex and then both people must negotiate for agreement. Signaling and negotiation often occur without words. One partner may send a message through his or her behavior—"I know she is interested in sex tonight because she put on perfume." A person may assume the partner will agree because he or she rarely refuses—"He always says yes to me." Partner consent may require social and physical interactions—"We spent the entire evening together at dinner and at the movie, so I knew it was possible."

But signaling and negotiating can be difficult for people who are shy about directly expressing their interest in making love. Masturbation, or even celibacy is easier than asking and being rejected. They may think they have sent a signal or two, but the message does not get through. There is no negotiation because the shy partner cannot effectively send a message of sexual desire. A husband and wife who had spent forty-two years with infrequent and unsatisfying lovemaking were reviewing how they communicated their desire to each other. The husband said it was not his style to just ask. He preferred to take a long shower, comb his hair, put on fresh pajamas and kiss her goodnight. If she was interested in sex, she wold kiss him back with more than a peck. He often went to sleep disappointed because she declined his offers. She was shocked upon hearing this. "My God, those were invitations to make love? We're a sorry couple!" I asked her how she signaled her interest to him. After a long explanation about how women her age were raised not to be forward, she giggled and explained that she turned on the little light on her dressing table only when she was interested. It was then his turn for shock.

One partner wants to have sex and effectively signals. The other is not in the mood. Under what conditions will the disinterest change into cooperation? Romance? Nagging? Sweet words? A plaintive look? Kissing? A promise of fellatio? A subtle threat? Every couple faces this challenge; some have enormous difficulty working it out.

Attaining Mutual Sexual Excitement

The final step in sustaining sexual activity is the creation of a high degree of excitement and orgasm in both partners. Partners must do more than just cooperate—they must become involved emotionally in the lovemaking.

To do this, both people need to clear their minds of other concerns and focus on the sensations that are occurring. Sexual play is an opportunity to enter the sensual realm and give up the usual sense of time. It is a feeling process, not a thinking process. Foreplay helps people make a transition from the thinking mode to the sensual mode, although this is not possible at every sexual opportunity. The sexual experience is most pleasant—wonderful, in fact, when both partners are fully able to concentrate on sensation. After a sensual experience, couples often look at the clock and are surprised how much time has passed.

Importance of the Sexual Equilibrium

The quality of healthy sexual experience continually changes because sexual motivation, partner cooperation, and sensual involvement are never the same. The sexual equilibrium is created from traits each partner brings to the relationship—gender identity, orientation, intention, desire, arousal, orgasm, and emotional satisfaction. The delicately balanced, ever-evolving interaction of these traits makes up the sexual equilibrium. It is the crucible in which sexual life is determined. If we understand these elements, we can more deeply understand sexual fulfillment or unhappiness.

Toward a Problem-Free Sexual Life

Our lives go better when we appreciate what is going on in them. It is important to sense the complexity of our sexual lives and act as though we are aware that:

- Three major forces determine our sexual experiences—our individual psychology, the quality of our nonsexual relationship, and our sexual equilibrium.
- Our sexual lives have a built-in capacity to change from episode to episode and over long periods of time.
- It is the interaction between partners that produces our sex life, not just one person's characteristics.
- Our motives for lovemaking are quite variable and highly private.
- Our partner's cooperation is crucial to our sexual life and must be carefully nurtured.

5

DEATH OF THE SEXUAL EQUILIBRIUM

As we have seen, our sexual lives exist in an ever-changing balance that can inhibit or enhance our sexual experiences. However, this equilibrium may grind to a complete halt and die although the partners are still capable of sexual excitement. When the sexual equilibrium has serious problems, sex usually becomes infrequent because the physical pleasures of arousal and orgasm are not powerful enough to override turmoil, disappointment, and pain. Couples are then at risk for sexual death. But if it occurs, it is usually a well-kept secret.

> "I'm forty-three years old and I don't know how long I can keep going sexually. My erection is already iffy and I don't often want to make love. Except for sex, we're happy in our marriage. Both of us have nice jobs, we're

healthy, our two children are great, and we have enough money. I know what the problem is, I know where it came from, but I can't do anything about it. Jane is harsh, she gets mad at me during sex. She is irritated by me. I don't last long enough or I'm not hard enough or I don't touch her in the right way—it's always something. We'll be in the midst of sex, I'll think things are going fine, and suddenly I hear, 'Why don't you do it this way?' I've learned not to ask her to stop yelling because she only gets more shrill and says, 'I'm not yelling!' Hell, I know when I'm being yelled at. It's a classic comedy scene, but it isn't funny. Jane grew up in a family that yelled all the time. When I visited them, I'd have a headache from all the picking and teasing. Her mother endlessly pestered her father, the poor guy, and her sisters screamed like banshees at the drop of a hat. Her parents are dead and, thank goodness, now I don't have to visit that house anymore!"

"Michael is impossible sexually. He's always nervous. I never know when he'll be hard, soft, fast, or anything. It's been this way from the beginning. He was a virgin at twenty-four. He has a low sex drive. He doesn't need sex like I do and he doesn't care that I do. He's too sensitive—if I sigh during sex he thinks I am complaining about him. I get mad because he won't do what I ask him to do or if he does, he quickly forgets and does it the old way again the next time. He's got a big sexual problem. Otherwise, he's a great guy, and I love him."

"Jane is never the cause of anything! It is always me or the kids or the waiter, whatever—I'm telling you, Jane, I'd have an easier time of it if you said things in a nice way. Why can't you say, 'I'd like it better here.' No, it's always, 'What is wrong with you!' or 'How many times must I tell you!' Maybe I don't want to make love because I don't know what I'm going to be hit with next. Jane, it isn't worth it."

Michael and Jane each briefly tried an affair. Michael was erect and appreciated. Jane was relieved to be with a man who wasn't rushed and uneasy. For about a month their new partners were satisfying, but they gave them up because the pain the affairs caused was greater than the pain from their sexual life. When their youngest child went from an "A" student to a "C-D" student in nine weeks, they knew it was time to stop.

Michael and Jane's uncomfortable sexual behavior persisted for many years. They kept hoping for better times, although they masturbated alone more frequently than they had sex together. Other couples might give up on such an unrewarding sexual relationship; their sexual equilibrium could disappear never to be revived. Indeed, Michael feared he was well on his way to sexual death.

The facts are quite clear: When a sexual equilibrium prematurely ends, a couple's sexual life withers. Therapists spend a large percentage of their time with such individuals and couples. And undoubtedly many others have given up sex and not come for help.

The truth about our sex lives is almost as closely guarded as the facts about our finances. Scientists meet many obstacles when trying to study sexual behavior: Sex is too private to discuss, vocabularies fall short of experience, many people lie about their sex lives, and many downplay the seriousness of their problems. Even more confusing, spouses sometimes cannot agree about what goes on in their bedroom. A man may say he is impotent; the wife insists he is not. A man may say his wife never has an orgasm; she is astounded at how wrong he is. A wife may say her husband ejaculates too fast; he denies it. A woman reports having sex three times last week; her partner insists it happened only twice.

In the 1988 Schein study mentioned in chapter two, several hundred adults filled out a questionnaire in a family doctor's waiting room. We discovered that 25 percent of these men and women, in all age groups, felt that they had significant sexual problems. In addition, half of them responded that they had sexual difficulties that they did not consider significant. Only one-fourth said that their sex lives presented no difficulties whatever.

A sexual equilibrium stops being active when a least one partner feels more comfortable avoiding sex. The other partner may not realize it, but the strong motive to make love that appeared early in the relationship can turn into a motive to avoid lovemaking. People in these situations say they want to make love; the truth, however, is that they are unwilling to bring their sexual bodies to their partners. They may not realize why, but they know they are unwilling. Such an asexual equilibrium may develop any time, whether a couple is young or has been together for many years.

Why Lovemaking Stops

Although the reasons the sexual equilibrium dies are unique to each couple, several general themes keep recurring. Among the newly married, sexual life may stop soon after one partner concludes that a disastrous mistake has been made in marrying the other. Before he or she realizes this, the motive to make love may have already inexplicably weakened. However, a more common reason for decreasing the frequency of sex is that there is nervousness in the sexual equilibrium. Persistent nervousness makes it impossible for partners to relax and concentrate on sensation. Some people think they cannot make love because of such problems as impotence, premature ejaculation, or contraction of the vagina. Actually, fear of their sensual selves keeps their motivation low and predisposes them to these specific sexual problems. Others with the same problems continue to make love, despite their difficulties.

Some couples, especially in middle age, stop making love because of nonsexual disagreements. If they have seldom been able to relax and enjoy their sexual equilibrium, problems in and out of the bedroom may become mixed together and hasten the death of their sex lives. This is what happened to Michael and Jane. Older people who have had long, satisfying sexual equilibriums often stop behaving sexually because of physical disease, medication, or effects of aging on the man's sexual drive and erection capacity.

The key element in all age groups is the motive to avoid lovemaking. When one partner develops a strong motive to avoid, the spouse's pleasure during the lovemaking disappears. Sex quickly becomes a mere mechanical act and soon it is not worth the effort. "I'd rather masturbate or simply forget it!" Some people can tolerate only a short period of disappointment before avoiding sexual behavior completely.

Joint Motive

Most couples who stop making love tell each other that it's only a temporary situation. Under the camouflage of their convincing statements, they make an unspoken agreement to avoid lovemaking; this marks the beginning of the end. The situation usually starts when some type of problem develops within the sexual equilibrium, such as low desire, fear of penetration, inability to tolerate arousal, or impotence. They may become demoralized after only a few months.

Whenever this couple anticipates sexual contact, one or both feel anxious, embarrassed, frustrated or angry. The partner without the problem feels unattractive, unloved, deprived, annoyed, and humiliated. Confused by the persistence of the difficulty, the problem-bearer feels responsible but helpless. "I'm tired of telling my wife I'm sorry I'm impotent." Sex becomes a dreaded experience because it makes them vulnerable to these unpleasant feelings. Since both partners really do aspire to a good sexual relationship, their self-protecting avoidance of sex is difficult for them to admit.

The couple enters into silent collusion to avoid sex. They are too busy, too tired, ill, preoccupied, or otherwise not in the mood. One partner's apparent hesitance allows the problem-bearer to ignore the real reason for avoiding sexual behavior. Each partner correctly blames the other for not wanting to have sex. Since it is not discussed, confronted, or effectively dealt with, sexual behavior becomes much less frequent and eventually ceases.

It seems logical to suppose that whatever caused the sexual problem in the first place—suppressed anger, guilt over an affair, depression—is the reason for the disappearance of sexual behavior. But this explanation is incomplete. It is the unspoken decision to avoid the unpleasantness of sex that leads to the end of sexual behavior—not the problem itself. Many couples continue to make love despite difficulties with desire, arousal, orgasm, or penetration, and some couples make love despite unresolved anger, an affair, or a depression.

Once stopped, sexual behavior may begin again under special circumstances—a vacation, a drunken evening, a large raise, the end of a big argument, the death of a parent. Most couples will quickly revert to avoidance, however, unless they acknowledge and try to understand the problem with their equilibrium.

Each partner in an asexual equilibrium may experience a surge of sexual interest in others. Fantasies increase; sometimes one or both persons seek new partners in an attempt to prevent the death of their sex lives. The unspoken message is "I want to be a sexual person with you or without you. I'm not going to allow myself to dry up!" Those whose morals will not let them take another person must content themselves with fantasies. They avoid sexually stimulating interactions and experiences because they find them too exciting, too guilt-provoking, and too dangerous. However, despite the wish to remain true to high standards, people in asexual equilibriums sometimes have affairs because living without intimacy can be a burden.

> After ten years of urging him to get help, fifty-year-old Marie convinced her husband that she was serious in her threat to leave him if he didn't see a therapist. He came to see me for help because of his lack of sexual interest. A year of their therapy only resulted in his going through the motions of sex. Sex was anxiety-provoking for him and insulting to her. After their therapy, her emotional state changed: She no longer had any interest in her husband as a sexual partner. She quietly set about having a sex life outside of marriage. Without words, the couple agreed to a new arrangement.

> For a decade, she protected his social role as husband and he never discussed her whereabouts on her nights out with her girlfriends.

One-sided Motive

When one partner's refusal to have sex ends the couple's sexual life, the other partner becomes the victim of the refusal. After three consecutive failures, a man stopped trying to obtain an erection with his wife. The wife initially remained silent because she did not want to hurt his feelings. Their sex life stopped, and six years passed without any discussion of their situation.

One-sided motives are not invariably caused by sexual problems. They are often due to the loss of respect for the partner. "When he lost all his money at the race track again, I lost all respect for him." "When she punished our son so unfairly, I lost my taste for her." A woman spent two years avoiding sex with her husband, whom she described as "insensitive" in and out of bed. She eventually refused him outright. He continued to occasionally ask, but after months of negative responses, he gave up.

Serious illness, either physical or mental, provides another one-sided psychological motive to avoid sexual behavior. The motive may arise in the healthy or the sick spouse.

> After years of regular and mutually satisfying sex, a stroke left a retired physician unable to use one side of his body. He had difficulty dressing himself, writing, controlling his emotions, and walking without an appliance. Although he was potent, medically stable, off medications, and able to interact with his family, his wife suddenly avoided sexual behavior. Her explanation was, "He is not the man he was. He has to be fixed up after he dresses himself. He's not healthy!"

> A fifty-seven-year-old woman with a worsening cough learned she had lung cancer. She continued to feel relatively well for seven months until she rapidly deteriorated six weeks before her death. Although sex used to

occur at least weekly, the first sexual episode after the diagnosis was the last. She wanted to have sex for as long as possible, but it seemed inappropriate to her husband. He knew she was dying. He was mourning for her and could not be with her in the same way. He feared having thoughts about her death during sex. Neither wanted to discuss her illness too much. His desire for sex with anyone disappeared. It was all that he could do to work, come home, and be with her.

It is important to note that throughout a spouse's serious, even terminal illness, other people behave sexually as long as possible.

A man with stomach cancer that had spread to his brain was having seizures and episodes of coma during his final month of life. During his last stay at home, he awoke with an erection and he and his wife made love. In the hospital before he lapsed into his final coma, he asked his wife to caress his penis. She gladly responded.

The ill spouse can be the one who decides to avoid sex. Despite interest on her husband's part and her quick return to strength, a woman with an excellent prognosis was so mortified by her mastectomy that she avoided any sexual interactions with her husband for over a year. Before she could respond to him, she had to deal with the emotional impact of her surgery.

People react to severe health problems, disfigurement, and impending death in various ways. In spite of weakness, weight loss, or the effects of medication on erections or orgasmic capacity, some couples continue to make love together until the end. For them, sex is reassuring, loving, a distraction from their misery, a means of maintaining self-esteem, and one more confirmation of the integrity of their bond.

Long-standing Avoidance of Sex

From a sexual perspective, the purpose of childhood and adolescence is to develop the capacity to enjoy adult sexual dimensions of living. These include sexual curiosity, masturbation as a means of learning about oneself, and enjoyment of increasingly intimate partner sexual behavior. The basic developmental task is to accept the body and its pleasures as something valuable. In doing this, young people have to learn how sex can both enhance and adversely influence their lives.

Most people progress toward these goals during adolescence and reach them during their twenties. Those who do not attain these goals develop a motive for avoiding sexual behavior. Their intense anxiety during physical intimacy, even with someone they trust, robs their new sexual equilibrium of its healing opportunities. Sometimes sexually anxious people had blunted psychological development. They may not remember having any sexual curiosity or desire, masturbating or being interested in physical intimacy. Usually, however, their lack of desire stems from a long-standing inability to acknowledge sexual discomfort. Their minds have blocked out the desire in order to avoid anxiety.

> Tony and Myrna had been unable to have intercourse during their two year marriage. He claimed that he never was interested in sex, never masturbated, and had no previous sexual experiences. He changed his mind within several weeks of following the therapist's suggestion to undertake a series of intimate touching exercises. His initial enjoyment of general body touching became overwhelming anxiety when he was asked to caress his wife's genitals. He then realized that his disinterest was protecting him from fear. Eventually it was learned that one of the sources of this fear was his repeated sexual play with a female babysitter when he was in the second grade. She fondled his genitals and taught him to reciprocate. After talking about this for several weeks, he was able to caress his wife with more ease and interest.

The tendency to blame the partner for a problem within the sexual equilibrium rather than to acknowledge one's own contribution is a forerunner of sexual death. This tendency occurs more often in people who are fearful of sexual intimacy. Whether they are not aware of this pattern, or they know about it but give in to it anyway, the impact is just as destructive.

Consequences of Sexual Problems

Blaming one's partner leads to anger and confusion about who contributes what to the couple's pain. Michael and Jane made no progress and almost ruined their good nonsexual relationship because they could not calmly discuss their personal contributions—they always wanted to list the other person's faults. Their discomfort in the early phases of their relationship was not unusual, but they dealt with it in a destructive way. There are thousands of Michaels and Janes, people who do not learn how to help their spouses feel more comfortable. However, this is not the inevitable outcome of sexual nervousness. Sometimes the sexual equilibrium works.

> A thin woman with a chronic cough, as well as chest, finger, and toe deformities had always worried about her "puniness." Thoughts of sex during her premarital years frightened her and were invariably linked to concerns about her unattractiveness. "No one will want me!" When she was twenty-two, she became engaged to a man who found her kindness, sensitivity to others, and sense of humor irresistible. After six months of marriage, she had no sexual difficulties and no time to worry about her appearance. When asked about the dramatic change from her earlier guilt over occasional masturbation and uncertainty whether physical pleasure was religiously justified, she said, "He thinks I'm just fine!"

Achieving a mutually satisfying sexual equilibrium is an adult developmental step to be cherished. A vital emotional nurturing comes from sexual behavior—our sexual equilibrium is worth protecting. Persistent sexual problems threaten people with the loss of self-esteem and an increased emotional distance from each other. Sexual problems have consequences. One of the most serious, as we have seen, is the premature death of sexual behavior.

Toward a Problem-Free Sexual Life

To maintain reasonably regular sexual activity within a relationship:

- We must find it in our best interests to make love.
- We must be able to deal with sexual nervousness, disappointment, and anger by discussion rather than avoidance.
- We must realize that our self-esteem, sense of closeness as a couple, sense of individual attractiveness, and fidelity are at risk when we avoid sex.
- We must be able to admit our contributions to a problem rather than quickly cataloguing what our partner does wrong.
- We must realize that our view of our partner determines how sexually comfortable he or she can be with us.

6

THE ELEGANCE OF SEXUAL DESIRE

Sexual desire seems to be a periodic bodily event like hunger for food, but it is indeed far more. It is a force that pushes us toward some individuals and away from others. It reflects our deepest privacy and signals changes in our inner world. Much of our essence as human beings can be seen in our sexual desire. Who we are, how valuable we feel, what we want with our partners, and how well we function sexually are delicately woven into its elegant simplicity.

Although everyone seems to know what sexual desire is, scientists have for years been frustrated by the inability to measure it. Many of the intricate pieces that comprise desire are known—the fundamental mystery is how the mind integrates these pieces.

For most of this century, the Western world has been influenced by Freud's theory that sexual desire is the result of the stirrings of an instinct called "libido." Since sexual feelings are an almost universal part of psychological experience, libido became a common explanation for both sexual and nonsexual matters. The sexual instinct was said to be sublimated, substituted, inhibited, expressed, suppressed, repressed, and unconscious. The resulting sexual behavior has been described as obsessive, compulsive, inverted, perverted, distorted, regressed, acted out, and, occasionally, as normal. Until recently, this explanation was the dominant view of sexuality as well as psychological development. Today we understand that this is too simplistic.

What is Sexual Desire?

Sexual desire is not just an instinct but a complex need that varies in intensity. It is a mental force, an energy that may appear before lovemaking begins and may accompany sexual arousal. Sexual desire only explains the tendency to behave, not the actual sexual behavior.

This view comes from my observations made over many years with people seeking help for their patterns of desire. Usually they describe too little sexual desire, but some complain of too much, and others are distressed by its unpredictable arrivals and departures. I have learned from patients who have talked freely about their experience and now understand that sexual desire is the psychological energy that precedes and accompanies arousal and accounts for our tendencies to behave sexually.

Although this energy is often baffling in its presence, absence, and intensity, it has a fundamental pattern that is well known. Health, well-being, good fortune, and inner contentment increase our tendency to be sexual. Desire is stimulated by joy, exhilaration, and personal triumph, and diminished by illness, misfortune, disappointment, depression, and a sense of failure.

Elements of Sexual Desire

Sexual desire is not merely a biological need. It is the interaction of three elements—drive, wish, and motive (illustrated in figure 5). The mind integrates these elements and produces something we know as sexual desire. It is a common mistake to confuse the three elements with sexual desire itself. In the examples that follow, the differences between drive, wish, and motive are emphasized despite the fact that they actually blend into one another.

> Elizabeth has become very frustrated with her husband's lack of sexual appetite. Two years ago she married a wonderful man. She had no complaints about their love-

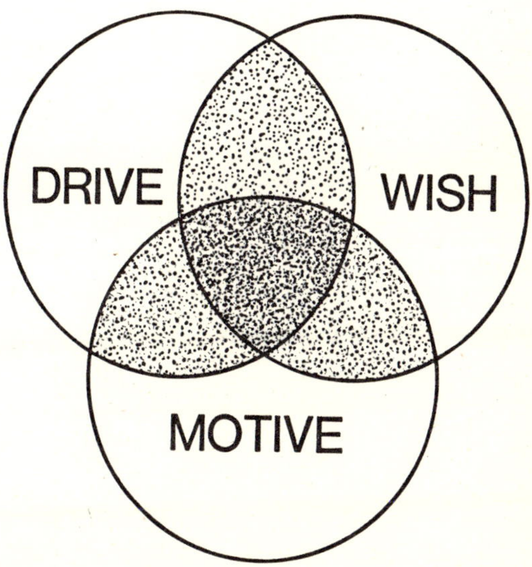

Fig. 5 Three elements of sexual desire.

making except for its infrequency of every three to four weeks. Her husband maintains that he cannot make love more often because he has to first feel horny. He began masturbating at age twenty and did it six or so times per year (drive). She told me that she expected in the early years of marriage (wish) to make love at least as often as she had masturbated, but she sometimes wants to make love daily because she loves him so much (motive). She feels aroused two or three times per week (drive). Lately, however, she has not even wanted to make love because she is so angry that he has not responded to her invitations (motive).

Allan has avoided lovemaking with his wife for many years. He claims he wants it to be different and often tells her he wants to make love (wish). However, he has no desire for her (motive). He masturbates weekly or so in response to spontaneously feeling excited (drive) or flirting with someone. He has an active sex life when he is out of town (motive).

Rose, who had a satisfying sex life with her husband during their forty-six years of marriage until his death six months ago, dreams about sex and occasionally notices that she feels excited for a few minutes without apparent reason (drive). She was greatly offended by a friend's sexual invitation when she was visibly grieving. She told him she did not want to have sex with anyone else because it would spoil the cherished memories of her husband (wish). Two months later, however, she responded with pleasure to his invitation (motive).

Sexual Drive

Most teenagers notice that they periodically become sexually excited for no apparent reason. They may feel genital tingling, become sensitive to attractive individuals, have erotic fantasies or dreams, masturbate, or seek out others for sex. Sudden sexual preoccupation can capture the mind and prevent concentration on other elements of living.

> "There I was studying for my calculus exam and getting a lot done when all of a sudden I started thinking of Brad. Brad's smile, Brad's shoulders, Brad in his bathing suit. There was no way I could study. Once again, I was on fire. I told my friends I had to take a nap. God, I can get so horny so fast!"

Some notice that these spontaneous experiences of arousal occur regularly—daily, weekly, or twice a week. Others find their sexual drive manifestations have no predictability. Since teenagers are also easily excited by visual and interpersonal impressions, the combination of sexual stimulation from within and outside the body may make them feel they are not in control of themselves.

When Freud suggested a sexual instinct, in 1905, its source was not understood. Now it is known that the hormone called testosterone is necessary to produce sexual drive in both males and females. There is evidence that a particular small region of the brain is the sexual drive center. Many medications are known to interfere with this center. Some are now used to treat people with too much sexual drive and there may soon be a medication to improve sexual drive.

After a vigorous beginning during late adolescence and young adulthood in both sexes, the frequency and intensity of spontaneous genital tingling, sexual fantasies, sensitivity to erotic cues in the environment, masturbation, and partner-seeking behaviors gradually decline to the point of virtual disappearance in late old age. Sexual excitability also diminishes, but does not disappear. The source of these changes is not understood, but may be due to the loss of cells in the sexual drive center and a decrease in the amount of testosterone in the body tissues.

When and to what extent the sex drive declines varies considerably from person to person. Despite the decline of drive, sexual behavior continues, and may even increase for some individuals throughout adulthood because the other elements, wish and motive, contribute to the tendency to behave sexually. Sexual drive is only the biological element of sexual desire; it is not the most important element of the three.

Sexual Wish

The sexual wish is the social aspect of sexual desire. Many older people whose sexual drives are infrequent and weak still have a strong wish to behave sexually. It is this wish that initiates their sexual behavior. The many reasons for this wish were established over their earlier years of adulthood:

- It makes them feel good physically
- It makes them feel loved, valued, or important
- It makes them feel vital or energetic
- It makes them feel masculine or feminine
- It makes them feel normal and useful
- It makes them feel connected to another and less alone
- It makes them feel they are pleasing their partners

Young people with frequent, strong, unexpected arousal and high excitability may nonetheless *wish* not to have sex. This wish, based on thoughts, ideas, and values, causes them to not express sexual feelings or to express them with discomfort. Who fails to remember the awkwardness of this time of life when one feels all revved up with no place to go? Young people may have many reasons for avoiding sex:

- They feel emotionally unready
- They do not know exactly how to do it
- They are frightened of experiencing intense excitement
- They do not like anyone enough yet
- They fear pregnancy
- They are afraid of getting AIDS or another venereal disease
- They have a strong conviction it is morally wrong
- They do not wish to disgrace or displease their parents

Sexual Motive

Sexual drives are physical while sexual wishes are based in thoughts. "I want to have sex!" may be either the body or the mind speaking. However, sexual desire is not simply an interaction between intellectual ideas and biological drives. The most important element, especially in adulthood, is motivation. When motive says, "I want to have sex," the person is emotionally willing to bring his or her body to the sexual experience.

When sexual life works well, drives, wishes, and motives all push in the same direction. An excited teenager who considers masturbation a legitimate way of removing spontaneous sexual arousal, can restore calm to his or her psyche, and then continue with other activities. But sexual behavior is not always the product of the three elements pushing together. A teenager who considers masturbation a terrible sin, punishable by present and future consequences, may have drive pushing in one direction and wish and motive pushing in another. Masturbation brings relief of sexual tensions but is followed by guilty tensions. The psyche is not calmed by the experience.

No one feels like making love all the time. The energy of sexual desire fluctuates between the extremes of urgency to behave sexually and rejection of sexual behavior. Rather than occupying the extremes, most people's lives are spent hovering around mild interest or changeable indifference. The most powerful influence on sexual desire is the emotional element—motive, not drive or wish.

In the chapter on the sexual equilibrium, the motive to make love was discussed in terms of what is accomplished by lovemaking. Now a more fundamental question about motive will be considered: "Why do some people bring their bodies less frequently than others to the sexual experience?"

Some people with sexual drive and the intellectual wish for lovemaking do not seem to actually want to make love. Long periods pass without sexual behavior, even when the partner is willing. Other people do not like to spend much time without making love. Sexual activity seems to them to be the cornerstone of their adult pleasures; life without frequent sexual activity is unthinkable. These individuals do not necessarily have high sexual drives. They value the sexual experience and have organized their private lives around it.

The tendency to organize oneself as readily willing or unwilling to engage in sex is rooted in the very fabric of personality. It is not certain how this aspect of our character is determined. There are at least one biological and four psychological factors that influence the predisposition—level of drive, sexual identity, past relationships, the current nonsexual relationship, and the patterns of self- and partner-regulation. These factors are inseparable.

Level of sexual drive. Humans can belong to low, moderate, and high sexual drive groups, but this is probably only partly correct. The categorization does have some truths, however. Those with high-drive levels become interested in sexual activity earlier in life and have more frequent activity for more years then those with low-drive levels. The sexual drive center is probably set at different levels from one person to another, much like a thermostat. Unlike a thermostat, however, no one knows how to reset it. As we reflect on a ten or twenty-year period, it often seems that the activity of the sexual drive center can be measured by the time that elapses between one orgasm and the time when the body asks for another. There are some people whose bodies speak monthly or less (low), once or twice weekly (moderate), or every other day or more (high).

The frequency and intensity of the sexual drive during adolescence and adulthood may have much to do with the development of sexual comfort. Those with frequent sexual drives have many more opportunities to grow comfortable with their sexual selves than those with infrequent drives. This may be a blessing or a curse depending on whether the developing personality is able to cope with the frequent bodily demand for sexual tension release. A fifteen-year-old with a high sex drive who is comfortable with his emerging heterosexual self may masturbate in privacy four or five times a week with ease and comfort. A similarly aged high-sex-drive homoerotic boy who has trouble coping with the sense of alienation may be quite distressed because his sexual feelings are a reminder that he is different.

Sexual identity. It is not possible to have sexual feelings without being aware of one's gender identity, orientation, and intention. The sexual experience is a confrontation with the self in which one's longings for a particular activity (intention), type of person (orientation), or experience of oneself (gender identity) are revealed. When the transsexual male is aroused, he wants, with all his heart, to be a female. The homoerotic woman longs for another woman. The excited masochist imagines being beaten and humiliated.

Those with unconventional sexual identities have a powerful psychological predicament—they must accept themselves. They either achieve comfort with their longings or experience dismay and conflict. People who are not able to accept themselves may be unwilling to bring their bodies to the sexual experience.

> Joseph, a thirty-six-year-old homoerotic man who was openly known among his family and friends as gay, had two brief impersonal sexual encounters in his life. He was baffled by his inability to ejaculate but was even more mystified by his avoidance of sex. During his infrequent masturbation, he often felt he was letting his father down by thinking of men. He felt "incredibly ashamed" during his two partner experiences.

Those with conventional sexual identities also have to accept the fact that they are sexual beings. This can be a difficult task for heterosexuals because many young people are not certain that it is correct to behave sexually—they have not yet accepted their sexual selves.

The discomfort from this lack of acceptance may lead a person to decide not to engage in sexual fantasies or behaviors. He or she may soon forget having made the choice, and then wonder about not being motivated toward sexual activities. Partners will eventually perceive this person as having a sexual inhibition or motivation not to be sexual.

> A forty-year-old recently married man sought help because his wife was in great pain over his sexual disinterest. "Sam is always busy with projects, but I'm never one of them." In therapy, Sam was eventually able to remember that when he was about twenty, he talked

> sexy to unknown women on the phone while he masturbated. He did this four times, and was very uncomfortable about it. "But, with the help of prayer and my electronics hobby, I was able to stop making those calls. Thank God that never came back to my mind. I haven't even thought about it in years."

Influence of past relationships. Past relationships have a significant influence on how motivated we are toward sexual behavior. Examples of the good and the troubled past creeping into the present cannot be ignored. Children raised in fortunate psychological circumstances, protected by loving parents who respect their individuality, are apt to participate in adult intimacies with the expectation of being treated well by their partners. Adults leaving a destructive marriage often worry that the new, pleasant partner may turn into a monster. Perceptions of our lovers are influenced by our previous intimate experiences. Past relationships produce trust or suspicion, warmth or defensiveness. It is not difficult to imagine a young child who was sexually abused by her stepfather being "irrationally" frightened at age twenty by sexual intimacy with a fine young man, even though she has no conscious memory of what happened to her when she was four.

Quality of nonsexual relationship. Willingness to have sex is linked with our feelings at the moment about our partners. The ease with which we enter into a sexual experience fluctuates considerably because our regard for our partners often changes subtly. If a person feels the partner is "always" self-centered and emotionally unavailable, willingness to be sexual likely diminishes. Many individuals no longer respect and love their partners. When love and respect cease, so does interest in sex with that person.

> A couple in their late twenties were not sure whether to continue their marriage. Laura felt her husband's personality was superficial: "He's a real showboat—a politician." She felt she could not relate to a man whose pleasures, temperament, and concept of fun were so different from her less social, more contemplative style. She did not know how their earlier intimacy had disap-

peared. Peter felt that no matter what he did, no matter how hard he tried, it didn't help. He felt hopeless that she could never love him as he deserved and he gradually withdrew. The more he withdrew, the more convinced she was of his superficial personality. The more she commented on his personality, the more hopeless he became about being loved by her. Although each stated that they experienced drive and wished to make love, they managed intercourse only once or twice a year for five years.

Patterns of self- and partner-regulation. Another factor explaining our sexual motives is how we regulate ourselves sexually. An aroused person has only a few options to deal with excitement: wait until the feelings and thoughts go away, force an interest in something else, masturbate, or have sex with a partner. The latter two are sexual ways of relieving tension and restoring internal calm. They are means of regulating the self through sexual behavior.

Orgasm can be useful in dealing with nonsexual disruptions of psychological comfort. It can distract a person from mild sadness or anger, induce sleep when worried, temporarily calm anxiety, or relieve premenstrual tension. A general willingness to behave sexually—that is, liking sex—implies comfort with a wide range of motives for seeking sex.

During the single years, a person may learn to regulate various feeling states through masturbation. When two individuals become a couple, each person has a more complex opportunity. Both may learn to regulate the self through the other and learn to cooperate with the partner for his or her self-regulation. When a person has had no experience with masturbation and has not learned to regulate the self through sexual behavior, cooperation with a partner who expects to use sexual behavior for self-regulation may be difficult. Since a sizable proportion of women do not remember teenage masturbation (according to many studies, including a discussion found in Sarrel and Sarrel's book), many young women cannot understand why their partners want to have sex so often. They do not intuitively grasp that their partners use sex to regulate emotions other than arousal. Some men use sexual behavior and their easily attained arousal as a distraction from their sadness, worry, or frustration.

Two people who agree to make love may not know that they have very different reasons for doing so. Those who maintain the illusion that their sexual behavior occurs only in response to romantic sexual feelings may feel betrayed when they discover their partner's motives. Here are a few examples of motivations for sex that may briefly operate within a regular sexual relationship. Some are for self-regulation:

- to ease the private pain of tomorrow's business trip
- to rid the self of the excitement stimulated at the office
- to substitute for words to express joy over being reunited

Others are for partner regulation:

- because the partner wants to
- because the partner has been insulted or disappointed today
- to convey the feeling that the partner is still valued in spite of mastectomy or stroke

Still others may be more mutual:

- because they like to have sex in as many cities that they visit as possible
- because they are simultaneously feeling affectionate and loving

Some, however, are purely manipulative:

- to minimize any suspicion of an ongoing affair
- to have another conquest

A person who is generally willing to behave sexually understands that having sex is all right for many reasons. Frequent sexual behavior within an established sexual equilibrium reflects the idea that partners can use each other to regulate themselves, although they may not know this is going on. This idea is not acceptable to everyone.

Cycle of Couplehood

Every culture searches for potions that increase sexual desire and cause more sexual behavior. Although there is a great deal of folklore about aphrodisiacs, no substance has been scientifically shown to perform the sought-after magic. The best means of increasing sexual involvement occurs from forming and maintaining relationships.

The establishment of a new intimate relationship, whenever it occurs in life, generates sexual desire. During new intimacies, the individual identities of the lovers are being reformed in terms of the other. No longer is the person purely individual; the self is replaced by a sense of oneness with the other. "It was very exciting—we kept discovering so many things we had in common, so many ways we just fit perfectly."

A slight degree of emotional distance between the couple generates desire. The sense of oneness is not perfectly stable; two people have to nurture their bond to keep the sense of oneness. Talking intimately, spending time together, intuitively understanding each other, and having sexual relations all increase the sense of oneness. When these are lacking, distance between them may grow and trigger sexual desire in one partner. This is a delicate matter because during the early days of emotional distance, the wish and motive for sex may be great but if the distance lasts too long, anger may erase desire. "We had everything going for us, but then he started getting really preoccupied with his work, so we lost touch. When he finally moved me up on his priority list, he had moved down on mine." Some couples fluctuate between too much loneliness and too much intimacy. Too much distance, independence, or aloneness provokes sexual desire. . . . which reaffirms the sense of oneness. . . . which allows for more distance. . . . which provokes the need to briefly return for more closeness. In chapter four, this closeness-distance-closeness pattern was presented as an example of why a person may want to make love.

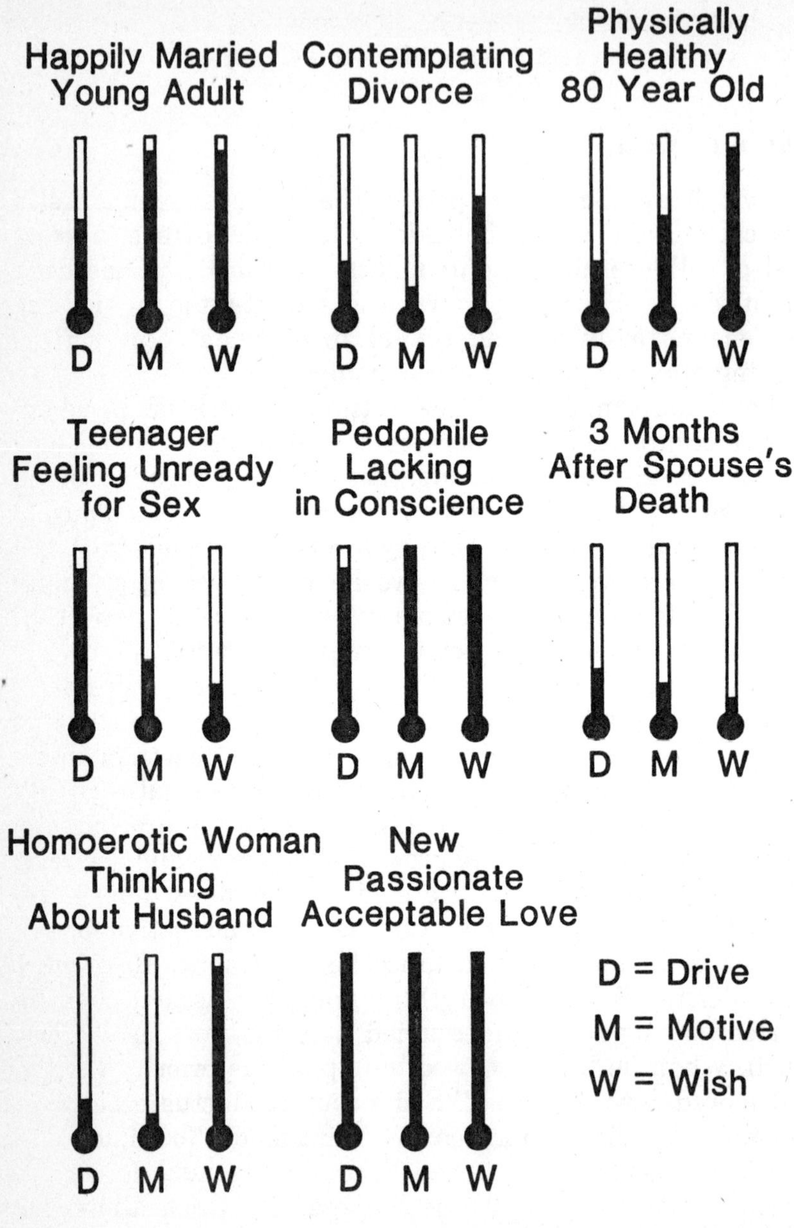

Fig. 6 Several combinations of the elements of desire.

Sexual Desire and Arousal

What is the relationship between sexual desire and arousal? First, we can reconsider what we know about the nature of sexual desire. It is the psychobiologic energy that precedes and accompanies sexual arousal, and accounts for the tendency to behave sexually. The energy of desire fluctuates because the three elements that comprise it—drive, wish, and motive—are changeable (see figure 6). These biological, social, and psychological elements interact to produce desire. They are also fueled by our sexual identity, our perceptions of how much we love and trust our partners, by the respect or adoration of our partners, our ability to regulate ourselves and our partners, and the extent to which our past relationships are woven into the present.

Sexual arousal is an emotion that simultaneously exists in the realms of psychological feeling and bodily experience. There is a complicated two-way relationship between sexual desire and sexual arousal. At first glance, desire simply leads to arousal, but this is not the entire sequence. Whatever arouses us—drive, watching people make love, being caressed—arousal increases the motive to want sex. The increased motive for sex then interacts with the wishes, "Do I want this? Am I ready? Is this okay with me?" Depending upon the answers, arousal either proceeds or diminishes. If wish and motive work together, arousal increases, inhibitions lessen, and orgasm eventually occurs. If wish and motive are in opposition, arousal lessens.

Arousal from any source provokes desire, at least briefly. Desire from any source makes arousal quicker and more intense. Sexual desire is not initially necessary for sexual arousal to occur. The caressing of foreplay, the act of intercourse, or a particular fantasy can enable arousal to orgasm in a person who had little or no sexual desire at the beginning of the sexual behavior.

Sexual desire is not the same as arousal, yet much sexual desire is the result of an early form of arousal. Arousal and desire stimulate each other and often with such speed that they seem to be the same event.

Toward a Problem-Free Sexual Life

We need to understand key ideas about sexual desire to more clearly understand ourselves and our partners:

- Sexual desire is not one indivisible mental or physical phenomenon.
- It consists of three basic interacting elements which sometimes work together, and sometimes against one another.
- When drive, wish, and motive work in sync, the ease and intensity of arousal is apt to be at a high point.
- Much of sexual life is conducted in some degree of conflict between these three elements.
- No satisfactory means of measuring desire has ever been devised and no one is able to fully understand its mechanisms, but happiness, contentment, and trust seem to be vital ingredients.

7

APPRECIATING MASTURBATION

The first outward sign of sexual desire in most people's lives is the act of masturbation. Sigmund Freud shocked the world around 1900 by observing that children had sexual feelings, interests, and behaviors. His views undermined the widespread belief that sexual thoughts began to appear in the mind of the adolescent. His research confirmed that sexual desire becomes part of the personality. The research of Freud's daughter, Anna, confirmed that young children feel sexual excitement, and that sexual desire is an important part of personality development. Her work, along with many others', suggested that an adult's sexual behavior may be directly influenced by how he or she dealt with childhood sexual excitements. A century ago, this example would not have made any sense.

> Brian, an impotent twenty-two-year-old who acknowledged masturbating several times a year beginning at age sixteen, recalled in therapy a pleasing bedtime ritual. In his sixth year, he was troubled by the impending breakup of his parents' marriage and his father's disappearance from his life. He recalled that his sadness and worry were often soothed by his mother's backrubs. When he was not upset, however, the backrubs generated genital excitement and erections which led to his feeling anxious and guilty about these private pleasures with his mother. The image of his mother's caressing his back lingered in Brian's mind for years, returned during his adolescent masturbation and made him feel sex was dangerous and not for everyone. As an adult, he was convinced that he possessed a low sex drive on the basis of his biology, but after recalling his feelings of excitement during childhood he began to doubt his theory.

Since all children have the ability to create or relieve excitement through masturbation, why will some indulge in it and others not?

Nineteenth-century American and European attitudes toward masturbation were decidedly negative, according to Tristram Engelhardt. Masturbation was considered evil and a source of physical disease, he writes. Even physicians believed that it produced the legendary warts and acne as well as tuberculosis, migraine headaches, anemia, birth defects, sterility, and impotence. Members of the medical community appealed to parents to prevent their children from endangering their physical and emotional health while, at the same time, American health faddists traveled the country warning teenagers and adults to desist from the vile practice of dissipation and self-abuse. Self-appointed experts recommended pelvic appliances to prevent access to the genitals, and a few zealous physicians even removed the clitoris to stop the practice.

Western antimasturbation rhetoric has quieted during this century. Now masturbation is considered so normal that its complete absence in a teenager is as worrisome as its presence was eighty years ago. Personal discomfort has not disappeared in response to cultural and parental enlightenment, however. Every child has at least a brief private struggle with bodily excitement, not only because of the remnants of nineteenth-century thinking in many parents, but also because of the socially forbidden wishes that accompany excitement.

Masturbation is known to occur during the first year of life and to continue throughout life. An eight-month-old, an eighteen-year-old, and an eighty-year-old do not masturbate in the same way, of course, but their masturbatory acts have the common ingredients of rhythmic stimulation of one's own body parts, tension generation and release, intense concentration, and pleasure.

The specific body part involved varies with age and personal preference. The infant begins to demonstrate these four characteristics with the mouth and moves on to the genitals, and rarely, the anus, umbilicus, or ears. Infantile and childhood masturbation are not tied to orgasm as is adolescent and adult masturbation. Orgasm may occur much earlier in girls than boys who usually cannot ejaculate until puberty.

Roles of Masturbation

Although masturbation plays divergent roles at different times in our lives, each of these roles promotes self-sufficiency. Masturbation is autonomy. Aladdin, the lucky boy in the *Tales of the Arabian Nights,* possessed a magic lamp that, when rubbed, would summon a genie to do his bidding. A psychoanalytic interpretation of this enchanting story suggested by Marcus and Frances was that the magic lamp is none other than the penis or clitoris. Rubbing the lamp, the physical side of masturbation, enables self-regulation of bodily and emotional feelings while the fantasies, the genie, permits the person to have his or her way. There is nothing in reality that cannot be briefly changed through fantasy—hunger is fed, victims undo their humiliation, spurned love is requited, the short become tall, the plain become gorgeous. The masturbatory retreat to wish-fulfilling unreality helps us to cope better with the harsher world outside our minds.

Early Childhood

The first role masturbation plays in life is to relieve distress. Infants naturally cope with hunger, discomfort, and fear by stimulation of their lips and mouths with nipples, teething rings, rattles, blankets, or other available objects until the distress is removed or they fall asleep. This behavior is reflexive; it is not taught. It does not feel right to most of us to think of this intense sucking of infants and toddlers as masturbation. However, this endearing behavior meets the four criteria and is, at the very least, its forerunner. When nerves to the genitals become better developed around nine months of age, the same intense, persistent, rhythmic stimulation will focus on the clitoris or penis. By the early part of the second year, the child usually has several body locations for self-regulation—the always accessible mouth and thumb, and the less accessible genitals.

Regardless of the body part selected, the child is soothing itself. Intense stimulation decreases its absolute dependence upon care givers and provides the child its first opportunity for autonomy. Many parents are relieved to realize that their child can briefly soothe itself while they are getting a bottle, answering the phone, or finishing some other activity.

Masturbation also has a role to play in the toddler's development of positive self-regard. Learning to like, value, and protect ourselves begins early in life and is crucial to the development of stable psychological health. Being able to give ourselves physical pleasure is part of this process. Physical pleasure helps to create the body image—rhythmic stimulation is one way to discover the body's physical limits. The endless explorations of fingers, toes, genitals, rattles, crib slats, mother's breast, and father's glasses help the infant distinguish its separateness from others, and understand the differences between itself and inanimate objects.

The ideal result of self-soothing, giving oneself pleasure,

and exploring the environment is that the child feels good about him or herself. If bodily pleasure can be generated when the child wants it, the child tends to think of herself as a "Good-Me." When parents smack their son's hands every time he touches his genitals, he may think of himself as a "Bad-Me."

Sometime during the second year, spontaneous and localized genital feelings occur. Before this time, genital sensations are externally stimulated by the child's own bodily explorations and caregivers' diaper changing and bathing. The child comes to recognize that the genitals can feel good on their own. Parents should take note of this by saying that touching the genitals feels good and is fine to do as long as it is done in private.

It may take years to distinguish the truly spontaneous genital sensations—sexual drive manifestations—from those that occur in response to interactions with others, but both sources introduce the child to sexual excitement. Masturbation, which began in order to soothe distress, now begins to result from spontaneous sexual feelings.

No one knows exactly what the infant, toddler, or older child thinks about during thumb or genital stimulation. The first experiences may not be accompanied by any particular thoughts. The earliest images may be of a soothing parent if the child is in pain, a full breast or bottle if the child is hungry, or a blanket if cold. These uncertain infantile beginnings evolve into an association between genital sensations and wish-fulfilling images during early childhood.

Fantasy is the means that children use to get their own way. They may be grandiose in their wishes and highly creative in expressing what they want. Fantasy is where children solve dilemmas and learn to compromise.

> When a boy earnestly tells his mother that he plans to marry her when he grows up, he is in for a rude awakening. His mother may graciously receive his ardent affection, tell him that she also loves him very much, and sensitively tell him how things are, but the son will be disappointed. After all, he has just been told that mother

> has been spoken for. Prior to telling his mother of his plans, his fantasies may have been preoccupied with playing "daddy" with mother. After his mother's rebuff, the moment may have a different outcome in his fantasies for a long time. Eventually, he will work out his hurt through fantasy, often soothing his wounded feelings with genital rubbing or thumbsucking. Soon, he will know how ridiculous the idea of marrying mother is. In a year or two, when he overhears his little brother telling mother his plans to marry her, he may think him quite stupid.

Although preoccupation with fantasy recedes dramatically as most people mature, fantasy remains an integral part of sexual behavior throughout life. Sexual excitement retains its link with creative imagination and personal problem-solving.

Older Childhood and Adolescence

The combination of imagination and sexual excitement eventually introduces the child to sexual identity. The dimensions of sexual identity–gender identity, orientation, and intention–are revealed through day- and night-dreams, imaginative reveries, and sexual images. The most undeniable revelations about sexual identity occur during adolescent genital masturbation, but these revelations can occur throughout life. Although a young person may feel guilty about provoking bodily excitement, conventional sexual fantasies at least provide evidence of "who I am" in a sexual sense. When masturbation involves cross-gender images, cross-dressing, homoerotic images, or fantasies of hurting or being hurt, the person is not assured about being normal. Atypical sexual identity fantasies may be confusing to a young child, but their significance becomes difficult to miss during adolescence.

Masturbation is a means of restoring inner calm and a sense of self-control to teenagers when their spontaneous arousal and intense sexual sensitivity overwhelm them. Teenagers soon discover its calming effects can be extended to other feelings. This use of masturbation to deal with anger, sadness, and worry feels like their private discovery. Many remain unaware for months or years that others also know that their bodies can be used this way.

When people start, stop, restart, and finally permanently stop masturbating varies enormously from individual to individual. The increased intensity and frequency of masturbation during adolescence is believed due to surges in sexual drive brought about by puberty. But not everyone begins masturbating during this phase of life. According to researchers such as M. Hunt and R. Clifford, as many as one-half of teenage girls in some cultural groups do not masturbate, even though most of them begin to experience sexual drive, but almost all boys masturbate during adolescence. Masturbation among teenage girls increased from about 40 percent after World War II to about 70 percent by the mid-seventies. There is a widespread belief that cultural conditions throughout the Western world are responsible for this phenomenon, as described by Clement and colleagues. Despite these careful efforts to study patterns of masturbation, it is difficult to draw firm conclusions because questions about masturbation produce more tendency to lie and distort answers than questions about other sexual topics.

The increase in sexual drive during adolescence is not the only reason for frequent masturbation. There are also social and psychological causes. Orphanages used to be very concerned about the relentless masturbation of some of their children. This behavior often was punished and schemes were hatched, such as bandaging the hands, to prevent it. Today, homeless children are told simply that masturbation is private and are not warned of dire consequences of self-stimulation. Their caretakers are usually taught that masturbation is self-soothing and is a common way for children to cope with abandonment. Such insight lessens their children's burdens.

The relentless masturbation of some homeless children suggests that the need to masturbate can be stimulated by loneliness long before the adolescent sexual drive roars. It is not a very far reach to wonder whether sexual desire at any time in life—the infant longing for a bottle, the aroused adolescent with no one to share excitement, the widower longing for his wife—expresses the hunger to be attached to some loving, need-fulfilling person.

Some children who are used sexually by adults may be unable to rid themselves of their need to masturbate to quell their recurrent excitement. Their vague memories may cause them to masturbate constantly and incessantly seek sexual partners years earlier then might otherwise be expected. My own research confirms such findings.

In addition, male homoeroticism often leads to frequent grade-school masturbation. Several studies of large groups including one by Marcel Saghir and Eli Robins have indicated that homosexual men begin masturbation much earlier in life, typically before puberty, and masturbate more frequently than heterosexual boys.

Homelessness, sexual abuse, and homoeroticism apparently cause people to often want to behave sexually. This observation raises the question whether those who think they have a high sex drive are correct. Rather than presuming they have a biological appetite for sex, there is also reason to consider them highly motivated to be interested in sex. Is it the brain-based sexual drive center speaking, or is it the personality-based motive to find a safe human attachment speaking? No one can be certain.

Adulthood

The roles masturbation plays during various stages of adulthood are slightly different. At all stages, it is used to cope with separation and loneliness. Masturbation is available to discharge the sexual feelings when there is no partner. Teenagers often regard masturbation as a preparation and rehearsal for the "real thing." Initially the "real thing" may be an opportunity to have intercourse, but soon it evolves into a relationship beyond sex. People are usually clear by young adulthood that they are really longing for a fuller relationship.

Once a psychologically intimate relationship is established and interrupted, masturbation is used to briefly recreate an absent loved person. If a lover is permanently absent, the recreation of the previous experience can be a double-edged sword. Adults fully understand that masturbation is not reality. Once the pleasurable sensations that accompany the fantasy are gone, the person is alone again. Some are able to use masturbation as a positive means of remembering and reexperiencing pleasure. Others consider the momentary pleasure a cruel reminder of what they cannot have and feel bitter after self-stimulation because the illusion of having a partner is not enough.

> Pauline, a widow who prided herself on her lifelong freedom from prudishness, gave up masturbation after "at least sixty-five years of experience." Her regular masturbation stopped during her twenty-five-year marriage to a man who valued sexual expression as much as she did. "We did everything together—even the unmentionable, oral sex. Several times after we were married, we had intercourse in the park just for kicks." Regular masturbation returned during the three years of her celibacy after his death. "In a strange way, it helped me grieve for Warren. I'd think of him, feel sad for a while, imagine I was having sex with him, and go to sleep." When she was fifty-one, she began a passionate relationship with Nick. She masturbated when he was out of town. This relationship lasted for twelve years until Nick died.
>
> She was too sad to masturbate for the first six months following his death. She told herself there still might be hope for finding another partner—"After all, I am still attractive, fun-loving, and adventurous." When she tried to imagine her next partner, Warren or Nick always appeared.
>
> During her convalescence from a heart attack at age sixty-seven, she masturbated occasionally, not so much because she was excited but "to check and see if I was good as ever down there." She was, but it never was the same. As she realized that she would not regain excel-

lent health, she lost hope of ever having another sexual adventure. Masturbation generated more sadness than pleasure. By age sixty-nine, four years ago, she concluded, "Who needs this depression?"

Doctor: So your sex life is over?
Pauline: I didn't say that. If a healthy man appears, I'll be ready! Do you have any relatives?

When adults become seriously ill or have surgery, they may often experiment with masturbation to see if they are "as good as ever down there." The health problem need not be closely related to the genitals as is a hysterectomy or hernia repair; it may follow any type of impairment, such as a stroke or gall bladder surgery. After open-heart surgery, for example, James felt himself in a dilemma. He had the urge to masturbate, but he feared it might be too much for his heart. After all, the doctor said to take it easy and not resume sex with Linda until the first checkup. By the fourth day at home, he decided masturbation wasn't sex.

Dangers

The dangers of masturbation are not acne, adult impotence, or mental illness. All the actual dangers come from the fact that our culture still widely misunderstands the positive value of the activity.

The first danger is that some individuals believe what they are told directly and indirectly about masturbation. They are taught that it is bad, then they feel *they* are bad because they masturbate, and they teach these ideas to their offspring. It is possible that negative ideas about masturbation play an important role in causing some adults to avoid sexual behavior.

The second danger is the possibility of excessive guilt and shame. Some degree of these feelings are normal and expected during childhood and adolescence because the fantasies that accompany masturbation are often thinly disguised hostile wishes that conflict with the young person's conscience. Children can usually deal with these on their own quite well. But sometimes, misinformation from adults about the act of masturbation can make the guilt and shame overwhelming. A vengeful four-year-old boy may imagine during his masturbation fantasy that his mean mother would fall and hurt herself because she sent him to his room; later he feels guilty about masturbating. A seven-year-old girl may masturbate to images of an exciting game she played with her father and then feel disloyal to her mother who she suddenly thinks hates her. A forty-year-old may fantasize raping his ex-wife and burning her house down, and then feel ashamed after he has an orgasm about his abnormal relentless rage. A seventy-year-old woman may feel guilty about her masturbation fantasies of making love with her invalid husband's physician.

Another danger is that masturbation gets blamed for the shameful content of people's fantasies and this inhibits them from enjoying the beneficial effects of sexual self-regulation. The content of these fantasies is actually quite predictable: in childhood, it involves sexual and aggressive thoughts about family members; in adulthood, it is usually about other partners, hidden sexual identity longings, and aggression; adolescence combines elements of both.

A fourth danger of masturbation has to do with the sexual equilibrium. A person always puts some interpretation on the partner's masturbation. Without any discussion, people often expect their partners to give up masturbation and use them instead to regulate sexual tension, sadness, disappointment, and other feelings. They may view their partners' masturbation as a form of competition, a means of excluding them, a sign of an inability to be intimate, or an indication of immaturity. When one partner learns that the other masturbates, he or she may feel jealousy, annoyance, or sadness. Spouses intuitively understand this and may keep their masturbation a secret to avoid upsetting their partners.

Usefulness of Masturbation

The facts about masturbation are quite positive; it is important that people, especially young people, understand them. Masturbation can be useful throughout life. Although it is a highly private activity and psychologically important to keep it so, it is no secret that people masturbate. The need to keep an individual's masturbation a private matter is not the same as keeping the culture in the dark about it. It would be helpful to adults and children if families, as well as the entire culture, acted as though masturbation exists.

Three important ideas about masturbation are not well recognized: (1) Masturbation is a vehicle for self-sufficiency throughout life, (2) masturbation is a means of guiding the child toward adolescent and adult sexual comfort, and (3) masturbation is an arena in which a person can rework a personal disgrace into a triumph.

> A sixteen-year-old boy, while delivering newspapers, allowed himself to be seduced by a woman in her late twenties. He was slowly and teasingly undressed by her and watched her undress. His excitement was matched by his fear. Their actual intercourse was over almost as fast as it began. He quickly left the scene in embarrassment but returned to it for years during masturbation. He felt humiliated by the powerlessness of the experience. He replayed the scene many ways but changed it so often that after several years he was not certain what actually had happened. His most common fantasies included his seduction of her leading to a prolonged intercourse, tying her up against her will and undressing her, and beating her up physically.

Masturbation is a window into the events, processes, and relationships that shape sexual desire. Sexual desire has a drama all its own during childhood. The drama typically reflects the developing child's mind and its changing relationship with others. The child may not know why certain images of masturbation keep returning, but these images involve what the child wants and needs. They are created from pleasant and traumatic, remembered and forgotten experiences. This is true for adults as well; the major difference is that adults have more life experiences from which to sculpt their images of masturbation.

Masturbation may be a window into sexual desire, but few permit themselves to peek into this private viewing place. Most people do not want to know too much about their masturbation images. Decoding masturbation fantasies in therapy tends to make them lose their excitement. It tends to expose us to our painful past. "I'm mad at you, doctor! Since we discussed my boxing hero fantasy, it seems silly. All that happened when I tried to use it this week was that I got mad at my father for leaving me and then I got sad all over again. It was a lot easier to just think about winning the girl because I was the champ."

Masturbation, like sexual desire, confronts us with our uneasy, fluctuating, contradictory selves. Most of the time we do not want to know too much about either; we just want to do it and have it.

Toward a Problem-Free Sexual Life

In order to help our children grow up to be sexually comfortable, we need to:

- be sure of our own attitudes toward masturbation
- understand the positive influences masturbation can have at every stage of life
- remember our own struggles over self-regulation and consider if there are better ways

8

DEVELOPING OUR SEXUAL IDENTITY

Why, in the privacy of thought, do many of us have moments of unconventional urges, interests, attractions, and curiosities? Each adult's sexual identity is formed from a mosaic of separate, but interlocking pieces. From one vantage point, this mosaic may appear to blend perfectly into a conventional form; for example, uncomplicated heterosexuality. But examining the same person's heterosexuality from a closer viewpoint will reveal the complicated nature of the composition.

Matters of sexual identity are often very subtle, so subtle, in fact that we usually are not aware of them as they operate within us. As long as we are linked to the right person—a person who fulfills our requirements to maintain our already established sexual sense of self—there is no need to even think about our sexual identity.

When, however, the reality of our partnership does not come close to fulfilling our requirements, minds respond with fantasy. If fantasy fails to make up for the missing ingredients, dissatisfaction and withdrawal from that partner follow. People rarely tell their partners when they do not meet these private identity requirements.

> A young married couple could not establish a comfortable sexual equilibrium. Heidi found sex physically and emotionally unsatisfying but had no idea why. Within two years of their daughter's birth, she began having homoerotic dreams and fantasies, and finally attraction to women, apparently in response to a friendship that developed in her daughter's play group. The couple tried to deal with her sexual disinterest by agreeing that each could temporarily choose new partners. Jon didn't know that her Tuesday dates were with a woman. His few experiences outside of marriage were unpleasant. When Jon wanted to call off the arrangement, Heidi wanted to call off the marriage. The hardest part for him to deal with was that his feminine wife was passionately making love to a woman.

The energy of sexual desire does not stand alone. It is always directed toward a person and an activity to confirm our deepest sense of ourselves. Ideally, courtship allows for the discovery of compatibility of our sexual identities, but in fact the details are often not sufficiently revealed by the time of the marriage. Relationships may suddenly end when the hidden aspects of sexual identity are realized.

> Norm, a quiet, kind, twenty-one-year-old mechanic, was too embarrassed to tell his fiancee of his periodic practice of dressing in girl's clothing. Their young marriage ended within three weeks of her walking in unexpectedly from work to find him lounging in nylons, slip, bra, and robe. She not only felt betrayed by his failure to tell her about this peculiarity before marriage, but she felt that

> she needed a husband who was "all man." During the ensuing crisis, she kept telling herself, "I'm a complete woman! I can't tolerate this!"

Not all the variability in sexual identity is as dramatic as the discovery of transvestism or homosexuality in a partner. Much of the unconventional remains in the privacy of thoughts and feelings and is not expressed in behavior.

Something happens quietly during early childhood that lays the groundwork for our sexual sense of self. If parents were asked every three years to predict their child's sexual identity, they would do so with more conviction each time. When the child is three, they may be able to describe a comfortable masculinity or femininity. They may know that their child of six will be heterosexual. They may be able to sense that their nine-year-old will exhibit ordinary sexual behavior.

Researchers are beginning to study how and when sexual identity develops, but progress is slow. Sexual identity is primarily subjective and is shaped within the child's mind when the child does not yet have much of a vocabulary and cannot be expected to fully understand what is happening within the family. When people are asked to describe their early life circumstances, it is usually apparent that memories of events cannot be trusted as accurate. Most of all, however, scientists struggle with the fact that the intellectual, emotional, biological, social, and sexual aspects of personality develop at the same time. Teasing them apart is very difficult.

Gender Identity Landmark

In a technical sense, the word "sex" refers only to the purely biological aspects of maleness or femaleness—for example, penis, ejaculation, vagina, lactation. The anatomical sex of a child is determined by chromosomes that chemically direct the development of genital organs and functions.

For many years, it was assumed that gender identity—the sense of oneself as male and masculine or female and feminine—was determined biologically. But now it is believed that how parents react to the sex of their infant is a vital cause of the toddler's early gender sense. Biology is influential, but it alone does not dictate gender identity. The interaction between infant and family can override biological influences (Money & Earhardt, 1972). Several dramatic, rare examples made the scientific world realize how strong an influence family processes may have: A male infant who was thought to be a girl at birth because of a genital abnormality grew up to have a female gender identity and then was discovered to have male chromosomes; a female infant who was erroneously declared a boy in the delivery room grew up to feel and behave in a masculine fashion.

One key factor is the family's belief about the child's true sex. This causes the child to label itself a girl or a boy and induces her or him to behave in ways that others will recognize as specifically feminine or masculine.

Inconspicuous social and psychological processes during the first two years of life usually lead to a firm conviction about being a girl or a boy. When the child is comfortable with this conviction, we say that core gender identity has been consolidated.

The formation of a gender identity that is consistent with the child's sex is a vital accomplishment. All later sexual development is influenced by the steps that helped the child settle on being boy or girl. Other problems with sexual identity and function are likely to occur when a child has a long delay in nailing down in his or her mind whether he is really a boy or she is a girl.

One-year-olds have a sense of themselves as either boys or girls that is probably similar to the ability to identify the nose or ears accurately. Having learned a name for a body part, the child comes to understand that it is part of "me." This gender sense replaces the natural tendency of all infants raised by women to develop an early feminine sense of self. It is believed that young babies think they are part of, and therefore the same, as the mother or female caretaker.

For gender identity that matches the anatomy to develop, the toddler must accept the label "girl" or "boy." Acceptance is easier when there is a comfortable relationship between child and parents. Trust and love are the bridges to appropriate gender identification. In order to accept the label "boy," the child has to accept being different from mother and accept the fact that his future is tied to maleness.

By subtly encouraging her son to be different from her, a mother promotes male gender-role behavior. Most boys have no persistent trouble with this. When the mother has a need to prolong the infantile closeness with her son, she may cause the toddler to be afraid of trying new things, taking part in rough-and-tumble play, and being a boy. Fathers usually play a subtle, supportive role in this process if they are loving models for sons to identify with, and if they take an active role in their upbringing.

> Caroline, a married woman with an effeminate five-year-old son, sought help for her "irrational" anger toward her nice husband. She feared that she had somehow created her son's problem. Her own father had left her and her mother when she was six months old to join the army and showed up again for several months when she was three. He committed suicide in their home when she was four. Her mother frequently spoke of men with considerable bitterness. Such remarks over the years became predictable, although her family realized their mother never recovered from her marital misfortune. Despite Caroline's objective appraisal of her husband's good character, she could not rid herself of the fear that he, "like all men," would prove unreliable.

For a girl to accept the label "girl," she has to take some pleasure in being like mother. If she feels secure in her attachment to her mother, she can accept the fact that her future is tied to femaleness. She does not have to undergo the disruption that boys do in order to achieve an identity separate from that of her caregiver. For this reason, serious gender problems are less common in girls than in boys. When girls have such problems, it is because they could not form a trusting bond with their mothers early in life and their fathers, if present, did not seem to be delighted in their femaleness.

> Cynthia, a teenager who eventually decided to live her life as a male, was adopted when she was three months old into a family with an older brother. Her adopted mother became depressed and unable to function after the baby arrived. The grandmother and the father filled in for eight months while the mother was recovering. The father remained Cynthia's primary parent afterward because she had become closely attached to him. She preferred his company and patterned herself after him. When the child's fearfulness of her mother abated during her fourth year, the family thought their troubles were over. The mother had no such problems relating to the son she adored. By the time Cynthia was five, the family was enjoying the tomboyishness of their daughter.

Like most personality characteristics, gender identity is not something that can be explained by simply pointing to the mother, the father, the child, or biology. All development occurs within a constantly changing family context. The child's temperament, skills, and capacities interact with both parents' temperaments, nurturing capacities, and interests in the child. It is through this interaction, not simply in the mother's, father's, or child's behavior, that gender identity is determined.

A loving family life encourages the child to accept the appropriate label and learn the differences between male and female behavior. Repeated warm interactions with both parents minimize any unhappiness with the label. For instance, when children discover that they cannot be both girl and boy, they are confused and disappointed. Two-year-old boys may play "mommy," put on her clothing, or declare that they will grow up to be a mother. These behaviors and the feelings underlying them are temporary, however, as the boy's misconceptions are quickly and routinely corrected. It also becomes clear to him that his emerging male gender-role behaviors please both his mother and father: "That's my boy!" "What a big boy you are!" Thirty-month-old Leslie, affectionately called "Les" by her parents, went through a stage for a month when she wanted to be called a boy and proudly told her parents and playmates that she was going to be a police*man*. Her worried parents went out of their way to praise her girlishness and patiently explain that it was not possible to be a boy since she was already a girl. These conversations always ended in a comment about their pleasure in having a daughter.

Uncaring parents and frightening events can discourage a child from accepting the biologically appropriate label. A father's drunken rages which terrify both mother and one-year-old son may cause them to cling to each other and frighten the boy about growing up to be a man. Another mother's harshness and disinterest may also leave her son frightened about maleness and uncertain as to how to elicit affection.

The formation of core gender identity does not suddenly happen; it gradually emerges from a seeming gender neutrality in early life. While a fourteen-month-old boy has more in common with all toddlers than with boys in particular, he has already begun learning about and identifying with males. His sense of himself as a boy will progressively appear during the next year or so. The sex of the child begins as a powerful factor in the parents' minds. By the first birthday it is becoming a powerful factor in the child's mind. Another key influence, therefore, on core gender identity is the quality of the child's relationships early in life. Parents can take certain steps to encourage the healthy development of core gender identity:

- consistently behaving as though the child belongs to his or her biological sex
- understanding the child's nonverbal expressions and being willing to meet his or her needs
- protecting the child from overwhelming separations from trusted people
- protecting the child from physical and psychological abuse

These factors are also important to other aspects of personality development in the young child—establishing individuality, learning to trust the people upon whom the child is dependent, learning to be patient, regulating mood, gaining control over sibling rivalry, modulation of expressions of anger, establishment of good self-esteem, self-protectiveness, joy in accomplishment, and pleasure in the body. It is not surprising that many people with atypical gender identity also have problems in these areas.

A very small percentage of children who develop conspicuous disturbances in gender identity were once treated by their families as though they were members of the opposite sex.

> A seventeen-year-old male, who was convincingly dressed as a very feminine girl, requested sex-reassignment surgery. When "her" parents were interviewed, the mother was so distraught she could not sit still. The father explained that his wife had raised their son as a girl for the first year and a half of his life. She had even converted his name to "Roberta." When the husband returned from the army and found the boy dressed in a pink dress with matching ribbons, he put an immediate stop to it. "But from that point on," he said, "Bobby always was a mamma's boy." Bobby's mother was a chronically depressed young woman with no close friends or relatives. She pretended that her infant was the daughter she had wanted. I suspect she engaged in this fantasy because she was loving her "Roberta" the way she felt she had needed to be loved when she was younger. But one can never be sure why people respond in unconventional ways.

For most children with gender disturbances, however, the processes that go awry during the first two-and-a-half years are not so dramatic as with Bobby. What goes wrong is probably ordinary family disruption and misery. The same circumstances that cause gender confusion in a few children probably produce different kinds of psychological problems in others.

The temperament of some children, however, may actually predispose them to difficulties with gender identification. Parents may continue to treat their passive, cuddly, adorable, and shy son as an infant much longer than their other sons. The extra closeness to his mother makes it more difficult for this child to become emotionally independent of her. Fantasizing that he is a girl may be his mental trick to soothe his worries about separation. The same mother's energetic, more outgoing son who does not like to be held will not tolerate his parents' attempts to keep him a baby. His temperament probably would not prompt such attempts in the first place.

Temperamental characteristics, the basic psychological features of a child, are caused by biological factors. However, these characteristics cause such swift emotional responses from others that they are usually wrongly thought to have a psychological origin. For example, an infant's sociability—response to strangers, tendency to greet the world, curiosity about the environment—begins as a biological trait and quickly causes parents to have a specific response. The difficulty separating temperament from response of the family to a child, and the effect on the child of this response illustrates why scientific understanding is slow to develop.

Once the core identity is established, the child will likely never lose his or her sense of maleness or femaleness. But gender identity, like other aspects of personality, continuously evolves. Each developmental step the child takes is an opportunity to create more layers of his or her sense of self along the gender dimension.

At each stage, however, gender identity depends upon different kinds of issues. Tolerance of separation becomes a major issue in feeling good about oneself—children must be able to comfortably leave their parents to go to school. This has a positive impact on the child's gender sense. Later on, ability in sports, interest in fashion, grooming, academic competence, and many other things will influence the child's growing sense of masculinity or femininity.

> Richard is a second grader who fantasizes he is a girl. He uses his awkwardness in kickball to prove he is not really a boy. He often declines to play at sports and seeks out "girl" games. His classmate, Mickey, is also among the less well-coordinated in the class, but he is more eas-

ily encouraged to keep trying. He notices that both boys and girls play kickball. Kickball is not a gender identity issue for Mickey, it is a skill issue. Richard sees almost everything in terms of his gender confusion.

There is no simple line of gender identity development once core gender identity has been consolidated. The evolution of gender identity is unique to each person because each child has unique interests and capacities. These become more apparent as the world broadens beyond the family for the older child and the adolescent. Children respond to social and political forces differently from one another and identify with a variety of people outside their families as they gradually construct their personalities.

Orientation Landmark

The earliest bodily pleasures may come from persons of either sex. Children, of course, prefer their mothers and fathers to strangers, but this is simply a matter of familiarity, trust, reliability. We do not speak of children in the first years of life as heterosexual or homosexual because orientation is not inborn. Within three or four years of basic bodily pleasures, many children seem to be attracted to, interested in, and aroused by one sex more than the other.

This change represents the second landmark of sexual identity development—the establishment of orientation. An unmistakable flirtatiousness is often noticed in children of this age. People observe with relief, "Ah, he is just like his father!" "Look at that little girl with her daddy!" Some preschoolers develop crushes on opposite-sex children and teachers during nursery school. These early landmarks of the psychological aspects of orientation—heteroeroticism (as opposed to the behavioral aspects of orientation—heterosexuality) are shaped by social and psychological processes that took place earlier. The timely formation of the appropriate core gender identity is the first step to becoming heteroerotic and subsequently heterosexual.

Children's erotic preoccupations are directed toward heterosexuality by their need to obtain and retain the approval of others. The culture continually steers children through messages from the family, the schools, the media, and peer relationships. The child learns to hide any homoerotic impulses or feelings when he or she sees the negative, anxious responses they produce in parents, teachers, and friends.

Longing for persons of the same sex occurs to most preschool children. To become predominantly heteroerotic, the child needs to get rid of these impulses. Exactly how the child accomplishes this is not clear, but the fact is that most children manage to do it.

Sexual interest in the opposite sex is evident long before adolescence. The dramatic disgust with which third- and fourth-grade boys appear to regard girls and vice versa is a temporary cover of disinterest that will soon give way to curiosity. Seeming lack of interest in the opposite sex and intense same sex friendships are grade-school markers of heteroerotic orientation. Children like to keep their desires and curiosities about the opposite sex private from adults and one another.

Origins of Homoeroticism

Estimates about the percentage of the population that may be gay range between 1 and 13 percent of men and 0.5 and 8 percent of women. These numbers are based on numerous surveys, including those of Lee Ellis and colleagues and Alan Bell and his co-workers. The privacy that envelops this subject and the question about how much homoeroticism is necessary before someone is considered gay keeps all these figures uncertain.

Many heterosexual adults are biased against homoeroticism and homosexuality and believe them to be a sign of psychological illness. Although current psychological theories about persistent homoeroticism point to unfortunate childhood development, these theories do not mean that homoeroticism is an illness. Mental patterns and behavior are considered a symptom of illness only if they convincingly meet two criteria: personal distress and impaired social functioning. After thoughtful consideration by both the American Psychiatric Association and the American Psychological Association, it was decided in 1974 that the weight of scientific evidence supported the conclusion that homosexual men and women could not be considered to have a psychological or mental illness on the basis of their orientation. Ronald Bayer has written about the background that led to this conclusion in his 1980 book, *Homosexuality and American Psychiatry: The Politics of Diagnosis.*

It is important not to confuse persistent homoeroticism in either sex with occasional homosexual behavior. Kinsey showed that about one-third of boys have at least one episode of homosexual behavior. Most of these boys grow up as comfortable heterosexuals. Isolated homosexual episodes among girls are probably less common than among boys and also do not predict homoeroticism.

Male Homoeroticism

Researchers have attempted to explain homoeroticism by biological as well as psychological theories. Although most of the biological theories have been refuted, the suspicion that at least some homoeroticism is due to biological factors still exists. It is certainly reasonable to think that biological factors do interact with social and psychological ones to influence heteroerotic and homoerotic orientations. Much prominent research, including Richard Green's *"The Sissy Boy Syndrome" and the Development of Homosexuality,* describes the interaction between biological and psychological factors.

A teenager who, unlike his athletic father, has no interest in sports, admits his homosexuality to his distraught parents after they find pictures of naked men in his room. This replaces their previous worry about their son's lack of sociability. Later, the usually sullen boy tries to ease his parents' anguish.

Son: But, Mother, I do love you—I have always loved you!

Mother: No, you don't! I used to tell your father when you were three that you didn't love me. You didn't want to be with me. You are so defiant of everything I say. I can feel it. You don't love me! What did I do to deserve this?

Son: I admit I don't like you a lot of the time. You are always pushing me to do things.

Father: I push you too, son. You are awfully stubborn.

Son: Yes, Dad, but that's different. You don't scream at me all the time.

Father: Don't you see that Mother has been trying to get you to do what was good for you? Mother and I did push you because you stayed in your room too much. When you were little, you played with your imaginary friends rather than be with your brother and sister downstairs. You're still like that today, except it's your records that keep you upstairs. You're always alone. That's not good.

Mother: Why did you decide you're a homo . . . sexual? I can hardly say the word. Let me take you to a doctor—maybe he can change you.

Son: No, Mother! I don't want to be changed. I've known since I was six. I used to be upset about it, but not anymore.

Mother: Six! Six! How could you know such a thing then? You were just in first grade!

Son: Stop yelling at me!—I don't know. But I knew I was different. I made friends with girls much better than boys. Kathy was my best friend at grade school. Boys made me nervous.

Father: Son, I want you to see a doctor.

Son: I won't go!

There are two major psychological theories that attempt to explain the origin of male homoeroticism. One is delayed formation of gender identity; the other is an unusual solution to the love triangle of the Oedipal phase.

The first theory seems to fit about two-thirds of homoerotic men who come to mental health professionals for any reason; this same proportion holds up in my more specialized practice as well. Both theories emphasize that the ultimate determination of orientation occurs within the mind of the preschool child. This involves not only the events or processes within the family, but also the way the child interprets and responds to them. The young child's mind deals actively with events and relationships to create his or her orientation.

Delayed formation of gender identity. Boys who linger in the warm aura of their mothers, remain dependent on them, and do not engage in independent activities appropriate to their age tend to be the ones who cannot resolve their fear of being hurt while playing childhood games. These same boys are unable to perceive their fathers' loving presence or their mothers' wishes that they behave as boys. A boy who is strongly motivated to stay physically close to his mother after age two is apt to be harboring a growing sense of himself as a girl.

Playful feminine gender-role behavior may not be noticed because most boys occasionally pretend to be the opposite sex. Mothers may dismiss a son's dressing up or playing "Mother" as cute, but such play tends to make fathers anxious and angry.

If there is continued delay in consolidation of male gender identity, these boys grow up to prefer the company and games of girls. Grade school boys tease and exclude them. Adults think of them as sissies. These children become progressively embarrassed about their feminine behavior as they grow older.

Joseph Harry and other authors have shown that most prehomosexual boys successfully rid themselves of their effeminate appearance in late grade school and junior high school. Only about 15 percent of homosexual males are noticeably effeminate in early adulthood. They have learned that their continuing confusion about their gender and their secret identification with girls should be kept hidden for social survival.

Male homosexuals' feelings of shame make it difficult to research this developmental process. Many do not want to remember their early feminization and subsequent defeminization. The painful past is over—it is enough that they are aware of their own efforts to become less obvious.

Oedipal complex. In most children, orientation is determined between the ages of three and six when they are particularly preoccupied with the triangular relationship with their parents. Sigmund Freud described these years as the Oedipal phase, named for the classic Greek story in which Oedipus unknowingly kills his father and marries his mother. The conflicts concerning such relationships came to be known as the Oedipal complex. Homoeroticism may have its roots in a person's instinctive attempts to find solutions to these Oedipal conflicts.

The Oedipal phase is the three-year-old's introduction to a love triangle. Before this phase, the son regularly experienced love, affection, and excitement with his parents in pure form. There was just he and mother or he and father. Relationships were a matter of two-person systems. As he gets a little older, he becomes sensitive to different implications of his father's presence. Now when he feels love and affection for his mother, he feels a sense of rivalry with his father. There are times he wants to have sole possession of her—he wants his father out of the way. And he thinks his father might want him out of the way also. Frightening monsters on the attack appear in his dreams. Although he feels guilty about his disloyalty to his father, the pleasure and excitement with mother may temporarily make it difficult to be just a son. Many mothers have cute stories about their sons' attempts to displace their husbands.

There is a less well-known dimension to a boy's Oedipal complex. He also loves his father, feels excitement with him, and notices that his mother is his competition for the precious time and affection with his father. Occasionally he may feel he would like his father to himself and may also want to get rid of his mother.

In order to develop heterosexually, the boy must give up his romantic or sexual feelings for his mother to maintain his father's love and protection. The result is that he affectionately loves his mother without sexual excitement. He loves and respects his father and strengthens his masculine identifications with him.

There are many times during the Oedipal phase when a worried, guilty, or frightened son needs his father's reassurance that his competitive urges are not threatening and that Daddy does indeed love him. A loving but otherwise occupied father can foster homoeroticism in his son if the boy cannot feel his interest and concern.

Problems in the mother-father-son triangle may cause the son to fear his mother and to need much more loving acceptance from father than is available. Harsh mothers may discourage their preschool sons from seeking comfort and excitement with females. Father's nurturance becomes most desired. The ultimate consequence of rejection by mother and the longing for more from father is a homoerotic orientation.

The complexities of the Oedipal phase can be simplified by saying that homoeroticism may result from being deprived of the father's interest and by realizing a strong fear or distaste for the mother.

Heterosexual, homosexual, or bisexual orientation is determined by a delicate balance of competing psychological forces. The child's perceptions of his parents, his reactions to these perceptions, and the actual behavior of the parents in response to the child interact during the preschool years to determine the balance.

Female Homoeroticism

Surprisingly little is known about how little girls' minds become programmed for homoeroticism. Three tentative suggestions—I hesitate to even call them theories—about the psychological process can be made. One is that the formation of a person's female gender identity has been delayed. A second is that the child is looking for a more nurturing mother. A third is that the young woman consciously has made an ideological decision to have sexual relationships only with women.

It is also possible that biological factors are involved in a few situations. Families usually have to accept a great deal of uncertainty when they ask why their daughter or sister has become homosexual.

Delayed gender identity. The typical child in our culture spends a great deal of time during the first year of life with women. The earliest copying behavior of both girls and boys involves mimicking women. Unlike boys who need to separate psychologically from their mothers early enough to develop another profound and lasting identification, girls have no compelling need to fashion a new sense of self. Their second year of life is different from that of boys.

The beginning of homoeroticism may develop if the girl perceives that she would be better off as a boy. At a time when the rules of the external world are not important and fantasy is readily confused with reality, the toddler can pretend she is a boy—a boy like her brother, the boy her father always wanted, a boy with the masculine nickname that somebody has given her, a boy because the older sister—the other girl—died very young. Girls may identify with the male elements in their family because the females are emotionally or physically unhealthy, are not available, or are too harsh.

It is difficult to develop a male gender identity, even under adverse circumstances, if her family gives her loving attention and encouragement to be a girl. However, some adversity disrupts the girl's attachment to her caretaker.

> Noreen, a very attentive mother, and her fifteen-month-old daughter were suddenly abandoned by her unfaithful husband. They were left in a new city without family or financial resources. Noreen was anxious, preoccupied, and disabled by depression for at least six months. She could only go through the motions of mothering. Her previous pleasures of mothering became a burden, as she had to go to work, find child care, and deal with her daughter's persistent crankiness. The nonverbal child could not understand the sudden change in her mother.

Girls with abilities that are usually valued in boys may find that their talent creates difficulties for their evolving feminine gender identity. Many college-aged women with superior athletic ability probably received or overheard comments that were confusing to their feminine identification. The ability to compete successfully in "boys' " sports may also make it a little harder for some girls to grow up feeling feminine.

One of the hallmarks of male gender identification among girls during their preadolescent years is the presence of stereotypic "boy" behaviors—that is, preference for rough-and-tumble games, the company of little boys, and "boy" toys. Such "tomboy" patterns can be seen before the first grade in some children and in grade school in others. Many, if not most, of these girls give up their masculine identification shortly after puberty. The masculine gender identity is replaced or covered over with a feminine one. The preference for "boy" behavior gives way to a feminine gender role, gender identity, and heteroeroticism.

Not all tomboys outgrow these identifications, however. Saghir and Robin and others have shown that the vast majority of adults lesbians were tomboys. Many can recall the childhood desire to wake up one morning and be a boy. The masculine identity of many lesbian women is persistent and leads to homoeroticism. However, the two gender identifications can coexist. Their feminine identification, which although not strong enough to permit heteroeroticism, is sufficiently strong to keep them pleased with their bodies. They are not interested in literally becoming men; they are comfortable as women. Their female bodies are not abhorrent. Their episodic male fantasies, if still present, are just thoughts.

Search for a nurturant mother. Frequent, prolonged separations from the mother can leave toddlers anxious and uncertain about their source of comfort. Near the end of the second year of life, when girls discover that boys have penises, some female toddlers blame their mothers because they don't have something boys have. For most girls this is a brief phase; it is outgrown with the aid of strong identification with their mother who is clearly a loving, undefective woman.

When this sense of the self as defective persists and the girl becomes preoccupied with it, the problem usually is not the fact that she has discovered the male anatomy, but the insecure attachment to her mother. If the mother continues to be inadequate in meeting the daughter's need for emotional nurturance, the child may begin a search for a new and better mother. During her Oedipal phase, her father's interest in her is not enough to overcome her hunger for a nurturant mother. She is too preoccupied with basic attachment to a female to respond to the triangular complexities of the preschool years.

This secret, poignant search takes an erotic form before adolescence. Crushes on same sex classmates and teachers appear. Although her gender identity is not male, she remains vaguely uncomfortable with being female. Homoeroticism may represent the continuing search for the missing basic ingredient of early life: a secure attachment to a person whom the child could experience as more nurturing than frightening.

> Alexandra, a twenty-five-year-old woman with very feminine characteristics, had been raised by a succession of housekeepers while her parents traveled for business and social reasons. She could not understand her homosexual behavior. There was no doubt in her mind about her basic homoeroticism, but she was confused by her angry reactions to her lover's sexual interest in her. Alexandra highly desired to be held by her lover and to lie on her breast, but anything else annoyed her. Her masturbation fantasies were a collection of images of being united with a nurturant giving person.

Ideological decision. This pathway to homoeroticism is unique to women. A woman with a conventional gender identity and heteroerotic development may become angry about being a woman in a culture she perceives as limiting opportunities for personal growth. She may feel that relationships with men are too demeaning. Such emotions are further encouraged by intense friendships with "sisters." Certain feminists feel that the only way to be true to the ideology of liberation is to become a lesbian. This pathway may begin as homosexuality and lead to homoeroticism.

This explanation is intriguing because it is a reminder that the past may not be the most powerful influence on the present. The tumultuous fears, confusion, and dilemmas of the present may provide sufficient motivation for new adaptations and developmental experiences. Could not an unsatisfactory heterosexual love relationship induce an adventurous, open-minded person to act upon the sexual feelings that arise in a new same sex friendship? What happens if the experience is not only pleasant, but better able to satisfy the woman's needs than any other? This may be another road to homoeroticism that begins with homosexual behavior.

Homoerotic Potential in Heterosexuals

Heteroeroticism in either sex is not always present in pure form. At various stages of development, heteroerotic individuals may experience homoerotic urges. All small children respond erotically—that is, with bodily pleasure—to either sex. Development usually requires them to suppress either the heteroerotic or the homoerotic experience. An occasional person does not suppress either and retains the ability to respond erotically and sexually with both male and female images and partners. This bisexuality is objectionable to many people because it suggests that a homoerotic "taint" is embedded in all heterosexuality.

I believe the most reasonable explanation for the homoerotic potential in heterosexuals harkens back to the child's original decision to identity with a male or female. We cannot be both. However, these wishes remain in our unconscious minds and periodically surface as curiosity, a dream, or an erotic fantasy. An older explanation, more popular among theorists, is that bisexuality or erotic interest in both sexes is part of the biological programming of the human mind. Either way, sexual identity is a mosaic.

Conventional and Unconventional Sexual Intentions

Sexual intentions—what one wants to do with a partner during sexual behavior—is the most private aspect of sexual identity. The most common themes of unconventional intentions are exhibiting one's nakedness, secretly looking at the nakedness or sexual behavior of others, hurting another person in a display of power, and being subservient to a controlling person. However strongly we reject such sexual pleasures in others, the potential to derive gratification from similar behavior is part of our human nature.

Extended lovemaking provides subtle gratification of some of these pleasures. There is opportunity, for example, to exhibit ourselves, to sneak usually forbidden looks at the partner's body, to dominate by providing intense arousal, to carefully bite or pinch in ways that enhance the partner's arousal. These actions may be so disguised and fleeting that they are not recognized as intentions or as forms of behavior that, when exaggerated, are considered forms of sexual aberration.

The diagnosis of sexual perversion is made by mental health professionals when unconventional themes recur with great intensity and are the major source of sexual arousal. These frequently involve aggression toward a victim as in child molestation, rape, exhibitionism, voyeurism, or masochistic behavior. Despite the lurid headlines in tabloid newspapers, most unconventional intentions are confined to fantasy or the bedroom with a consenting partner.

Aggressive sexual intentions originate in events that traumatized the child, according to Robert Stoller of U.C.L.A. and many other theorists. The childhood experience is reversed: The original victim, the child, becomes the victor in fantasy. Humiliation is avenged—over and over again.

> A three-year-old child goes to surgery without any emotional preparation or discussion of what to expect. He is undressed, tied to a cart, and etherized while screaming for his mother. Later in life, he masturbates to the enigmatic fantasy of tying up and stripping partners.

> A five-year-old boy is forced to put on a dress several times by his grandmother as punishment for being unruly. Later in life he discovers that he has his most exciting sexual experiences when he has intercourse wearing a woman's garment. Without the garment, he cannot feel interest in his wife.

Conventional sexual intentions reflect a positive, trusting attitude toward one's sexual partner which is based upon the belief that other people can give us pleasure and will not hurt us. If past experience has not taught this, the mind may harbor hatred, fear, and vengefulness. Adult sexual intentions may involve some subtle accounting system that balances reassuring and frightening childhood experiences.

Children who have been consistently well treated may also develop aggressive sexual preoccupations because children cannot understand traumatic events. They may be angry at things that are not their parents' fault. Those who are more angry than others by temperament may be vulnerable to aggressive intentions.

These intentions may arise suddenly during adulthood in response to disappointments in intimate relationships.

> Harold was horrified when he began masturbating to fantasies of punching his partner in the face. He had never been preoccupied with this kind of erotic image before. The mystery disappeared when he came to realize just how furious he had been with her recently because she had seemed callous and indifferent to him.

When the source of an unusual intention is recent, the mystery is relatively easy to unravel. Most serious problems with intention remain unclear because the sources are many years old. They may also involve parent-child relationships rather than specific traumatic events. These situations often cannot be recalled because they occurred too early in life, are too subtle to put into words, or produce too much pain for the person to reconsider.

In the subsequent chapters on impairments of sexual function, the relationship between desire and hidden identity wishes will recur because sexual identity, desire, and function are inseparable in our minds.

Toward a Problem-Free Sexual Life

In order to maximize the chance that our children will develop conventional forms of sexual identity, we need to:

- be pleased with their biological sex
- emotionally connect with them and remain interested in meeting their needs
- protect them from prolonged separations from trusted people
- protect them from physical and psychological abuse
- vigilantly communicate to them our sense of their worth

9

PREMATURE EJACULATION

The issues involved with orgasm, though less complicated than those with desire and sexual identity, have their own interesting twists. This chapter on premature ejaculation and the next one on women who cannot have orgasms discuss the common problems of sexual beginners that many people never outgrow. Individually, the chapters highlight the unique psychological experiences of each sex; together, they emphasize the accomplishment of mutually satisfying sexual behavior.

There is a basic life-cycle scheme that carries the typical male from uncontrollable ejaculation when young to difficulty attaining orgasm when old. In order to experience the entire cycle, a man usually begins having sex by his early twenties and continues into his seventies. By the middle of the cycle, men generally have learned to choose when they ejaculate. Middle-aged men sometime smugly feel they have "arrived" sexually because orgasm feels terrific and intercourse occasionally lasts a long time. "Enjoy, enjoy," I say, "the biological clock is ticking!"

There are considerable variations in the evolution from rapid ejaculation to consistent ejaculatory control to difficulty attaining orgasm. Aging of the nervous system underlies the psychological struggle with the timing of orgasm. The low ejaculatory threshold, the sensitive trigger mechanism, and the perception of the vagina as sensually overwhelming are characteristics of efficient youthful nervous systems. The gradual slowing of the nervous system contributes to ejaculatory control by more mature men and to orgasmic inhibition by men in the final decades of life.

As many as one-third of young adult and middle-aged men think they ejaculate prematurely, as Ellen Frank and her coauthors discovered in their study. By this they usually mean that they are disappointed about not being able to choose the moment of ejaculation during intercourse. They usually want to last long enough to bring their partners to orgasm, which they feel is their responsibility.

When the subject of premature ejaculation is raised the usual question is, "How long should intercourse last?" There is no correct answer to this question since it is based on men's mistaken perspective on sexual performance. This perspective is a dangerous oversimplification that only adds misery to the worried heterosexual man who suspects that everyone he knows lasts much longer than he does during intercourse. He is convinced he is a sexual cripple. If his partner believes the only thing standing between her and sexual pleasure is his premature ejaculation, her attitude corresponds nicely with his defective sense of self. Their explanation for their sexual dissatisfaction is that she is a victim of his defectiveness.

Misleading answers to the performance question sometimes given by "experts" are "two minutes," "five minutes," "fifteen minutes," and "until the woman has her orgasm." The right answer, however, is "Stop counting!" I much prefer to look at the timing of ejaculation from the vantage point of the sexual equilibrium. This perspective takes into account the man's capacity to monitor and pace the development of his arousal, the partner's capacity to tolerate a high level of sexual arousal, and the quality of the couple's nonsexual relationship. This approach is useful in helping many individuals and couples quickly outgrow their concerns about premature ejaculation and gain ejaculatory control.

The Passion-Control Dilemma

Genital stimulation presents a man with a passion-control dilemma. He must choose between prolonging the intercourse or giving in to his escalating arousal. Most men think they can solve this dilemma by trying to make their passionate feelings last longer but control and passion are opposites. The natural dichotomy between passion and control cannot be defied because passion is by nature brief but intense. Men who successfully negotiate the passion-control dilemma achieve a level of controllable pleasure until they allow themselves to be swept away by intensity. They find themselves in a position neither totally passionate nor totally controlled.

Even when the man has good ejaculatory control, he has no guarantee that his partner will have an orgasm. His capacity for prolonging intercourse, however, does provide her with an opportunity to use both the controlled and the passionate moments of intercourse for her own pleasure. If she will not or cannot have an orgasm, his control does not enhance her experience; it only diminishes the intensity of his. Since sex is carried out with an equilibrium, ejaculatory control cannot be considered apart from the partner's sexual characteristics.

The mechanics of intercourse are important to the timing of ejaculation. The man may avoid passion at first by simply being still in the vagina, pacing himself slowly, or having his partner move in a manner that does not create friction along the shaft of the penis. The woman-on-top position is often the best in which to delay the escalation of his arousal because it provides weight constraints to his pelvic movements and allows the couple to avoid male-centered intercourse. The woman is free to move her entire body along the head-to-toe horizontal plane rather than just move her pelvis along the shaft of the penis, and this often helps the woman to attain orgasm.

When a man decides to come, he usually thrusts in and out of the vagina along the shaft of his penis at an increasing pace. The vagina fits his penis like a glove, providing a warm, wet friction. His thrusting typically stops when he triggers the first reflex of ejaculation. He then pushes deeply into the vagina where the pleasurable pelvic muscular contractions can be experienced without distraction.

Ideally, the man's focused pursuit of his pleasure is highly exciting for his partner. In fact, his orgasm may trigger hers.

> "I know I am a lucky man. From the first time we made love when we were dating, Jackie has responded to my orgasm by having an orgasm. I was deeply attracted to her physically and mentally before we had sex, but when she always responded to my orgasm that way, I knew I would never leave her. She is unlike any woman I ever was with—she is a jewel."

While Jackie's response is very lovely, it usually does not happen for most women. Men have to learn a few things about their partners. Intercourse that focuses on male thrusting would be ideal for women if this movement also provided the major source of the woman's intense arousal. However, most woman achieve orgasm if the clitoris and the vagina, or the clitoris alone, is stimulated during intercourse. This does not easily happen during in-and-out thrusting alone.

A woman who is deliberate in pursuit of her arousal, who knows how to do what feels good while her partner is intensifying his arousal, has much to teach. She demonstrates that a woman can be responsible for her own orgasms by learning to do what arouses her, by teaching her partner how to cooperate with her pleasure, and by enjoying his intensity.

The couple must learn each other's patterns. They must cooperate to maximize each other's opportunities for intensity. The intercourse motion that maximizes her clitoral and vaginal stimulation—the bump and grind of the burlesque queen—is not the same as the motion that most passionate men unthinkingly adopt. The complexity involved in learning how to cooperate with each other's pleasure is infinitely more than the demand to last two, five, or fifteen minutes. The time that intercourse actually lasts is largely irrelevant for well-adjusted couples and the duration varies greatly with their moods. It is sometimes passionate, sometimes controlled.

Most men who worry about the timing of their orgasm should be more concerned about how to have more mutually passionate sexual moments rather than more controlled intercourse. The first step in doing this is a mental one for both partners. Men must grant their partners the responsibility for orgasm; their partners must accept. And both men and their partners need to understand the principles of the red screen metaphor that were discussed in chapter three.

Women who blame their failure to achieve orgasm on the duration of intercourse usually are surprised to learn that others can attain orgasm within moments of beginning intercourse and that arousal to orgasm can continue to escalate despite their partner's ejaculation. The penis does not immediately become soft upon ejaculation when foreplay has been extensive. The slowly softening penis can continue to provide sensations of containing the man within. In addition, by slightly elevating his pelvis when in the woman-on-top position, the man can make his pubic bone more available. Her clitoris is lying over his pubic bone and its slight elevation provides a hard surface, a platform, against which she presses her clitoris. She need only put pressure on the pubic bone to continue her drive to orgasm. Another way to accomplish orgasm is for the woman to press her pelvis to his by holding his buttocks tightly. This is more tricky to accomplish in the man-on-top position because the man has the greater mobility and from moment to moment does not know exactly what the woman needs to maximize her arousal. She does!

Unfortunately, some women erroneously assume that their partner's orgasm inevitably signals the end of sexual opportunity. It is understandable how the frustrated woman can feel shortchanged. She feels like a victim, and does not understand what she might do to help herself.

The most destructive consequence of blaming her unhappiness on the duration of intercourse is that she traps herself in the gloom of helplessness. A helpful alternative to these "victim" and "villain" roles is the clarification of each partner's contributions to their difficulty. There are certain tactical errors that men make that prolong the problem of premature ejaculation.

Tactical Errors

The first is that the premature ejaculator does everything he can to minimize his excitement. He instructs his partner not to touch certain body parts in stimulating ways; in turn, he will not touch her in erotic ways because it excites him too much. He is a lousy lover, not because he comes too fast, but because he makes himself and his partner follow silly rules.

However, these rules make a great deal of sense to him. He believes his problem is not being able to tolerate excitement so he tries to make sex less exciting. During sex he thinks of baseball, the stock market, a depressing scene—anything to distract himself from the pleasure of her body. Her excitement frightens him because it triggers his own. Even if he understands that it is absolutely normal for her excitement to intensify his own, he refuses to deal with this knowledge.

The premature ejaculator's second tactical error is that he does not effectively monitor his excitement in the vagina. In therapy, several men have described this experience as zooming from minimal excitement to orgasm in only a few seconds. This is usually not true, however. More likely the man spends so much time distracting himself from excitement that he does not notice the gradual build-up of his arousal.

Third, the premature ejaculator spoils the intensity and pleasure of his orgasm. He does this out of shame and frustration, as a seemingly well-deserved punishment for his inadequacy. When he knows he is about to come, this pleasure turns to frustration. He then ruminates about his inadequacy, which keeps him from noticing the lesser muscular contractions that lengthen the duration of orgasm. He finally apologizes to his partner who, after several repetitions of this pattern, is either crying, fantasizing the most painful way of murdering him, or writing off all possibilities for their mutual sexual pleasure.

The premature ejaculator does not understand the best way to tolerate sexual intensity is to experience sexual intensity. Avoiding these exciting sensations until the moment of intercourse is a colossal error.

The first experiences with sexual intimacy can be overwhelmingly exciting. Many young men are unable to have prolonged intercourse or be touched genitally without having an immediate orgasm. Repetition of the pleasure and intensity, learning to value the brief passionate moment for its own sake, and having his partner enjoy the power to arouse him makes it possible to have longer sexual intimacies. Within several weeks or months, the man is able to extend the duration of intimacies. His nervous system no longer responds as quickly.

Ejaculatory control is learned, acquired or developed. The difference between premature ejaculators and those with good control often is only a series of errors in reacting to sexual intimacy. New tactics can be learned even late in life. Rapidly ejaculating men must make love with a positive view towards the uniqueness of what they and their partners feel. They need to stop their concern over performance and begin seeking pleasure and intensity rather than control. They must no longer react to their orgasms with disappointment and apology. They must feel every last muscular contraction of their orgasms and allow their partners to hear their pleasure. In short, they must become better lovers, not better performers.

Joys of Ejaculatory Control

Couples who are concerned about premature ejaculation are missing something special in their lives. Men who have acquired ejaculatory control can sometimes experience a prolonged period of high excitement that enables them and their partners to feel sensations and emotions not previously felt. This high level of excitation is not the same as the passion felt during the drive to orgasm as the threshold for triggering ejaculation seems to be higher. Although men still have the passion-control dilemma, they are able to enjoy being in the vagina without being overwhelmed. This is what men sense they are missing when they worry about premature ejaculation. It is important to remember, however, that most couples do not achieve this state of grace with any great regularity. Too many factors inherent in daily living conspire against them.

Single Premature Ejaculators

Single men without steady partners may find it difficult to maintain control with each new lover. Intercourse with a new person is both more exciting and more fraught with anxiety than sex within an established sexual equilibrium. It is the horse race again with Fear running first. Luckily, the same principles useful to men in well-established sexual relationships apply. Single men can establish a much better pattern by immersing themselves in the experience without being preoccupied with performance, by sensual adventurousness rather than avoidance, and by willingness to discuss the experience with their partners.

If the nightmare of meeting a woman who insists upon a fifteen-minute performance comes true, the not-quite-established couple has a great problem on its hands. Often such a woman's disapproving impatience is enough to frighten him into silence, flight, or both. He needs to be very cautious about this moment, considering how she said what she said. What was the tone? What was her intent? Did her negative comparisons with previous partners reveal anything else beside his humiliating inadequacy? What is lovemaking like for her? Why is prolonged intercourse at this stage in their relationship so important to her?

The woman has quite a dilemma herself. If she comments about his rapid ejaculation during intercourse, she is apt to increase his anxiety. If she says nothing and the pattern persists over several months, she may be setting herself up for despair. Many not-quite-established couples break up without discussion because the women are too frustrated. Some women hope it will get better with time; others tell themselves sex just is not that important.

If the single man who is worried about premature ejaculation can be comfortable talking about lovemaking with his partner, she may find this open, honest conversation a good reason to continue their relationship.

> Mark made love to Jean in a predictable way—a few kisses, a few minutes at her breasts, a slightly longer period of caressing her clitoris followed by man-on-top intercourse. He preferred to be the more active partner in giving sexual pleasure because he was afraid of coming before intercourse if she did too much to him. Jean shocked Mark once by asking him if he was coming fast in order to hurt her. He tried to reassure her that it was just because he was nervous and they were new at this as a couple. "No, no! It's just the opposite, I'd give my right arm to be able to have sex for a long time for you. I want to please you!" Jean also admitted to being nervous and the subject was dropped until a week later when she told him that she would not be able to tolerate his brief intercourse. "Sex is too important to me to spend my life being disappointed every time we make love." This filled Mark with a sense of helplessness and dread because he always had been "fast" in the vagina and although it was early in their relationship, he was already thinking about marriage.
>
> Mark was helped to rethink his tactics of lovemaking. Jean needed no arm-twisting to be on top and to have more of her body stimulated. When Mark learned about changing how he manually stimulated her vagina from in-and-out, intercourse-simulating movements to slight lateral deflections, he was amazed at how excited Jean became. He soon relaxed and felt he was a more powerful lover. Not only did he begin to last longer during intercourse by not thrusting the entire time and using his

pubic bone, but neither of them worried any longer about how long he lasted. Two months later, they decided to marry.

Causes of Premature Ejaculation

Most people are anxious when facing the first time in any social situation such as the first date or the first starting position on a team. Men especially are afraid of disgracing themselves. The important rite of passage of intercourse is just another social role. Many, but not all, nervous systems respond to anxiety by lowering the threshold for ejaculation. This means that the more frightened a biologically susceptible man is, the faster he ejaculates. The question for a man who continues to ejaculate too quickly then can be translated into, "Why am I still anxious about intercourse?" Usually, he answers, "Because I come too fast!" But this leads him nowhere. He must look for causes beyond the obvious.

The basic question is "Why is the vagina so exciting?" Part of the answer lies in the genetic programming of mammals. Human beings are the only animals that attempt to prolong intercourse. In some monkey species, intercourse with ejaculation is over in six seconds. Elephants ejaculate on their way to the vagina. Horses and bulls are lightning fast. The neural wiring of human beings' sexual capacities are partially influenced by our kinship with lower animals.

The idea that the man should last longer for the woman's sake is a very civilized one that recognizes that the woman's needs are apart from him. It is part of our modern social heritage. Wanting to prolong intercourse goes against our genetic programming as mammals, however. The tension between our social and biological heritage is the larger framework for the passion-control dilemma. It is reasonable to believe that some men are endowed with a different biologic heritage than others. These "mammalian" men respond almost as efficiently as elephants, horses, and bulls in terms of sperm delivery and find that the vagina provokes an excitement that is beyond explanation and control.

It is not yet possible to identify the actual biological contribution to quick ejaculation. Perhaps chemicals near the sexual drive center are in a balance that sets the threshold of ejaculation too low, and someday a drug may be found that will raise the threshold. It follows, then, that changing sexual tactics may alter the chemistry of this area of the brain. This biochemical view should be considered along with powerful psychological forces that are capable of lowering the ejaculatory threshold by causing anxiety and other feelings. Feelings may change the biochemistry of the brain, which in turn lowers or raises the threshold.

Sometimes the explanation of premature ejaculation seems to be an unrecognized fear and distrust of women, sometimes it is the avoidance of directly expressing resentment, sometimes it is a camouflage to hide the woman's sexual discomfort, and sometimes it defies explanation.

> Lee, a man who acquired good ejaculatory control with one girlfriend within a month, eventually married another woman. At first, he had trouble lasting long enough for her to reach orgasm, but carefully changing his tactics he again achieved good control. However, after his wife complained "for the hundredth time" that he did not make enough money, he decided "the hell with her" and began coming too fast again. This is not a "mammalian" problem; it involves a man angry with his wife.

> After many years of good ejaculatory control, Edward had a heart attack. He was so scared about resuming intercourse that orgasm occurred almost immediately upon entering his wife. His fear of another heart attack took the form of uncontrollable ejaculation.

> Gordon, who had lived in three foster homes as a child, was unable to last more than a few seconds in his girlfriend's vagina. Although she tried to reassure him, he became very anxious that she would leave him because of his poor performance. For him, the vagina symbolized parental abandonment.

Arthur, who said his mother ruled him "with an iron fist" by never allowing him a voice in childhood decisions, was unable to learn ejaculatory control. Although his wife was a sweet, nondemanding person, he valued his freedom so much that he would not allow himself to be in a woman's control.

After years of therapy, Paul showed improvement in many aspects of his life except for his premature ejaculation. He had limitless ejaculatory control outside the vagina. Once inside, however, he was always immediately overwhelmed with excitement. Neither of his therapists could get him to change the style of his male-centered intercourse. Though he stated he badly wanted ejaculatory control, he refused to cooperate with the suggestions for learning it.

Andrew learned ejaculatory control rather quickly in therapy. His wife then became depressed and refused to have sex with him any more.

The causes of premature ejaculation are neither uniform nor simple. They must be sought individually for each man and must be considered in relation to each couple's sexual equilibrium.

Toward a Problem-Free Sexual Life

A man who ejaculates too quickly needs to:

- realize that he cannot cheat the passion-control dilemma
- realize that lasting longer in the vagina may not help his partner to attain orgasm
- stop avoiding stimulation during lovemaking and begin exposing himself to pleasurable sensations
- stop making rules for his partner and allow her to behave in a way that increases her arousal
- stop apologizing when he ejaculates, just feel and enjoy each pelvic contraction
- learn to be a better lover outside of intercourse

10

WOMEN WHO CANNOT HAVE ORGASM

This chapter discusses three problems that many women have with orgasms: never having had an orgasm, not being able to have orgasms with a partner although able to with masturbation, and no longer being regularly orgasmic although having been once. These patterns are sometimes referred to as orgasmic inhibitions. Chapter 11 discusses another widespread concern, women who are easily orgasmic except during intercourse.

When a woman cannot allow herself to do more than help her partner's arousal, she has earned the label "orgasmically inhibited." The number is not known with certainty, but many clinicians and researchers (such as Helen Kaplan, Ellen Frank and her colleagues, Murray Yost and I) estimate that possibly up to 20 percent of adult women cannot attain orgasm with ease or regularity. Even if this figure is closer to 10 percent, it is a common problem. And it is a serious one: Sexual behavior should be a cooperative system of helping each other reach the point of orgasm. The self-esteem of both partners is related to their orgasms.

> Twenty-four-year old Martha sought treatment for orgasmic inhibition a year after marrying a man she loved "intensely, beyond words." She felt both of them were being cheated by her inability to relax as she became highly aroused. She compared the sudden loss of pleasant genital sensations as her husband caressed her to a curtain being pulled in the middle of a play. Reading how-to books had not helped.
>
> Martha's manner became painfully shy when she introduced the topic of her widowed mother whom she described as a limited, clinging, manipulative, and obnoxious woman—"not a nice person at all!" Her anger at her mother was quickly followed by a hollow sounding self-accusation for "selfishly" getting married and leaving her mother alone. At the fifth meeting with me, she announced that she was cured. Several months later, she continued to be easily orgasmic.
>
> After our fourth session, Martha had an exhilarating all-night talk with a much older sister who confided that she had been "frigid" early in her marriage. The sister's disdain for her mother never passed, but the guilt that preoccupied her during her early twenties finally had. This previously estranged sister also revealed that she, too, missed their gentle henpecked father a great deal. Martha's orgasmic inhibition lifted when she realized that she had good reason to be disappointed and angry with her mother, and was justified in "moving on and growing up."
>
> Betty, a forty-two-year-old accomplished woman with good self-esteem, had begun to date an eligible man, Stan, several months earlier. She was readily aroused

> but not orgasmic as they progressed to genital intimacies. She dismissed the first few intercourse experiences as getting used to him, but soon realized that she was unable to reach orgasm no matter what she or he did. This problem took her by surprise since she was no longer in the midst of the terrible grief she felt following her husband's sudden death three years earlier. Betty described Stan as kind and considerate, and thought she could grow to love him. However, she had questions about him. "Why was he divorced? Why does his son avoid him? What am I getting into?" She worried that her uncertainties showed her tendency to make her husband more perfect in death than he was in life. "I can find something wrong with everyone if I look long enough!" On the other hand, she had been sexually at ease with her husband from the beginning and almost always orgasmic.
>
> After some discussion, Betty explained her mysterious new orgasmic inhibition by herself: "Maybe I'm not ready to commit myself to one man again." Later, she reached another conclusion, "Maybe he is not the one man I want to commit to." To me, her orgasm was a gift that she was unready to give and a sign of her apprehension about her attachment to Stan. Orgasm, for Betty, symbolized total commitment. She and I agreed that her inhibition was an intuitive message to go slowly.

Both Martha and Betty were baffled by their orgasmic inhibitions. Martha was surprised to discover one could love intensely, yet not be sexually free. Betty was shocked by the fact that her past sexual ease and comfort could not be readily transferred to her new partner. If Martha and Betty had been able to compare experiences, they might have discovered they had very different reasons for the same problem.

Cultural tradition cloaks female sexuality in mystery. Many inhibited women think they are missing something in their anatomy, as Martha did for a time. They are surprised to hear that every woman is biologically capable of having orgasms. Even those who have been regularly orgasmic, like

Betty, do not always understand why it is easier for them. "That's just the way I was. I didn't give it much thought. Isn't everyone?" We've learned, too, that men don't know as much about female sexuality as we once thought they did. The male's personal knowledge of orgasm comes mainly from his struggle to delay it—male and female experiences with orgasm are quite different.

However, Sigmund Freud's 1926 description of female sexuality as a "dark continent" no longer applies. We now know much more about orgasmic attainment and its inhibition than ever before. We are living in an age of enlightenment about female sexuality.

The Orgasmic Experience

Orgasm is not the whole point of sexual life. It is one of several landmarks in the process of female sexual development. After a woman has had an orgasm with a partner, she may be able to enjoy greater ease of arousal, orgasms in a variety of ways, more frequent orgasms, and an increasing sense of sexual freedom, curiosity, and willingness to be innovative.

Orgasm with a partner is a natural, completely normal phenomenon, the result of progressively focusing attention upon pleasurable sensations. The capacity for this reflex is prewired into the nervous system. However, in order for a woman to have an orgasm, she must be able to accept the legitimacy of these sensations, and she must understand and be comfortable with her body. Many women still have personal prohibitions against the experience of intense physical pleasure with a partner, even though they are able to have regular orgasms. These prohibitions, which may take years to completely disappear, occur because the woman's drive to orgasm requires a concentrated, single-minded attention to her own sensations. This "self-centeredness," being for oneself, is at odds with what many women consider to be their role in relation to men. In addition, it reveals a part of her she may be shy about showing to another person, which means she has to trust her partner and believe that her partner values this behavior.

Most orgasmic women know about the clitoris and accept

responsibility for using it to bring them pleasure. Men do not intuitively know where or what the clitoris is, how and when it may be touched, and what it is like to have one. A woman who depends upon her male partner to know all about clitoral stimulation could easily lead a life of sexual frustration. She must give up the illusion of male expertise, even if he is "more experienced." Growing up in a sexual sense means taking responsibility for one's sexual anatomy, function, and pleasure.

Orgasm, although it can occur during sleep, usually requires physical and mental work. Especially during intercourse, it is a result of her activity, not simply lying there passively receiving stimulation. She must actively focus her attention upon genital sensation and produce pelvic muscle contraction during the drive to orgasm.

> Once while giving a lecture to a medical audience on female orgasmic attainment, I described the intense contractions of abdominal and pelvic muscles and the prolonged facial grimace that is part of the final concerted drive to orgasm, and lightheartedly said, "So if your partner has been sweetly smiling, purring with pleasurable sounds and looking her most beautiful self—she's probably faking it!" Almost everyone laughed, except one male physician in the tenth row who turned beet red.

The most difficult way for a woman to have an orgasm is during intercourse, the so-called coital or vaginal orgasm. It is easy to physically please the man—she only has to let him continue his drive to orgasm in her vagina. But if she is to get pleasure for herself, she must do what feels good for her. In any intercourse position, the woman must consciously take care of herself in order to attain orgasm.

For example, many women enjoy the on-top position during intercourse—this position is not reserved only for men. Since there is no weight to constrain her movement, she can more easily combine stimulation from bumping and grinding her clitoris against the partner's pubic bone with vaginal sensations of thrusting.

When a woman becomes orgasmic with a partner for the first time or after a long period of time, many of her behaviors change because she now accepts herself as a person entitled to a sensual experience. She grants herself the freedom to experience her sensuality and no longer stops the stimulation when the subjective sense of being carried away begins. (Martha discovered who was "pulling the curtain.") She cooperates with intensity, rather than fighting it, and no longer switches to nonerotic thoughts when highly aroused.

Some women genitally stimulate themselves to increase their intensity, particularly during intercourse in a rear-entry-to-the-vagina position. Those who have trouble accepting supplemental clitoral self-stimulation either think it insulting to the man or that it defies some unwritten rule that the man is supposed to trigger the woman's orgasm. But most men are relieved not to assume the entire burden of the woman's orgasm and find it exciting to watch a woman stimulate herself, either alone in masturbation or cooperatively with them. Knowing that she can induce her own orgasm frees a woman from absolute dependency upon the male partner.

Childhood Sources of Orgasmic Inhibition

The reason many women cannot have orgasms with a partner is because they lack knowledge about sexual anatomy and function. This lack of information begins in early childhood and may sexually cripple women for the rest of their lives. Reading a book, hearing a lecture, or having a frank discussion can steer some people to regular orgasmic attainment, but these simple means do not help everyone. Many women do not get better, as Martha did, and never know the personal joys of sex.

Inhibition exists in all people to some extent and has at least five sources: the girl's evolving relationship to her body, her temperament, the expected difficulties of growing up, the dangers of premature pregnancy, and the threat of venereal disease. These combine to produce the woman's sexual comfort or discomfort when she enters an intimate relationship.

The Child's Relationship to Her Body

The infant's sucking is the earliest form of personal bodily pleasure. Later attempts to mouth anything and everything are also examples of infantile bodily or sexual pleasures. Witnessing the preoccupation of the baby with these and later intense anal and genital experiences, we can understand why they are considered forms of sexual experience.

Sexual difficulties as an adult may be rooted in the child's early management of these excitements. The young child is almost completely dependent upon her parents for learning the rules of the world. It only takes a few times of being slapped on the hands or given a disapproving look while she is rubbing her vulva before the girl may conclude that her genitals are bad parts of her body. Since preschool children often have genital urges, there are many opportunities to teach them negative attitudes toward bodily excitements. Thankfully, some girls do not get the intended message; they only learn that this behavior frightens their parents. In spite of that, they live comfortably with their emerging sexuality.

Anxiety about bodily pleasures is transmitted from one generation to the next. Parents may not yet have lost their own personal discomfort about bodily excitements when their daughter begins to discover her sexual self. The little girl's self-explorations may make them uncomfortable and the cycle begins again. To help her—and themselves—be more at ease, parents can talk about it in simple terms: "What you feel is called a sexual feeling. You are feeling it in your genitals. It makes you feel good. It is okay to touch your genitals, but do it when you are alone, because sexual feelings are private." Parents should convey that they know that the body's sensations are comforting and rather nice. Nothing more complicated is necessary for the young child.

A calm introduction to bodily pleasures leads to ease in masturbation during childhood and adolescence and prepares the way for orgasms with partners. Masturbation provides an opportunity for a completely controlled sexual experience. Thinking only of herself, the girl can pace her excitement, stopping whenever she chooses. In this way, she loses fear of sexual arousal.

Temperament

Each child processes thoughts, feelings, impulses, and parental demands in temperamentally different ways. Some children are "easy." They have no trouble obeying their parents and seldom create conflicts. Others are "difficult." They are fussy babies who often have separation problems and engage in a prolonged struggle over toilet training.

Children also have temperamental differences about being comfortable with bodily sensations or believing that bodily pleasures are sinful. These temperamental differences may account for persistent sexual inhibition as much as what goes on in the family. For example, sexual play between a brother and sister may or may not interfere with the girl's adult sexual life. Often it is temperament that explains different outcomes in children who have the same difficult environment.

> Judy and Trudy were ten months apart in age. Judy was an outgoing adventurous person who was well known to be defiant in response to her parents' requests. She was protective of Trudy who tended to be shy, obedient, and fearful of new circumstances. They relied heavily on each other for support during the four years that they coped with their mother's alcoholism, which began when they were entering puberty. Judy had occasional sex with partners in her senior year of high school and enjoyed it very much. Trudy fled from sexual opportunities until she was a senior in college. She then found sex with her boyfriend anxiety provoking and without pleasure. She thought her sexual fearfulness made sense. "It is just the way I am. Things are hard for me. I'm not like Judy."

Expected Difficulties in Growing Up

A person may develop sexual inhibitions even when a loving, respectful family does everything right. This is because growing up is not easy and even normal development has its problems—conflicting wishes about body urges, uneasiness about forbidden excitements, guilt feelings over other matters.

People can feel uneasy about masturbation at various stages of life, even without a parent who says it is wrong. Every adult sexual inhibition is not the result of a difficult parent-child relationship.

> Grace, the oldest of three daughters, is a talented fourteen-year-old girl from a very loving home. Her parents are financially comfortable and have never had any serious marital distress. This good student, who has many friends, has an ambition—she wants to be a figure skating champion. For many years she has applied herself with discipline and diligence to this goal. She feels as though her sexual feelings are the enemy of this dream. She finds her sexual drive frightening, even though intellectually she knows better; it threatens her self-control and single-minded devotion. She is afraid that if she gives in to her bodily urges, she may ruin her chance for greatness.

Dangers of Premature Pregnancy

Our culture works hard to teach girls about the dangers of irresponsible sexual behavior. Parents may be delighted if their daughter is sexually inhibited and hope that the fear of pregnancy is strong enough to keep her from experimenting with genital intimacies. Often, however, this fear is not quite that strong. It does not stop genital petting and intercourse—it only stops enjoyment.

> "I was so scared I was going to get pregnant in those years I didn't know what to do. I didn't want to stop our—you know what I mean. I was too embarrassed to see a doctor about birth control. I wanted to have intercourse but I was so tense we didn't try it for a long time. Now I can look back on my first big pregnancy scare and laugh. Pat came outside me, on me. I kept remembering the jokes about sperm being world-class swimmers. For two weeks I had these horrible worries about being late with my period and being banished from my home as a disgrace to the family."

The sexual inhibition that families encourage is supposed to magically disappear when the marriage ceremony takes place. This dramatic transformation actually does happen to some women; more often, however, much female sexual inhibition is caused by the failure to outgrow fear of premature pregnancy.

Fear of Venereal Disease

When the topic of teenage sex comes up in the home or school, parents and teachers almost always mention the risks of sexually transmitted diseases. Although medical information about diseases such as syphilis, gonorrhea, and herpes is available, these facts are often taught with moral messages in order to scare adolescents away from intercourse. However, using fear to prevent teenage intercourse and venereal diseases has not worked well—scare tactics probably do more to inhibit sexual pleasure and cause fear of being punished through disease than to prevent intercourse.

Fear of AIDS does prevent intercourse, however, because the stakes are higher. AIDS threatens the lives of women who have sex with men whose backgrounds they don't know. Parents, teachers, and teenage girls have begun to realize that the most devastating danger of sexual activity is no longer premature pregnancy—it can be premature death. We don't yet know whether this will result in more orgasmic inhibition, but I suspect it might.

Meanings of Orgasm

We cannot discuss the three patterns of orgasmic inhibition without mentioning the important symbolic meanings that women unknowingly give to orgasm. These meanings have a number of sources. Many psychotherapists emphasize that they can be traced to the influence of parental relationships on the girl's emerging gender identity. Many feminists focus on the difficulty of growing up sexually healthy in a male-dominated society. Both therapists and feminists are concerned about the mounting evidence that many girls are sexually abused—for every girl who can clearly remember such instances, there is at least one other who has unclear or no memories of them. In this section, the common meanings of orgasm are described in order to understand how powerful this symbol is for women who are unable to have orgasm.

If a girl or woman can have orgasms during masturbation, she is forced to realize that she actually is a sexual person. Her masturbation fantasies show her that her sexuality is defined in terms of particular elements, such as men, intercourse, and admiration.

Orgasms achieved with a partner have two vital meanings: the woman's emotional independence from her parents and her capacity to trust her partner. Many women who never have orgasms with a partner are emotionally trapped in some old dilemma with their original family. Like Martha, they are often angry or disappointed with one or both parents and feel guilty about harboring resentment towards those they are supposed to love. Women who can concentrate on their own and their partner's pleasures are, in a sexual sense, free of their parents. They do not necessarily love them any more or have less resentment toward them; it is just that their bodily pleasure is no longer tied to family issues. This is a highly individual matter. Not all women in Martha's situation would have trouble with orgasms. But she did. However, after an all-night talk with her sister, she was able to untie marital sex from guilt about her bitterness toward her mother. Others might have done the same thing on their own.

Adolescent sexual behavior can be an act of defiance. Having orgasms with a partner usually requires a sense of readiness, gradually achieved by increasing, genuine emotional independence from parents. Much adolescent sexual activity occurs before a girl feels capable of such independence. She may feel too guilty about her behavior to enjoy it, too unready for the giant step of physical intimacy, too uncertain about her role in sex to assert her right to pleasure, or too needy of simply being loved, held, and cared for to even consider these more luxurious self-expressions. Orgasm, therefore, is a symbol of the girl's personal emotional accomplishment—her growing separateness from her parents.

The other common vital meaning of orgasm is trust of the partner. Many inhibited women have orgasms with masturbation but not with their partners. They do not feel secure with their partners even though they know them to be trustworthy. This paradox is often the result of distrust and apprehension from an earlier, unsafe relationship. Besides depriving the woman of orgasms, this distrust can eventually seriously injure her partner's self-esteem.

> Joanne had a recurrent masturbation fantasy involving sexual intercourse with either of two unidentified men, after they fight each other into mutual utter exhaustion. Her early life was spent with a mentally ill father who terrified the household with his frequent rages. Her husband, a gentle man who rarely raised his voice, could not understand her emotional distance from him. She acted as though she were terrified of any sexual or psychological intimacy. He sought help for his anger and sadness over being alone in his marriage when he found himself contemplating suicide.

This woman was able to have orgasms with her husband after one year of psychotherapy, during which she dealt with her fear of trusting her husband with any of her feelings; she and the therapist rarely discussed sex. After some life experiences, however, there is a limit to how trusting any individual can be. For the following woman, the meaning of orgasm as a personal possession was so important that her partner simply had to understand that she would not, and likely could not, trust anyone enough to have an orgasm with him.

> Bev, an experienced prostitute, had never been able to have an orgasm with a partner. She was orgasmic by herself and was expert at faking it with her customers. She developed a live-in relationship with a man who had helped her over many tight spots. His painful deduction that she had been faking orgasm for five years led her to tell him why she felt she would never have an orgasm with her partner. Although she admitted that their relationship was as close to love as she had ever felt, she

> insisted that her orgasm belonged to her alone and that she could not share it. He stopped pushing her on the issue after she told him that when she was twelve, her heroin-addicted mother gave her a Seconal and made love to her so that a man could watch for a fee. She reassured him that there was nothing wrong with his lovemaking and that she actually enjoyed pleasing him.

Whether from a lack of trust or a lack of emotional independence, orgasm symbolizes fear for orgasmically inhibited women—for example, fear of discovering angry feelings toward a parent or a lingering, intense, childlike love for their fathers. They may be afraid of losing control of their excitement because this emotion can make them aware of some guilt-laden memory.

> Tricia, a happily married woman, responded to sexual intimacy with brief arousal followed by anxiety. After several months of sexual nervousness, she began to remember lying in bed with her father to comfort him through his depressive spells when she was a teenager. Although no sexual activity occurred between them, she was secretly excited by their closeness during these naps. Ten years later, these memories were interfering with her lovemaking. She had much difficulty acknowledging that she imagined a physical intimacy with her troubled father, but the emergence of bits and pieces of this fantasy produced her anxiety with her husband. She suffered from her memories and from the fact that orgasm had come to symbolize her incestual guilt.

This person's actual experience is not as important as the fact that her mind constructed a special meaning for orgasm. For her and for many inhibited women, orgasm is frightening because it has come to symbolize something else that is frightening.

Society can either encourage or inhibit the woman's discovery of her sexual self. There are two compelling explanations for the fact that so many women initially have difficulty discovering the naturalness of orgasms with their partners: We are not correctly educating young girls about sex, and we are not providing them with parental relationships that let them feel comfortable with their emerging sexual selves. Changing women's roles have led to widespread recognition that their sexual needs involve more than just pleasing a male partner. Articles and other information about orgasm have encouraged many women to more fully discover their sexuality. Self-help books, such as Lonnie Barbach's *For Yourself: The Fulfillment of Female Sexuality,* have been very useful in helping women become regularly orgasmic. However, some women need more than factual information. Those with persistent problems of distrust, unexplained apprehension, or embarrassment over their excitement may require some type of therapy. Even the most experienced therapist, however, cannot help everyone to achieve orgasms with partners.

Sexual Fantasies

The sexual fantasies of orgasmically inhibited women are especially interesting because they provide clues to their requirements for arousal and to the sources of their inhibitions. Some fantasy themes recur over decades and seem absolutely necessary for orgasm. Orgasmic inhibition may come from the fear of allowing a fantasy to form or of knowing what the fantasy means.

Claudia: I can only have an orgasm if I imagine myself nuzzling at an older woman's breast when I am very excited. Does this mean I am gay?

Doctor: I don't think so. The fantasy reassures you that you are safe at a time when you are frightened by the intensity of your feelings.

Claudia: But why is it always a woman?

Doctor: Please, you tell me.

Claudia: You mean I am with my mommy, so to speak? But my mother wasn't around that much in my life to comfort me!

Doctor: I think that's the point. Sexual intensity scares you and you've created a comforting mother to help you feel less anxious. You carry a good mother with you in fantasy.

Claudia: That's weird. Are you sure?

Doctor: Not absolutely, but let's hold onto this idea and see if it relieves your worry. Maybe we'll understand your image of the breast differently in the future. But, you've never told me anything else that indicated that you are attracted to women.

Claudia: That's for sure!

This power of fantasy to gratify wishes and soothe worries works for many women—they use images and scenes to increase sexual excitement with a partner. Women who believe they are too fat may fantasize about being thin; those who are tired of making love with their husbands may turn them into movie stars. Fantasies are very private and need not be discussed with the partner. Even so, many women avoid fantasy during lovemaking because this mental act feels like infidelity or because their erotic images seem sick to them. This is often the situation when a woman is preoccupied by images of masochistic experiences.

> Fran, a woman who had lived with a gentle man for over a year, was thought by him to be sexually unmotivated and totally unresponsive. What her boyfriend did not know was that she masturbated frequently to images of being spanked, yelled at, and being "taken" by sinister communist troops. Occasionally she imagined herself tortured with hot irons or pierced with needles. She could not remember an orgasm without such highly arousing themes. She felt trapped by her problem. She felt her erotic life was "disgustingly depraved" and needed to be kept free from her intimate relationship. But she had limited interest and capacity to enjoy anything but her masturbation.

Over several months of weekly discussions, Fran began to understand that she was reliving her childhood experiences of humiliating physical beatings and the sense that her naughtiness had caused her parents' divorce. She was not able to share any excitement with her partner until she spent almost a year in therapy. Even then images from her once elaborate masturbation fantasies still appeared, although her attitude toward them became much more accepting.

Of course, most fantasies that help women attain orgasms are far less memorable. They are romantic and involve being treated as an important, beloved person by a powerful and respected partner. While some may be able to see the childhood longings for an improved relationship with parents in such fantasies, these scenarios have more to do with the present and the woman's intuitive knowledge of what she needs to allow her sexuality free rein.

> Mary Lou, who took ballet as a child, developed a favorite fantasy that she used both in masturbation and during lovemaking with her busy husband. She is a dancer, whirling on stage to the delight of her audience. Afterwards, she is greeted with flowers and great admiration. She is finally alone with her rich powerful suitor in her star dressing room and they make passionate love on the divan and floor.

Loss of Orgasmic Ability

Usually the loss of orgasms is due to psychological and social problems, but there are also physical reasons for orgasmic difficulty. The most common physical cause is medication. When a drug is responsible for the problem, orgasm may still be possible but the woman has to work too hard for it. Antidepressants, tranquilizers, pain medications, and drugs of abuse can interfere with the brain's coordination of orgasm. The problem quickly disappears when the drug is discontinued or the dosage is lowered.

> Carol, who masturbated to orgasm several times a week and had orgasms during intercourse with her husband, was given a drug to combat symptoms of depression. When the dose was increased beyond 80 mg, she no longer could achieve orgasm. At 60 mg daily, she could

have an orgasm but had to work harder for it. At 40 mg, she had normal orgasms, although her depressed mood and general anxiety level were worse.

Most diseases that interfere with orgasmic attainment do so indirectly through energy depletion or depression. Women with heart or lung disease or severe anemia may not have orgasms easily because the effort induces too much shortness of breath. Women who are depressed about their loss of health and attractiveness may not feel intense sexual excitement because they concentrate on their impairments rather than their sensations.

Disease and surgery rarely are direct causes of loss of orgasm. When they are, it is usually because they interfere with the transmission of sensations from the genitals to the spinal cord and brain. Multiple sclerosis, diabetes, vascular disease of the pelvis, hysterectomy, and operations on the sympathetic nerves may cause orgasms to disappear in some, but certainly not all women with these conditions.

An endless variety of temporary situations can induce orgasmic difficulty: unexpected pregnancy, abortion, spontaneous miscarriage, death or serious illness of a parent, loss of a job, worry about spouse's health, disagreements with a child, a court appearance, and so on. The sexual problem usually disappears when the crisis passes or the problem is solved.

Most women who stop having orgasms over a long period of time are either suffering from depression, involved in deteriorating relationships, or both. Lack of sexual desire is a fundamental problem in depressed women. Deteriorating relationships are usually caused by unexpressed or unresolved anger over disappointments with the partner. Orgasm often becomes a symbolic gift to the partner, but in a deteriorating relationship, the woman may feel so annoyed with her partner's behavior outside the bedroom that denying the gift becomes a matter of pride and dignity. The unspoken retort is, "Not after what you did!" Her continual failure to attain orgasm usually jars her partner's self-esteem.

After considerable discussion about the pros and cons of a mid-career move for the sake of the husband's profes-

> sional happiness, and three specific promises about what would happen once they did move, a childless couple uprooted themselves, leaving behind family members and friends. Gail had expected to feel lost and unhappy for several months while she settled in, but after eighteen months of aggravation, depression, and an inability to have an orgasm with her husband she sought help. The mystery of her lost orgasms was solved when she recalled that he failed to follow through on any of his three promises to spend time with her, to actively help foster new friends as a couple, and to not object to the expense of flying to visit her sisters or calling long distance. She had never lost her ability to have orgasm during masturbation.

This woman was concerned about her lost orgasmic capacity because she was unaware of her motives for withholding orgasm. However, many formerly orgasmic women are unconcerned because they understand their situation—it is a matter of pride, power, and punishment.

Toward a Problem-Free Sexual Life

A woman who has never been able to have an orgasm needs to know:

- that she is physically capable of having orgasms
- that there is hope because other women in her situation have become regularly orgasmic
- that clitoral stimulation is very important to intense arousal
- that masturbation is helpful when learning to tolerate high levels of arousal
- that she must take responsibility for her own orgasm

- that it is important to talk to her partner about what she likes and doesn't

A woman who can easily have orgasms alone but not with her partner needs to know:

- if she doesn't trust her partner enough to share her orgasm
- if this lack of trust is related to the partner's behavior or to childhood experiences
- if her masturbation fantasies are too private to have in the partner's presence

A woman who once had regular orgasms needs to ask herself these questions:

- Could the medicine I'm taking be playing a role?
- Am I in good health?
- Am I too resentful of my partner to share my orgasm?
- Am I too depressed to have an orgasm?
- Am I too guilty to allow myself this personal pleasure?

Many women concerned with their orgasms seek brief psychotherapy.

11

WOMEN WHO CANNOT HAVE ORGASMS DURING INTERCOURSE

Fact: More than half of regularly orgasmic women do not have orgasms during intercourse. This is one of the most puzzling aspects of women's sexual experience. Even though most women attain orgasm through hand or mouth stimulation of the clitoris, many fear that something is wrong with them if the man's penis cannot drive them to orgasm. Many such couples find their sex lives physically and emotionally fulfilling, but occasionally worry that their lovemaking must be second-rate because they cannot bring about the woman's orgasm during intercourse.

A woman may wonder: "Do I not love him enough to come during intercourse?" "Am I physically abnormal?" "Am I sexually inhibited or psychologically unhealthy in some way?" "Do we not fit physically together well?" Her partner asks himself comparable questions, and even when the woman and man discuss this together, it is difficult to come up with reasonable answers.

Over much of this century, mental health professionals—the "experts" on sex—had a strong conviction on this subject: These women were sexually inadequate. In the 1970s and 1980s, this conviction weakened considerably as our culture became aware that no one discipline is entitled to have the last word on sexual matters. However, even though a great deal has been learned during the last two decades about having orgasms, it is still a mystery why some women can readily climax during intercourse, while for others it is rare or even impossible.

The differing opinions on this subject can be grouped into three categories: (1) It is a serious neurotic symptom, (2) it is just one of many normal variations of female sexuality, and (3) it is a minor sexual learning disorder. We shall review the background for each argument and discuss them further. However, this author takes the position that the third view is the most reasonable.

A Serious Neurotic Symptom

The first opinion is that women who cannot climax during intercourse suffer from a serious neurotic symptom. This belief is based upon the psychoanalytic theory of the development of femininity originally described by Sigmund Freud in 1905. His theory suggests that the problem stems from an early life disruption of the normal sequence of her evolving sense of femininity. In those days, there was no such phrase as "gender identity." The development of femininity meant the shifting of "libido"—the focus of sexual instinct—from one body part to another. Freud and others believed the normal sequence was that the preschool girl's sexual excitement would shift from the mouth to the anus to the clitoris in early life, and finally would move to the vagina during adolescence. The sign that feminine development had occurred normally was that the sexually active woman was able to have orgasms during intercourse. This implied that the transfer from the clitoris to the vagina had taken place sometime during adolescence or before, and that therefore the woman was sexually mature.

In 1951, during the heyday of this theory, Edmund Bergler estimated that 80 percent of women could not have orgasms during intercourse, especially with the man on top. He labeled their inability "frigidity," and concluded that its high frequency showed how difficult it was for girls to pass through their early developmental stages in a healthy manner.

Bergler and other psychoanalysts had two explanations for the inability to transfer sexual excitement from the clitoris to the vagina. One was the unresolved Oedipal conflict in which the adult woman is still trapped in subtle dilemmas involving triangular relationships between her and mother and father. The other was penis envy—the idea that some toddlers are unhappy about being girls when they discover that their genitals are different from boys'. These explanations build on each other. The woman's inability to have orgasms from thrusting in the vagina could come from both her envy of boys' "better equipment" and her later competition with mother for a special place in father's heart.

This theory had an enormous power over many couples' lives for most of this century. Countless women spent years in therapy trying to resolve their childhood conflicts so they might finally grow up and have an orgasm the "mature" way—during intercourse. And even today, many couples unequivocally accept this. "I guess my therapy didn't work because I still don't have vaginal orgasms. Kevin thinks it's no big deal, but I wish I could have dug deeper and worked out my early life problems so I could come in the normal way."

Men do not have to understand Freud's theory of feminine development to think that their partners' inability to come during intercourse is the result of the woman's inhibitions. If, while the man is concentrating on his pleasure in her vagina, the woman also feels intense pleasure, his only concern may be who will achieve orgasm first. In addition, when a woman has an orgasm during intercourse, her partner is assured about the adequacy of his penile thrusting and ultimately, his masculinity. Moreover, it is a small step beyond this to think that her orgasm means that she cares for her partner.

The theory of "inadequacy," which suggests the presence of significant unconscious or neurotic conflict, bears a suspicious kinship with a male-centered view of female sexuality. This theory defines normal femininity in a way that is most convenient for the man: It gives *him* the power to cause her orgasm, and if she cannot climax during his thrusting, it is because *she* is defective.

This view finally has been called into question by many mental health professionals. It has also been ridiculed by the women's movement which has no patience for its circular reasoning and its familiar male-centered domination of women. However, many women, because of the ideas that predominated in our culture when they were young, still believe their sexual response is defective even though they have sexual desire, are easily aroused, and are regularly orgasmic. Thankfully, many others have learned by themselves to listen to their bodies, not to their culture.

A Normal Variation of Female Sexuality

Even before the women's movement, the first major challenge to the psychoanalytic theory came through science. In 1966, William Masters and Virginia Johnson published the results of their sex research in their classic book, *Human Sexual Response.* After measuring the sexual responses of hundreds of women, they concluded that there was no truth to the theory that women had two distinct types of orgasm, an immature clitoral one and an authentic vaginal one. They believed that orgasms, regardless of the means of stimulation, consist of the same bodily responses and that the clitoris is the key. Although women's reports of their sensations may differ from one orgasm to another, they experience the same rhythmic muscular contractions in the pelvis whether orgasm is attained during intercourse, masturbation, partner manual stimulation, or with a vibrator.

Masters and Johnson explained the three forms of clitoral stimulation that occur when orgasm is achieved during intercourse: the bumping of the clitoris during deep penile thrusting, the woman's tendency to move side-to-side during deep penetration in a grinding fashion, and the effect of the downward pressure exerted on the inner labial lips as the penis moves in and out of the vagina.

Masters and Johnson proclaimed that "an orgasm is an orgasm is an orgasm!" and announced that it was as normal to have an orgasm from direct clitoral stimulation—the efficient way—as from indirect stimulation during intercourse—the inefficient way. This relieved many women, who could not understand why intercourse never led to orgasm, and their partners, who secretly felt their masculinity was flawed.

However, some people refused to accept Masters and Johnson's conclusions. Among the skeptical were women who recognized that they had two distinct orgasms: a superficial clitoral one that often was more physically intense, and a deep pelvic or vaginal one that was less intense but more emotionally fulfilling.

Many psychoanalysts also remained dubious, insisting that women's sexual responses require privacy and could not possibly be studied in a laboratory. They argued that after they helped some women with their emotional difficulties in psychotherapy, their patients began to have orgasms during intercourse. In these clinical situations, the analyst, the patient, and her partner were convinced about the separateness of the two orgasms and the superiority of the "vaginal" one. For example, in 1974 Dr. Natalie Shainess argued that there was only one authentic feminine sexual response and that was the vaginal orgasm! However, these arguments and authoritative pronouncements missed the point of Masters and Johnson's research which was to disprove the assumption that one way to have orgasms was immature and the other was a sign of psychological health or sexual maturity. These distinctions were value judgments, not scientific facts.

The new and the pre-1966 positions were at odds. Masters and Johnson's emphatic restatements that the basic objective bodily response during orgasm was the same, even though the woman's subjective experience of orgasm was different, did not change the minds of skeptics who continued to believe that one means of attaining orgasm was normal and the other immature. Even now, many people, including mental health professionals, hold fervently to the clitoral vs. vaginal or immature vs. mature distinctions.

A Minor Sexual Learning Disorder

The inability to have orgasm through intercourse is neither invariably a sign of deep-seated neurotic conflict about femininity nor simply a normal variation. The main reason why many women cannot have orgasms during intercourse is that they and their partners have not learned how to use their bodies more fully.

The popularization of the "G" spot in the early 1980s helped to clarify this theory about why many women have not learned to climax during intercourse. The "G" spot was alleged to be a quarter-to-half-dollar-sized area on the upper vaginal wall about two inches from the opening (as illustrated in figure 7). Supposedly, only the lucky women who responded uniquely to its stimulation possessed it. Many women reported finding their spot and having an unusually intense orgasm. The sensations were described as initially mimicking urinary urgency followed by a voluptuous orgasm. The "G" spot became the most likely source of the vaginal orgasm.

This "breakthrough" had its skeptics. Why had women not discovered this long ago? Why had this location not been discovered by the thousands of investigations of the vagina performed by anatomists, physiologists, gynecologists, and pathologists since the microscope had been invented?

The answer is that there is no anatomically distinct "G" spot. It is true that when this area of the vagina is stimulated, voluptuous sensations often result. These sensations are due to the mechanical distention of bladder and internal clitoris tissues (most of the clitoris is not visible from the outside). It is also true, however, that if the opposite wall of the vagina is stimulated, there can be voluptuous sensations from the distention of the vaginal and rectal wall tissues. And indeed, if the side walls of the vagina are stimulated,

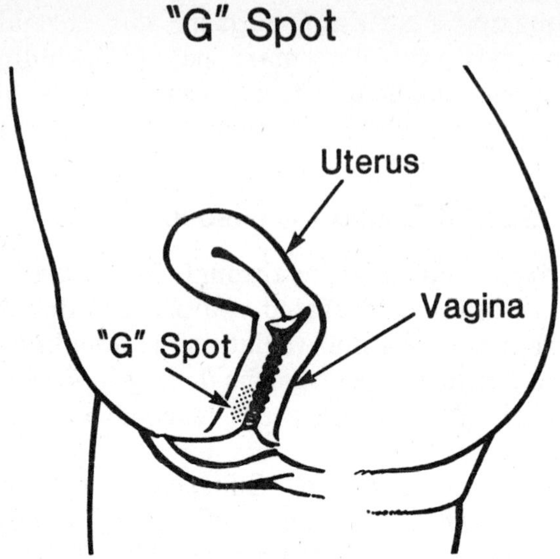

Fig. 7 Voluptuous sensations can be provoked by gentle lateral pressure everywhere in the vagina, not just the "G" spot.

slightly different sensations result from the vagina and the peritoneal lining of the tubes, bowel, and ovaries. No doubt, the idea of the "G" spot helps us to realize that arousal depends on the type, duration, and location of external and internal genital stimulation.

The "G" spot is voluptuous because it combines vaginal, bladder, and clitoral stimulation. The opposite wall is voluptuous but different because it substitutes rectal for bladder and clitoral stimulation. Other theories summarized by J. Singer and I. Singer in 1972 included the notion that the bumping of the uterus, ovaries, tubes, and bowel is the source of orgasms achieved during vigorous intercourse, triggered by sensations that arise in the thin outer lining of these organs known as peritoneal tissues. Most women find it difficult to discriminate between these sources of genital stimulation because sensations from the vagina are not well localized. However, whatever genital areas are stimulated, the same sequences of muscle contraction result. If the majority of the intense stimulation occurs within the vagina, the woman and her partner may feel they have just achieved the "vaginal" orgasm. If the stimulation centered on the clitoris, they may think they have just had a "clitoral" orgasm. In fact, the woman has had an orgasm—period. There are multiple pathways to trigger orgasm. That is why I believe that the inability to have orgasm during intercourse is a minor sexual learning problem. Individuals and couples place meanings on these separate pathways and think that there are different types of orgasms. If there are different types of orgasms, there are far more than two—sexually adventuresome couples may trigger orgasms in a dozen different ways. Masters and Johnson were simply saying that however it gets triggered, the same bodily events occur.

How to Have an Orgasm During Intercourse

If a woman wants to try to have an orgasm during intercourse, she must pay more attention to pleasing herself than him during some moments. She should know that the vagina is much more responsive to lateral or side-to-side movement of its walls than to in-out stimulation. Intercourse triggers orgasm because either the woman's motions distend her vaginal walls laterally and stimulate her adjacent tissues, or the partner's thrusting produces the same sensations. Many women who are regularly orgasmic during intercourse have discovered that with the deep penile containment, they can mimic the burlesque queen's bump-and-grind motions to bring themselves to orgasm. While this is easier when the woman is on top, some women can do it on their backs as well. Other women who have orgasms during intercourse learn how to move their clitoris against the male's pubic bone in a head-to-toe plane while containing the erection deep in their vagina. "I used to believe my wife needed my penis during intercourse to come, but the more I pay attention to what happens when she is climaxing, the more I think it is not so much my penis, as this bone. What a letdown!"

A woman and her partner must discover and rediscover what feels best and do it. The body does not lie, nor does it function according to any particular theory. It is there, available for discovery. It is both partners' responsibility to discover the patterns of her body. The challenge is to learn how to use genital stimulation to provide various routes to orgasm—including the ones that simultaneously make the man and woman feel good about themselves. Many women and their partners have simply not yet learned to do this.

A woman's inability to have an orgasm during intercourse is a minor learning problem. There are many individual ways to achieve orgasm. Some women find a way that works and stay with that pattern most of their lives. Others are more curious and sexually adventurous and come in many different ways. Not everything is possible for every woman. However, since she is part of a sexual equilibrium, her partner's attitudes, knowledge, behavior, and capacities also contribute to her sexual experience.

Toward a Problem-Free Sexual Life

If a woman wants to have orgasm during intercourse, she should:

- believe in her body and its sensations rather than in experts and theories
- pay more attention to pleasing herself than her partner some of the time during intercourse
- educate her partner about what does and does not please her
- know that the vagina is more responsive to side-to-side stimulation than to in-and-out movements
- take responsibility for moving her pelvis during intercourse in ways that feel good, rather than in ways she thinks are normal or proper

12

MEN WHO ARE UNABLE TO HAVE INTERCOURSE

Impotence, the inability to achieve or maintain an erection, is a common problem for men of every sexual orientation. Today, because of recent treatment advances, physicians and mental health professionals are able to help many impotent men and their partners. Men become impotent for a variety of physical and psychological reasons. All of these need to be clarified so that the man, his partner, and their professional helper can make a wise choice together about how to proceed with therapy. This requires frank, thorough discussion of very private matters. Anything less is ill-advised.

Impotence is not the same as a problem with desire, ejaculation, satisfaction, or fertility; these often require separate treatments. A treatment for the inability to have an erection was developed in England by G. S. Brindley in 1983 and is effective almost beyond belief. Medication can now be injected into the penis to cause an erection that lasts several hours or more. A floppy erection appears within a few minutes of the injection and then becomes firm after engaging in foreplay or simply waiting twenty minutes for the full effect of the drugs. Now that this treatment is available, reliable, consistent potency can be restored to men who have been impotent for many years. It may feel like a miracle to them and their partners, and it has certainly been much appreciated by physicians who could not restore potency with other methods.

Jim had never had a potency problem until his mid-fifties, when his erections became unreliable. Although occasionally he could have normal intercourse, most of the time he would lose his erection during or just before vaginal entry. On rare occasions, he could not get one at all. His attempts at lovemaking with his wife, Helen, became less frequent with each embarrassing sexual incompletion. Within a year he avoided sex entirely rather than risking frustration.

He thought about trying a new partner but, after thirty years with the same person decided not to. Anyway, he was sure that the problem was not in his relationship with his wife.

Helen assumed that the potency problem was a symptom of his resentment over her doting relationship with their mildly retarded son. Jim freely acknowledged that this was a major annoyance in their relationship, but could not understand why this should cause impotence now and not years earlier. He argued that something was physically wrong: "I don't want sex in the same way anymore. I am never horny!" While he intellectually wished to make love, the possibility of failure kept him from trying. He was dismayed by the inability of several doctors to find any definite physical cause; their opinion was that his impotence was due to marital resentment.

His doctors agreed with him that his lack of morning and masturbatory erections and his brief semi-hard erections with Helen suggested physical disease, but his general vigor, normal physical and laboratory examinations, and the fact that he did not smoke, drink, or take medications pointed them away from a physical explanation. Jim finally agreed to Helen's suggestion that they seek marital therapy because he wanted to do something about her obvious frustration and he did not know where else to turn.

On those occasions when disagreements about their son were thoroughly aired, his erections were firm enough to have intercourse. These encouraging experiences were invariably followed by more erection difficulties. "Things have to be perfect between Helen and me for us to have intercourse—hell, that's not how it used to be!" Over several months, Helen became more accepting of the idea that something was the matter beside resentment. She sensed that their time for intercourse was over and contented herself with trying to help him become more affectionate. Jim, who had only shown his affection during intercourse, insisted that he was too old a dog to learn new tricks.

He eventually had a laboratory test that showed that he had a physical problem—many small obstructions within the blood vessels leading to his penis. Soon after this, papaverine and phentolamine injections became available. The urologist injected these drugs directly into Jim's penis. He was relieved to feel only momentary pain as the needle went in. In twelve minutes, he had the first erection that he could feel confident about in two years. He and Helen raced home to use it. Everything worked normally except that he did not lose his erection after ejaculation. He tried to make up for lost time by having intercourse again, but ran out of interest and energy before a second orgasm. Within several months he had learned to inject himself at home. Now, at age fifty-nine, with an assist from one or two weekly injections, Jim is affectionate again in his own way.

Jim and Helen's story is not unusual. Thousands of other people may be able to benefit as well from these injections.

For many couples, they are an improvement over the other physical treatments for impotence such as the surgical implantation of a prosthesis, the use of a tourniquet at the base of the penis, or a vacuum pump applied to the penis before sex. A review of the causes for Jim's impotence will show clearly how these injections actually helped. However, as we shall see throughout this discussion, no one treatment—individual psychotherapy, couple's psychotherapy, pills, injections, pumps and tourniquets, or surgery—helps everyone.

Jim's vascular disease prevented enough blood from getting to the penis when he felt sexually aroused. After several unpleasant experiences, his anxiety about failure made it difficult for him to relax and feel aroused. The less aroused he felt, the fewer neural commands his brain sent to his blood vessels to route blood to his penis. He became trapped in a cycle of performance anxiety: worry leading to less blood flow which led to more worry, and so on. Resentment about their son decreased his motivation for sex and made it difficult to concentrate on sensation, adding to the performance anxiety cycle. In addition, like many men in their fifties, Jim seemed to have a diminished sex drive. This may be because of changes in the sexual drive center in his brain associated with aging. This loss of drive was another factor in his decreased interest in sex. Jim's motivation for sex returned when the injections assured him he had no reason to fear failure. But even though he regularly has had intercourse, he has not become "horny"—his sexual drive center cannot go back to its youthful condition.

Jim's impotence was caused by a combination of physical and psychological factors. The physical ones included his vascular disease and loss of sexual drive. The psychological ones included his performance anxiety and his resentment. Together these factors led to the temporary halt of Helen and Jim's sexual life. The injections were enough to reverse the effects of the vascular disease and the performance anxiety.

No single treatment is effective for impotence because many different problems produce the symptom. Papaverine and phentolamine injections, like the surgical implantation of a penile prosthesis, only cause a mechanical erection. The man and his partner must be able to supply other necessary ingredients to have emotionally satisfying lovemaking.

> Don never had a reliable erection with a partner. During his twenties, with a dozen or so women, he could either obtain no erection or suffered through a nervous intercourse without ejaculation. He sustained potency for only about two months before and after his marriage at age thirty-five—he and Missy had intercourse perhaps five times. He avoided sex so completely for the next four years that she frequently thought to annul their childless marriage. At his physician's recommendation, Don began psychotherapy. Progress was slow because Don rarely knew what he was feeling and had almost no childhood memories. When his wife joined the sessions, his inability to allow himself to feel any emotion became apparent. Then, one year into their therapy, the injections became available.
>
> Don was amazed: Within ten minutes he had a fully firm, stand-up erection which he quickly used for his first intercourse in four years. Both he and Missy were delighted. However, the plan to use the injections until Don would spontaneously engage in lovemaking ended abruptly when Missy refused intercourse immediately after the second injection. She screamed that he hadn't talked with her about anything personal, hadn't been affectionate, and that she didn't know whether she wanted to be married to him. Don was devastated and decided that he had been right all along—his wife was dangerously emotionally unstable. Missy concluded, "he is happiest when he is avoiding me."
>
> This injection incident brought them back to the brink of divorce, which they averted by avoiding each other for a while. Missy took a second job, which made her too tired to want sex very often. Don bought dark room equipment to keep himself busy in the evenings. When Missy said she was willing to try a third injection, Don kept forgetting to schedule it. He soon realized that his forgetting was caused by his fear of another scene.

Don has lifelong psychological impotence and, like other men with this problem, is uncomfortable with himself as a sexual person. He has very limited abilities to know what he feels and to talk about himself personally. These traits make it hard for him to relate to Missy in a way that allows her personal self-expression. "Telling Don about me is like talking to someone who doesn't speak English!" Don's experiences with the injections have taught him that there is more to sex than a rigid penis and have made clear Missy's requirements for affection and psychological intimacy. He now knows he is fearful of intimacy with anyone and worries that he may live the rest of his life alone if he does not overcome his avoidance of emotional contact. His reasons for going to therapy have expanded considerably from his wish to fix his penis.

Studies such as those of Kinsey, Finkle, Babbitt and Rubin, suggest that there are vast numbers of impotent men like Jim and Don. The medical profession has had difficulty deciding exactly how widespread the problem is because men are uncomfortable discussing the subject. The available information, however, suggests that this problem increases dramatically as men get older, especially over forty. Young men are rarely permanently impotent, although brief episodes of impotence are common. Men in their seventies may be unable as often as they are able to sustain intercourse. On the study in which my colleagues and I surveyed patients in a family doctor's waiting room, one out of four men between eighteen and seventy-nine admitted that they have periodic difficulty attaining and maintaining erections.

Physicians used to classify impotence into four types: lifelong psychological impotence, new onset psychological impotence, organic impotence, and mixed organic and psychological impotence. Lately, however, this classification system is being replaced by a listing of all the identifiable psychological and physical factors contributing to the difficulty. For example, in Jim's case they were vascular disease, effect of age on his sex drive, performance anxiety, and resentment. All these need to be identified before any therapy is undertaken.

Psychological Causes

Sometimes impotence is purely psychological in origin. The simplest way for a man to tell whether his impotence is psychological is to think about the pattern of his erections after the impotence began. There is little chance that it is caused by physical factors if he has fully firm, lasting erections that reliably occur under any circumstances—for example, with masturbation, in the morning upon waking up, in the middle of the night when awakened from sleep, with the partner prior to intercourse, with a different partner, or when reading about or seeing others behave sexually. Don, a classic example of pure psychological impotence, had frequent, lasting, stand-up morning erections and masturbated regularly with a good erection.

Recognizing psychological impotence from the pattern of erections is easiest in physically healthy men under forty-five who are not depressed. As a man ages, becomes depressed or develops a chronic illness, his erections may never be completely firm, a fact that could make him think he has a purely physical problem. However, his impotence is probably largely psychological if it follows any of these patterns:

- lasting, stand up, firm erections until penetration is attempted
- no erections with partner, firm erections with masturbation
- consistent erections with one partner but not another
- consistent erections with men but not with women
- erections with a particular fantasy but not without it

When a man is impotent, he asks himself, "Why don't I have an erection?" This is the wrong question. If he were to ask, "What am I feeling when I am not erect?" he may be able to answer: "I feel scared," "I don't want to make love," "I feel angry," "I feel humiliated," "I am preoccupied," "I feel guilty," or "I don't belong here!"

A man is psychologically impotent because he is unaware of or unwilling to admit to such feelings. If he were more honest with himself and his partner, he might describe himself as frightened, disinterested, angry, or guilty rather than impotent. This realization can help immensely. It takes the mystery out of impotence and directs the man's attention to the reason for his feelings.

> Bob, a thirty-eight-year-old father of two boys, said he was served with divorce papers without any idea that his wife was planning such a move. Several weeks later, he learned that she had been involved with her college boyfriend for the last four years of their marriage. He stridently objected to the divorce and even begged, but she went through with it. Once single, this handsome, hard-working, pleasant man was able to have as many dates as he wanted. He coped with his loneliness by filling the evenings with female companionship. Almost everyone he met was willing to sleep with him. "Ironically, I now have what I dreamed about when I was a teenager: I'm a rooster in a hen house!" Without exception, however, he was unable to complete intercourse. Bob professed to be without a clue as to why his penis was not working.

Bob's penis was able to say things that he could not: "I'm not ready for such intimacy; I don't want another disaster." "I'm still too angry; I don't want to make love." Bob does not need injection therapy or the surgical implantation of a prosthesis. He needs time and opportunity to appreciate what he thinks and feels. Bob's erection pattern demonstrates that he has psychological impotence—"I can hang a wet washcloth on my morning erection." His impotence is caused by the disruption of his marital bond, not by a lifelong discomfort with sex. He wants to love someone and be loved by her. He is just going through the motions of being a rooster.

Common Causes of New Psychological Impotence

Most men with psychological impotence once were potent. Their problem is caused by at least one of these four social circumstances: loss of partner through death, loss of partner through divorce, deterioration of the nonsexual relationship, and job or career difficulties.

Loss of partner through death. The death of a loved partner ranks among the worst of the many events that may befall a man. Whether expected as with a terminal illness, or without warning as in an accident, the wife's death forces the man into a period of grief, confusion, and despair. Psychological impotence due to this personal tragedy is relatively easy to understand.

For a brief time after the wife's death, most men are unable to be involved with another woman; in fact, just the idea may be offensive. Eventually, the pain of being alone and the need to get on with living propel men into social arrangements that quickly present the possibility of physical intimacy. Such opportunities are hard to turn down, and, ironically, may result from male pressures on the woman.

A widower's penis may have a surprise in store for the unwary man. This body part may not cooperate with any foolish thing he attempts. The man may be mysteriously impotent, but the mystery comes from the fact that he is not aware of his guilt, the strangeness in being with an unfamiliar woman, or his emotional unreadiness for this degree of intimacy.

When it occurs within several months of the wife's death, he can readily understand his impotence: "I guess it's too soon." This explanation is difficult to accept when impotence occurs years after the death, when the emotional pain of loss has been reduced to a wistful remembrance of the ease, warmth, and love of the marriage.

> Alex, a physically healthy, energetic man, buried his wife of forty-nine years on his seventieth birthday, following several years of her physical deterioration from kidney disease. After a miserable eighteen months of loneliness and grief, he began to accept invitations from friends which led to female companionship. He eventually met a woman he thought was lovely, charming and well-suited to him. He had erections with her while necking but nothing but frustration in the bedroom. I

> insisted he tell me only about his wife and marriage during each of three sessions. After crying so much that he promised to buy me another year's supply of Kleenex, Alex was able to have intercourse.

Widowers are typically in a hurry. If their wives die young, the men need a mother for their children. Later in life, they feel that they do not have much time left. But when they try to "get on with it," their nervousness may make it impossible to relax and concentrate on sensation. These men have to understand the timelessness about their marriage bond. During a long marriage, many men develop a sense of themselves as belonging to their wives. Their wives become an inseparable part of their identity. This does not change.

> "That first year was miserable—not only was I alone, I didn't know me without Lois. Our house was suddenly 'my' house and its familiarity was somehow strange—every room was different because she was not in it. I imagined Lois there more times than I want to admit."

Occasionally, I hear the new partner of a widower accuse him of still loving his wife, as though that were an act of infidelity to her. I try to emphasize to her that death, rather than terminating love, often briefly intensifies and perfects it. New partners may worry that the erection problem means that their man's affection is insincere. They insist that his thoughts, feelings, and attachment to his wife never be mentioned. "One just does not discuss past lovers with a partner!" one woman firmly said. "I don't mention mine and I am sick of hearing about his Adrienne!" If such a rule continues, the man will be forced to hide this aspect of his inner life from his lover. That hardly sounds like intimacy to me.

I suggest widowers and their new partners patiently acknowledge and honor the past. The power and tenacity of a love that grew over thirty or more years is not erased by just a few years of grief. I worry that this widower's impotence is a signal that the man is prematurely sealing off his feelings about his wife. I try to have him appreciate the depth and meaning of the past relationship and suggest to his worried partner that his continuing love for his wife is simply an indication of his capacity to love. It is easy for both partners to be impatient.

Loss of partner through divorce. The loss of a partner through divorce is more complicated than loss through death. In addition to the sadness and regret that accompany any partner loss, the divorced man has to deal with his anger at his ex-wife, recriminations about his failures in the relationship, and anxiety about his children and his finances. Most divorces prove painfully complicated and produce new dilemmas.

The divorced man often quickly seeks a simpler, more satisfying emotional union with a woman. He does this to gain comfort from his emotional pain and to take advantage of his freedom. Inexplicably, he may find himself anxious and impotent when he should be relaxed and sensual.

> "I met her in a bar, we danced, drank a lot, and went to my apartment. I was nervous. I couldn't believe how nervous I was. I kept thinking, who is this woman? What is she doing here? After a while I just knew I was not going to make it with her that night. I was right."

Most men are surprised by their intense pain. They anticipated certain events—telling the wife, telling the children, moving out, being lonely, and even being upset at times. But they usually do not predict the persistence of their distress, anticipate their hatred, guilt, and shame. The additional, unexpected irony for men with dependent children is that divorce does not mean freedom from the ex-wife. A relationship, often very difficult, continues long after the marriage ends.

The next woman inherits certain prejudices based on experiences with the wife. "Will this one hurt me too?" "Will this one reduce me to lying?" "Will this entanglement end in my being abandoned, cheated upon, or found wanting?" People carry their pasts into new relationships. Men's impotence is an expression of their fear of hurting and being hurt by women. Instead of experiencing sexual arousal from the sight and touch of their new partners' receptive bodies, they feel nervous, worried about performance, and confused by their humiliating lack of masculinity.

It takes some men a long time to recognize that their penises are not machines that function under any circumstances. Most eventually learn that their genitals are attached to their hearts.

I have great respect for impotence after a divorce. Impotence is the mind's way of counterbalancing negative emotional forces. A man's heart may be so filled with vengeance and so preoccupied with hurting a woman that he fears his fantasies or nightmares will be fulfilled. He is afraid that his excited penis will destroy the partner. His temporary impotence is a civilized means of protecting his partner and himself. His mind is keeping him away from women until he is able to dissipate his rage and be kind once again.

> Julian, a gentle fifty-year-old man, went through a long, depressing period. He perceived that he was the victim of his cruel materialistic wife, who by cunning and guile took most of his assets and turned his three daughters against him. He insisted as a matter of principle that, though he knew what she was up to, he would not stoop to being anything but kind lest it prove destructive to his girls and he further diminish his self-respect. He was not ready to date for two years and not able to have intercourse for another year. Although he steadfastly avoided the usual ugly responses to the divorce process, his dreams and fantasies were preoccupied with sadistic imagery toward his wife and other females. Julian was able to have intercourse regularly, but only after his internal rage quieted.

Deterioration of the nonsexual relationship. Couples whose relationship problems have caused impotence usually do not want to admit to themselves or each other that sex had lost its joy and intimacy before the impotence. The erection difficulty is preceded by disagreement, which makes both partners less receptive to lovemaking because they are annoyed and emotionally withdrawn. They go through the motions of lovemaking in the hope of ignoring or erasing their tension.

The man is the sexual symptom-bearer of their relationship because erection is necessary for intercourse. The woman often has comparable arousal problems but is better able to hide them. Her inadequately moistened vagina can receive him more easily than his unrigid penis can enter her.

> A couple in their forties had been impotent for half of their twenty-year marriage. After spending six months in therapy, it seemed less clear to them what the problem was—well, sometimes the explanation seemed clear to them. Neither liked the explanation because it forced them to confront something they had been sweeping under the rug for years: They had profoundly different approaches to raising children. Janice thought and acted in a limit-setting, confrontational manner with their three sons while Fred was indulgent and believed that children do best when obstacles are not placed in their paths. Fred made up for Janice's harshness by being more giving than even he thought was wise. He repeatedly spoke to her about how the boys were treated, but no lasting progress was made. Fred deeply resented Janice's manner. Janice deeply resented Fred's undermining her efforts with the boys, his tendency to take their sides in any dispute, and his I-know-best attitude. His resentment robbed him of his desire for Janice and his potency; her resentment robbed her of her desire and receptivity. Although they each said they loved each other, after every disagreement, neither was sure what love is.

Most distressed couples are not aware of when and why their relationships deteriorated. There is no quick explanation of why they fail. One common source of rapid sexual deterioration in a relationship is that one partner has a secret. This makes it difficult for at least one of the partners to understand why the relationship is failing and prevents problem solving. Secrets are dangerous because they inhibit spontaneity and intimacy. A husband's secret affair may lead to impotence with his wife soon after he becomes involved with another woman. The reasons for his impotence may be that he is too preoccupied with the other woman, he feels too guilty during sex with his wife, or he has lost his motivation and cannot be aroused.

Another secret may be the wife's affair. Her husband becomes impotent soon after she becomes involved with another person. Is this because the wife's receptivity has changed and she really is not as good an actress as she thinks? Can the man sense his wife's limited emotional involvement during lovemaking? Sometimes a man who is certain that his wife is faithful dreams she is not. Therapists are often expected to pick up the pieces of relationships that have contained secrets for many years; unfortunately, they cannot work miracles.

> Larry, a forty-nine-year-old businessman who had been emotionally distant from his family in his single minded pursuit of financial success, immediately became impotent when his wife told him that she had been having an affair. Her disclosure emerged during a truth-telling session in which he admitted several periodic "meaningless" infidelities. The impotence persisted for six months before he sought help to find out why he could not get an erection.
>
> He was aware of the following feelings but did not like the idea that they provide answers to his question:
>
> - He was furious with her for her unfaithfulness.
> - He wanted to preserve their relationship at all costs.
> - He felt responsible for her infidelity because he refused her repeated pleas for more closeness and time with the children.
> - He thought turnabout is fair play.
> - He was bothered by her comparisons of their sexual relationship with her "incredible" lover.
> - He felt damaged and defective.
>
> "Can't you just fix me?" he repeatedly asked throughout his initial psychotherapy sessions.

Most secrets, however, are not as dramatic as infidelity. Many simply involve unstated resentments and convictions that the spouse is "impossible" or "hopeless," as with Fred, who thought Janice's attitude toward their sons was beyond help.

Job or career difficulties. The sexual identities of many adult men pivot upon their ability to perform a task for money. When a job is lost or threatened, some men react as though they no longer have the right to have sex with their partners. The feelings of failure associated with the work environment are easily transported into the bedroom. This leads to anxiety and preoccupation with the firmness of erection instead of concentration on the pleasures of creating and receiving sensations. When a long strike is settled, a personal job crisis is resolved, or a worried-over promotion finally comes through, some men find that their mysterious impotence disappears.

> A man whose marital, family, and business life had been quite successful, became impotent for almost a year after he made a bad business decision. While selling off some of his assets in anticipation of retirement, George misjudged the financial capabilities and moral integrity of one of his purchasers. The result was a quarter of a million dollar loss. While he still had considerable means with which to retire, he was preoccupied with his being duped and having to curtail some retirement plans. His wife, who was more worried about him than the financial loss, could not get him to stop ruminating about it and calling himself "stupid." Initially, neither of them understood the relationship between the business loss and his impotence—both thought something was physically wrong. George had a few therapy sessions in which he was able to acknowledge that he did not feel he deserved to make love because he lost the money. His potency returned.

> After his union struck the company, thirty-year-old John's potency waned. Now with a toddler and a pregnant wife, his short-lived strike benefits and low paying temporary job were not nearly enough to keep his financial head above water. Nine years earlier during his first strike experience, he spent his savings traveling out

West with two buddies. "It was great!" Now he felt unmanly and was preoccupied with letting Lucy and his daughter down. When the company announced that wages had to be cut in order to keep jobs, John began to despair about his hope to be the first man in his alcohol- and divorce-ridden family to maintain a stable home. Scenes of his father's irritability and violence during periods of his unemployment kept coming to his mind. He knew he never wanted to put Lucy through what his mother experienced. Lucy felt that her husband was wonderful but a little depressed. "Wouldn't you be if you couldn't work, doctor?" The four-month strike was settled when his new daughter was six weeks old. A three-year contract was signed and his income was nearly the same. His potency reappeared.

For many men, the ability to work, to earn enough money to maintain a lifestyle of their choice, is intimately connected to their self-esteem, the sense of mental balance, and personal contentment. While the loss or the threatened loss of a job does not rob every man of his potency, employment problems can change sexual behavior. Some men may react to these threats to their social worth by increasing their sexual behavior, while others, like John, may find sex nearly impossible.

Less Common Psychological Factors in Impotence

Virtually all heterosexual men succeed at having intercourse at least once by the time they are thirty. Those who do not suffer from an incapacitating degree of anxiety during intimacy and an inability to establish a comfortable relationship. Most of these men have unconventional sexual identities—strong, persistent wishes to be or to dress as women, homoerotic orientations, unusual sexual intentions. In the presence of a receptive partner, they are so overcome with nervousness that there is no excitement.

A twenty-five-year-old timid man could not have an erection with his girl friend for one year. After several

> months of psychotherapy, Ron was able to erect and attain an orgasm during oral stimulation, but still could not have intercourse for another year until he began to talk about his mother. He described her as a screaming, unpredictable paranoid who embarrassed him every time he was with her in public. He left home at eighteen and intentionally has never seen her again. Ron thought his impotence was due to homoerotic feelings, but I thought that his "homosexuality" was less powerful an explanation than his fear of finding his frightening mother in any woman.

Some potent men teeter on the brink of impotence during much of their lives. The following man was quite successful in using fantasy to allay his worry.

> Tim, a prissy man who described himself as being markedly effeminate as a teenager, became impotent again with his wife of fifteen years when he began working with a male assistant. This attractive young man reminded him of a homosexual love he shared during his senior year in high school. "Just being around him unnerves me." Tim had been impotent for most of the first year of his marriage. "I couldn't tell you why, doctor, but all I knew was that I was scared of Sheila. It made no sense to me. Sheila is a wonderful woman. I just got over it after a while." For years when he had any softening of his penis during intercourse, Tim fantasized about his high school friend.

Lifelong impotence or lifelong teetering on the brink of difficulty is usually an expression of the man's inability to overcome his distrust of closeness. This usually focuses on his fear of women, but often the fear of intimacy with anyone is apparent.

Physical Causes

An impotent man should suspect there is a physical reason for his problem when his erection pattern meets these three criteria: First, he can never get more than a slightly elongated, floppy erection at any time—when he masturbates, wakes in the night or in the morning, reads erotic literature, has sex with a different partner, or engages in a variety of sexual techniques. Second, he has a previously diagnosed disease or is taking medications known to lower the sexual drive or impair potency. Third, there has been no significant change in his emotional life before his erection problems began.

> Carl, a fifty-eight-year-old homosexual physician who has happily lived with Zachary for ten years, has not obtained more than a slightly elongated, soft erection for many months. Under no circumstances does his penis fully erect for a moment, even when he feels sexually aroused. X-ray evaluation of his lower aorta and the arteries to his legs and penis has shown vascular obstructions that account for his impotence and the pain he feels in his leg when he walks fast. Carl smokes much less since his heart attack two years ago, but he is drinking a little more. "I find whiskey soothing when I worry about dying." Although he was potent before and after the heart attack, his erections have been becoming less firm for about three years. Despite his health concerns, he continues to function well in his practice.

Carl fulfills the three criteria that suggest the possibility of a physical cause for impotence. His penis never becomes fully firm when he is sexually aroused. He has a disease that adequately explains the problem. The social, economic, vocational, and intimate aspects of his life had not shifted before his potency waned. Pure cases of physically caused impotence are very rare. Carl is not one of these; his emotional response to his heart attack and his fear of death also contribute to his problem, but not as much as the vascular disease in his pelvis.

All the possible physical causes of impotence need to be understood in order to find the correct therapy approach. A brief discussion follows.

Medication Side Effects

The most common reversible organic causes of impotence are medications that impair sexual drive and erection capacity. These medications fall into several categories: drugs for control of high blood pressure, pain medication, antidepressants, tranquilizers, and female hormones given for cancer of the prostate. Physicians deal with medication-caused impotence by lowering doses or switching to other medications. Anyone who suspects that medication might be the cause of his impotence should discuss this with his physician.

Hormone Deficiencies and Excesses

Men who have inadequate levels of pituitary, thyroid, adrenal, or testicular hormones may be readily cured of their impotence and low sex drive by correct amounts of the missing hormone. Most of these problems have a gradual onset in midlife and cannot be diagnosed without laboratory tests. Men with known hormone problems should periodically see their physicians to be sure they are currently receiving the right dose of replacement therapy. Occasionally impotence and low sex drive are due to an excess of the hormone prolactin. The drug bromocryptine can quickly restore potency to these men.

Neural and Vascular Diseases

The physical conditions that may interfere with potency can form a frighteningly long list; however, most of them involve difficulties with the nerve supply or blood supply to the penis.

Diabetic males are susceptible to impotence. Either the nerves that coordinate the routing of blood to the penis and retaining it within the penis stop working properly, or the insides of the arteries that carry blood to the penis become blocked by arteriosclerosis.

Diabetes is not the only cause of blockages within the arteries to the penis. The diseases of large and small arteries, atherosclerosis and arteriosclerosis, can also decrease blood flow to the penis and prevent a sustained erection. Cigarette smoking can induce spasms of the pelvic blood vessels which further decrease the rate of blood flow to the penis. Lately it has been learned that some impotence may be caused by disease in the veins of the penis rather than its arteries. These men have trouble keeping blood in the penis—they get erections but cannot keep them. Urologists are experimenting with new diagnostic tests and surgical techniques in the hope of helping these men.

Surgery and Radiation

Surgical replacement of the last portion of the aorta, removal of the rectum and sigmoid colon, or the entire prostate gland usually impairs potency. These operations are done for serious diseases such as atherosclerotic blockage of the aorta, aortic aneurysm, cancer of the large intestine, cancer of the prostate or testicle. Radiation treatment to the deep pelvis may have the same effect as surgery by damaging the nerve or blood supply to the penis. Injection treatment, penile prosthetic surgery, and the pump can restore potency in these situations.

Chronic Illness

Chronic diseases of the heart, lung, and kidney are quite common among people as they age. Chronically ill people may find that the most basic activities of daily living can use up their physical resources and that sex requires too much energy. However, energy depletion rarely is the only cause of impotence. Medications and psychological responses to the illness are also factors. The psychological impact of a colostomy, severe skin difficulties, crippling arthritis, or a stroke can be as destructive to potency as the physical factors.

Alcoholic Excess

Exactly how alcohol causes potency problems is a medical mystery. When a chronic alcoholic is impotent, doctors often assume that the alcohol impaired his ability to have an erection. Paradoxically, when a heavily drinking man loses his potency after he dries out, doctors assume that the alcohol made him potent by removing his anxiety about sex. It is difficult to tell in any particular man's situation how much is psychological and how much is physical, because alcohol may have a tarnishing effect on his personality, social relationships, nutrition, and many different organs. The toxic impairments on the alcoholic's liver, brain, heart, nerves, and hormones each contribute something to the drinking man's impotence.

Peyronie's Disease

Peyronie's disease is a condition in which painless fibrous nodules appear in the penis and cause the erection to change shape. These nodules form for unknown reasons and distort the chambers that usually hold the blood during erection. Severe distortions of the shape of the erection interfere with intercourse because the erection is bent at strange angles and the penis is not firm throughout its length.

Coping With Impotence

It is vital to understand that intercourse—not sex—requires an erection. There is much more to the physical and emotional aspects of sex than just having intercourse. The emotional nurturing, reexperiencing the relationship bond, removing built-up annoyances, and enhancing self-esteem that occurs within a long-term sexual equilibrium are all possible without genital union. As is true with women, it is useful for the impotent man to continue making love without trying to have intercourse. This allows him to be preoccupied with sensation rather than with failure and to rediscover the emotional and physical pleasures of sex. This idea takes getting used to, however, because many men equate sex with intercourse and narrowly view foreplay as a warm-up for "the real thing."

Making love without trying to have intercourse can markedly decrease the man's performance anxiety. Repeated lovemaking without intercourse is enough to cure some men of psychological impotence. However, those who still feel rage, despair, guilt, and other intense emotions when they want to feel sexually aroused cannot expect that this technique will make everything better. These men still have to go through the painful process of facing why they are impotent and directly dealing with their personal dilemmas.

It is important for the man and his steady partner to understand why erection is not possible. Those with strong organic reasons such as diabetes or vascular disease need to know about them to preserve their self-esteem. Their partners need this information to avoid misunderstandings such as "You don't love me anymore!" "You must have somebody else!" and "It is my fault, I was never good enough in bed for you!"

Here are some useful facts for couples with impotence:

- The man can achieve orgasm without having an erection.
- The woman can achieve orgasm by hand, mouth, vibrator, or self-stimulation.
- The man can get self-esteem and enhancement of his masculinity from helping his partner achieve orgasm.
- Many people engage in sexual behaviors other than intercourse even if they are not impotent.

Some people with irreversible organic impotence adjust well to affectionate, reassuring cuddling with only occasional orgasms. As their sexual drives wane, the reassurance that they are loved and valued becomes more important than having intercourse. This is simply not enough for others, however. For them, urologists have the three technologies of injections, prostheses, and the vacuum pump. While these initially offend many people's sensibilities ("I don't want to be a bionic man!"), they should not be quickly dismissed.

The injections are efficient, relatively painless, and safe. As of the late 1980s, three side effects have been noted—prolonged erection, nodule formation, and elevation of liver enzymes. Prolonged erections can be prevented by using the lowest dose of medication that is effective. The nodules, which occur in about 50 percent of men within twelve months of injections, are painless and usually do not cause bending of the erection. The abnormalities detected in liver function tests are mild and have produced no symptoms of liver disease. Nodule and liver enzyme abnormalities occur most frequently in men who use the injections more than once a week. Physicians consider the benefits of injections to far outweigh the risks of side effects, which are usually mild and clinically insignificant. However, Stanley Althof, Louisa Turner and my other colleagues at University Hospitals in Cleveland have recently shown that about 40 percent of men who agree to begin the injection treatment change their minds within the first year because of their distaste for the procedure.

The prostheses have steadily improved during twenty years of surgical experience. A study by Steege and his colleagues in 1986 showed 80 percent of the men and 60 percent of the women partners were happy about the results of the surgery; however, other studies show that satisfaction with the results is not that high. According to Leonore Teifer and Arnold Melman, at least 20 percent of men require an additional operation within four years.

The vacuum pump is a simple device that lowers the air pressure around the penis, usually quickly causing a semirigid erection to form. A tourniquet is then placed at the base of the penis. This erection may last up to thirty minutes. When the tourniquet is removed the erection immediately fades. Side effects have not been reported with this method.

Impotent men, their partners, and their physicians must be careful about undertaking prosthetic surgery, injection treatment, or any new, experimental medical or surgical treatment. Prosthetic surgery or injections are best undertaken when the following criteria are met:

- Irreversible organic factors are present.
- Surgery or the injections present no significant medical risk.
- The man and his partner are both in favor of the procedure.

- Sex has continued despite the impotence.
- Prior to the impotence, the sexual relationship was satisfying to both partners.

After deciding that a specific method may help, the physician can usually leave the choice between surgery, injections, or the vacuum pump up to the man or the man and his partner.

Experimental operations that tie off leaking veins within the penis or those that attempt to bring a new blood supply to the penis still need additional research. Men and their partners who are thinking about undergoing these procedures should discuss the most recent studies with their surgeon before the operation. Urologic and vascular surgical technologies change quickly.

As we have seen in Don and Missy's situation with injection therapy, simply having the capacity for intercourse does not mean it will happen. Intercourse is the result of many factors within the couple's sexual equilibrium. A man may erroneously think his impotence is causing the tension in the relationship and believe that everything will return to normal if he can have intercourse. However, implants or injections may not make his partner receptive. And these technologies will not overcome a man's lifelong wariness of women.

Toward a Problem-Free Sexual Life

A man who has lost his potency should:

- ask himself if he is *unable* or *unwilling* to have sex with his partner
- see a physician to undergo a careful evaluation and to discuss his own impression about what might be causing the problem
- try making love without attempting intercourse for several weeks to rid himself of performance anxiety
- see a mental health professional if the impotence is purely psychological or both psychological and organic and does not clear up spontaneously
- not rush into a mechanical means of fixing the inability to erect without a thorough discussion of the options and their advantages and disadvantages with the partner and the physician or psychologist

13

WOMEN WHO DO NOT WANT SEX

I have been waging a personal war against the term "frigid" for a dozen years or so. Some days I feel victorious, other times I know the battle is hopeless. My vendetta began when, as a young psychiatrist, I realized I had assumed that some unfortunate women and their partners suffered from a disorder called "frigidity." Patients used the term with me and I used it with them until I realized that "frigidity" is largely an illusion. "You see, doctor, my wife is frigid and in order to stay married to her, I had to seek sexual release elsewhere." "Well, I have frigidity; I can't change that. It's just one of those unfortunate things."

When I went to the medical literature to find out more about this disorder, I came away confused. All authors agreed that frigidity was a serious and widespread problem, but there was no consensus about its causes or its best treatment. It was not even clear who should and who should not be labeled "frigid." All the decades of psychiatric writing and research did not accomplish much on this subject.

Two other events set my mental war in motion. I was quite impressed by several articles that characterized the notion of frigidity as vague, disparaging, and sexist. About the same time in 1970, Masters and Johnson's research in *Human Sexual Inadequacy* suggested that a new way of understanding sexual problems was at hand.

Even when I began to teach this subject, I did not understand why "frigidity" and "frigid" were destined to remain in common use. I now understand that people use these terms to deceive themselves and their partners. Men are apt to describe their partners as frigid when they cannot comprehend the unexciting or unattractive aspects of their own behavior. The words help them escape responsibility for their contributions to the sexual equilibrium. An unsuspecting woman may accept her partner's label "frigid" because she thinks he knows best and because she is still too frightened to acknowledge her growing negative feelings about him. She begins to think of herself as being frigid. The label also can be used dishonestly, such as when a woman who is richly and easily responsive with her lover encourages her husband to think of her as frigid.

Even when such instances of self-deception and dishonesty are ignored, there still remains a set of problems that has been characterized as frigidity. Unfortunately, I know of no word that communicates sexual disinterest and unarousability as powerfully as this one, but I will avoid it and just describe the problems and my perspective on what contributes to them.

Women with arousal problems cannot easily slip into a sensuous mode. They are unable to relax and to concentrate on sensations associated with being caressed and caressing. They come to dread sexual behavior because, at the very least, it is unpleasant and anxiety provoking. These women describe themselves as lacking sexual desire, by which they usually mean that they have a strong motive to avoid sexual behavior with a partner.

> Peg, a warm, loving mother and extremely well-organized real estate salesperson, hated sex. She avoided it until Phil "made a federal case out of it"—her guilt and worry moved her to comply before he blew his top. She had sex more freely when she was not under stress, but her life always contained unexpected problems. Early in their marriage Peg faked pleasure until Phil told her he knew. She could briefly feel arousal during breast stimulation, but she quickly left the scene of her sensations and began to consider the demands she faced tomorrow at work. "Demands, demands—the story of my life!"

Women with psychological arousal problems are similar to psychologically impotent men in their avoidance of the sexual experience and the broad range of reasons for the avoidance. And like psychologically impotent men, they may feel sexual drive and may attain orgasm during masturbation.

It should be clear by now that in either sex the emotion of arousal requires freedom from interfering feelings such as anxiety, guilt, anger, or fear. Women who do not want sex cannot abandon their tenacious hold on ordinary consciousness. Sensuousness and arousal are not welcome and, somehow, do not seem to be in their best interest. Many harbor the conviction that life is better lived without sex. "Why bother?"

Arousal problems mean that women do not experience the normal bodily changes that occur with sexual excitement. They do not produce much moisture in the vagina. During sexual behavior with their partners, none of the other typical signs of arousal occur. There is no clitoral enlargement or thickening of the inner genital lips. Their pulses do not speed up, their nipples do not enlarge and harden; gooseflesh does not appear on their arms and reddening of their upper trunk never occurs. The most important missing ingredient is personal pleasure.

Women Who Used To Become Aroused

Most women with arousal problems were once normally able to feel sexual excitement. This means that women and their partners must constantly monitor their personal feelings and the quality of their relationship in order to keep the sexual equilibrium healthy. In therapy, the reason for a woman's loss of arousal usually does not remain mysterious very long. She may not initially want to acknowledge it, but generally it soon becomes obvious.

Common reasons for a woman to avoid sexual behavior include rejection of her partner, reaction to her partner's new limitations, depression, and medication.

Rejection of the Partner

Lovemaking may be rejected soon after the woman senses a serious flaw in her partner. The intensity of her new negative attitude can be confusing if it appears before she fully grasps the reasons for her unwillingness to be sensual. The partner may never figure it out.

> Jody was in her late twenties and had enjoyed sexual behavior with her husband before and for a year after marriage. This ceased after an argument over the use of a charge card that ended with his calling her "a dumb bitch." Although Glenn apologized the next day and said she could use the card again, she was gravely offended. For three months, she was unable to feel aroused during their lovemaking, returning in her thoughts each time to his angry, name-calling face. During these months she often reconsidered the argument that frightened and reduced her to tears. Not only was she not dumb, in many money matters she was at least as smart as he. Calling her a bitch meant he viewed her with little respect. She wondered what could be next. Removing the charge card humiliated her; she felt as though she were the irresponsible child and he was the mature grownup. Could she love a man who said these things to her?

"How many times can I be sworn at before I no longer love him?" When she tried to explain the impact of the fight to him, he thought she was overreacting. She then felt dismissed.

Many divorced women report that their inability to become aroused evolved in stages. First was their lessening degree of arousal, soon followed by a heavier reliance on fantasy during sex to maintain arousal. Then they felt less motivation for sex, which led to less sex. Finally, they stopped being able to feel excitement.

Such arousal difficulties are the mind's way of alerting the woman and her partner to a serious relationship obstacle. The obstacle is the woman's perspective on his recurring behaviors—for example, unilateral decision making, thoughtlessness, depression, avoidance of emotional expression, failure to acknowledge her worth, infidelity, heavy drinking or drug abuse. It does not matter whether her perceptions are entirely correct; they are her perceptions and, in her mind, they have a powerful reality. She responds to them by withdrawing her arousal. She no longer wishes to share her excitement with him. He is rejected.

The man's pleasure in her arousal has an important role in this sequence. Her withdrawal affects him; he senses she no longer is with him emotionally during lovemaking.

Bea discovered her husband's infidelity, went through several years of anguish, prayer, and therapy, and preserved her thirty-year marriage. There were several nice sexual experiences with her husband thereafter, but four years later they were both describing her as "frigid." It seemed easier to accept this than to rehash their feelings about this most difficult period in their lives.

Many men feel that they are being punished and decide that their partners' vindictive nature is the basic problem. They use the word "frigid" because it describes coldness and cruel withholding. The man's role in provoking the woman's rejection is easily overlooked, despite her repeated attempts to have him change the provocative aspects of his behavior.

Sylvia: You know, I'm grateful that you've helped Steve and me to get along better, but I feel very uneasy about it. You haven't said anything to Steve that I haven't said to him many times.

Doctor: I think that's true. But what does this mean to you?

Sylvia: It means that he doesn't think what I say is important but what you say is because you're a doctor. I don't like that!

Steve: Maybe it was because I could see it more clearly when an objective person said it. After all, you were yelling at me half the time you said those things. You made me feel defensive.

Doctor: Steve, what about the possibility that there has been something in your tone or manner that demeans Sylvia? She could have an important point here. Maybe it has been hard for you to listen to her opinions because you don't respect her enough.

Steve: Maybe so, but I don't think it is just that.

Doctor: Perhaps not. Anyway, Sylvia has been quite clear that she feels more regard coming from you to her in the last several months.

Sylvia: I hope it lasts.

Doctor: Me too.

Steve: (laughter) Me too.

The inability to be heard is responsible for some women's inability to feel aroused. The insistence of many divorcing husbands that their wives are frigid is sometimes laughable. When a bitter, demoralized man describes his ex-wife as a "frigid bitch," he is at that moment unable to acknowledge any personal role in her loss of arousal. This is only a public statement, however; he may privately regret that he refused to consider her views.

Divorcing women's ideas that their arousal problems were caused by something in the marriage are supported by their turning to masturbation, their ability to become easily aroused with other men during marriage, and most telling, the complete disappearance of the problem after the divorce.

Reaction To Partner's New Limitations

Women may have to adapt to significant impairments in their partners' mental, physical, or sexual capacities. The new condition changes how they feel about the partner and this changes their relationship. A wife may not aspire to the pleasures of the bedroom because she feels they are no longer possible. In her mind, sex is linked to health; without good health, she has no motivation to behave sexually with him. The partner's new serious physical illness—for example, a disabling heart attack or Alzheimer's disease—commonly produces this dilemma. "I've lost my appetite for sex since Leo's had chest pains and shortness of breath." "I don't feel the same about him—he is confused. And even though I know I ought to enjoy what little we have left while I can, I just can't."

The loss of motivation and arousability may occur because the partner's impairment fundamentally changes the nature of their relationship. A traditional wife may no longer be able to believe that her husband is protecting her; it is obvious that he is now the dependent one.

> A forty-two-year-old lawyer had a series of health disasters. The development of insulin-dependent diabetes, a seizure in his wife's presence, the diagnosis of a brain tumor, and brain surgery that left him speech-impaired all occurred during twelve weeks. A year later, she was finding one reason after another to decline his sexual offers. His inability to function as a lawyer, their new financial problems, and her terror of another health problem were her explanations for her arousal difficulties during their rare attempts at sex. She preferred masturbation.
>
> "Sean isn't the same, I'm not the same, we're not the same," she stated sadly but emphatically. "Now I work every day; I take care of him. I just tell him I'm too tired from working. He doesn't need to know the truth!"

The man's impairment may be entirely sexual. Men who develop premature ejaculation, become intermittently impotent, have difficulty ejaculating, or lose sexual desire may cause their partners to give up all hope for a normal sexual life. During lovemaking the woman shows signs of performance anxiety—that is, she vigilantly awaits the appearance of his sexual problems—and goes through the motions of sex without excitement. Before she knows it, she no longer can be aroused when she wants to.

> Marilyn, who had been sexually responsive in two previous relationships, initially reacted with reassurance and patience to her fiance's inability to obtain an erection. They did what they could together; she was content because they were otherwise quite well-suited. Soon he was having erections that disappeared when he tried to enter her vagina. She considered this reasonable progress for three months. But when no further gains were made, she ceased to be able to get excited with him. Instead of pleasure during foreplay, she felt angry, hopeless, or insulted. When she started experiencing waves of doubt about her personal worth and attractiveness, she put a stop to their lovemaking with an ultimatum: "You either stop procrastinating and seek help or we are not a couple!" As a result of therapy, his erections became normal, but Marilyn was stuck with an inability to feel arousal for several months until her buried feelings were unearthed, expressed, and appreciated by both of them.

New health situations are not usually perceived by the woman as the man's fault in the same way that marital deterioration is. The woman does not respond with the same angry rejection. She may be frustrated by life's new unfair burden and find that she has trouble feeling aroused.

Depression

Many of life's traumatic circumstances are accompanied by sadness, helplessness, hopelessness, lack of energy and pleasure, and sleep and eating disturbances. These are symptoms of depression. Decrease in sexual arousability must be added to this list. Professionals often have difficulty separating unhappiness over life circumstances from depression because both can create arousal problems. The arousal problems of an unhappy woman may ease dramatically when the source of the unhappiness is removed—for example, when her husband finally agrees to adopt her young child from a previous marriage. When improvement of some life circumstance does not make the unhappiness go away, it is reasonable to consider consulting a mental health professional for more specific diagnosis and therapy. Psychotherapy and/or medications may be helpful in ending the depression and restoring capacity to feel arousal.

Medications

It is likely that sexual arousal is affected by many medications, but this has been difficult to document. Most women have learned to expect that their degree of arousal will vary with each sexual opportunity. When medications do interfere with their arousal, they may be slow to realize that this is not just another one of those times. Those who immediately know that medication is causing sexual difficulties are women who are otherwise almost always aroused with their partners. Most of the medications in the following list are the same drugs that produce impotence in men. Apparently they affect the brain's ability to sustain the arousal, but the mechanisms for this are not scientifically known.

Antidepressants. Most women who take antidepressants are given drugs called tricyclics; some receive monoamineoxidase inhibitors. There have been a few reports that antidepressants such as imipramine and phenelzine may interfere with arousal. It is often difficult to recognize a drug's effect because the depression itself may diminish arousal capacities even before medication is given.

Tranquilizers. The major tranquilizers are powerful drugs used to treat psychotic forms of thinking and mood disorders. These drugs may interfere with arousal mechanisms in some women by inducing the pituitary gland to secrete an extra amount of a hormone called prolactin. This is the same hormone that is secreted in large amounts by nursing mothers who often notice less sexual desire and arousability.

The minor tranquilizers are widely prescribed and abused for treatment of anxiety and stress associated with daily life. It is possible that a few women who take these drugs find it more difficult to be aroused. These may be the same women who also report feeling more depressed when they take the minor tranquilizers. Physicians usually can switch tranquilizers easily for women who report this side effect. However, the loss of arousability is a good opportunity for them and their doctors to reconsider the need for medication.

Central nervous system drugs. Sedatives, pain medications, and anticonvulsants are widely used and prescribed singly and in combination with other compounds. Some of them may interfere with arousal capacities. New arousal difficulties in a woman on medication should always make the woman and her physician think about sexual side effects of the medication.

Alcohol and other substances of abuse. Drugs such as alcohol, marijuana, cocaine, heroin, methadone, and quaaludes have a reputation for possessing aphrodisiac qualities. However, this is not completely true. In low doses, especially in the beginning of their use, they may enhance sexual arousal because they take away anxiety about intimacy and pleasure. However, many women who use such drugs regularly or in high doses actually have trouble sustaining arousal. These substances are powerful central nervous system agents that may paralyze the normal function of the sexual drive center. It is simple to pass from the antianxiety effect to the sedative effect, in which one is not quite "with it" during sex, to the stage of no arousal.

Physical Diseases

Serious physical illness, the use of medications, depression over loss of health, the partner's lack of sexual interest, feelings of lessened worth and personal attractiveness, and lack of energy often combine to dampen a woman's arousal. These psychological reactions may occur in response to a wide variety of diseases. Reversible hormone imbalances, such as too little or too much thyroid or adrenal hormone, may interfere with arousal. Multiple sclerosis, brain tumors, substance abuse, cancer, Alzheimer's disease, and diabetes can also interfere. Severe vascular disease in the pelvis may interfere with the ability to increase blood flow and interfere with lubrication. Even medically minor problems such as Monilial or Trichomonas vaginal infections which often produce genital itching and abundant vaginal secretions may lead to sexual avoidance, fears of painful intercourse, and interrupted arousal.

When a woman loses her sexual responsiveness, the first question she should ask is, "Am I physically healthy?" If she is not, she and her physician should consider the disease she has, the effects of the medication she takes, and her and her partner's psychological response to the condition. Medications can be changed, feelings about being ill can be brought into the open with physicians and partners, women can be helped to stop abusing street drugs, and medications can relieve many depressions. The loss of sexual responsiveness need not be permanent. Everyone—women, men, physicians—must remember that physical diseases that are known to impair arousal do not impair in every case. Most women with diabetes or multiple sclerosis, for example, do not lose their ability to be aroused. But more important is that the loss of responsiveness that accompanies physical illness is often a psychological reaction to being ill or medicated, and not to the disease itself.

If she is physically well, as most women with arousal difficulties are, she can either hide the source of her problem from herself or identify the reason she has rejected her partner, perhaps with the help of a mental health professional.

Women Who Have Never Been Aroused with a Partner

Most women who have never been able to maintain arousal with a partner nonetheless have felt the beginnings of excitement. While they are frightened by this emotion, their minds gain control of their fear by dampening its initial stirrings. Their intolerance of arousal deprives them of the richness of the sexual experience with partners they may deeply love, and the partners are also deprived.

This problem limits the quality of the relationship. Disappointment and anger become part of it. Each partner wonders, "Is this all there is for me?" The sexually inexperienced woman may blame her inability on her partner's behavior and yearn for a more passionate one because she does not understand why she cannot feel aroused. The partner, deeply affronted by her lack of arousal but too embarrassed to say so, may become destructively critical of other aspects of her behavior. Some couples in this circumstance quickly stir up problems for themselves that lead to an asexual relationship; others quietly accept their sexual limitations. Infidelity may be on both partners' minds to "prove" that the other is at fault.

> Barbara and Gil were commercial artists who felt uneasy about sexual life. She had a low self-regard and was preoccupied with her physical imperfections. ("She's crazy, she is quite attractive!") He could not forget an experience five years earlier with a girl who stopped him during intercourse and said, "You have no idea what you are doing!" Within several years of marriage, despite many shared nonsexual pleasures, sex had all but disappeared. Barbara cried that she was twenty-nine and had never known any sexual pleasure.
>
> During a picnic, after much wine and with Barbara's permission, Gil and a mutual friend necked briefly. Gil was so taken by her excited response to him that he continued the relationship in private. Barbara, who knew that her sexual dread kept Gil feeling sexually inadequate, did not object. His experience was so reassuring that he became attached to this woman and could not stop their relationship. Barbara was tempted but never accepted their standing invitation for a sexual threesome. She and Gil sought help for their marriage when neither could tolerate the new tensions because they did not want to break up.

Unconventional Sexual Identity

The sexual equilibrium of a woman who cannot feel aroused with her young husband often contains her secret of unconventional sexual identity.

> Erica could not relax and enjoy her lovemaking with her new husband. Not only was she not interested or arousable, she felt that sex with Kent was inappropriate. "Don't ask me to explain why!" she would often say as though she meant she could not because she had no idea. But Erica knew that she was predominantly homoerotic. After several years of fidelity, she began a "sexually torrid" relationship with a female partner and finally told Kent the other meaning of "Don't ask to to explain why!"

Another secret of women who cannot be aroused is the presence of strong unconventional intentions. The most common one involves masochistic suffering or degradation, but sometimes it involves humiliating others. These wishes are rarely acted out in a direct fashion, but they are so erotically charged that they keep the woman's arousal confined to masturbation.

The most dramatic identity secret of unresponsive women is the wish to live as a man. Married women who harbor these thoughts usually cannot abide the idea of making love as a woman. They not only want to make love with a woman, they want to make love as a man. In this way they feel normal.

I do not wish to overemphasize the relationship between lifelong arousal problems and unconventional sexual identity. Even when some unconventional women are with the "right" partner, they may not be able to feel aroused. There are lesbians, for example, who cannot be aroused with a female partner. Any woman can have arousal problems.

Childhood Experience

Childhood experiences often surface when people begin to discuss their arousal difficulties. After many therapy sessions with women who have never developed tolerance for arousal, I find myself asking the same two questions: "How did this person become so fearful of her sexual arousal that her mind automatically rejects it?" and "What is it about showing her arousal to a partner that makes her feel so vulnerable?" Certain common impressions have emerged. In some combination, they may begin to explain why these devastating problems exist.

Physical and psychological abuse. Despite increased interest in female sexual abuse, a different form of trauma is probably more common, persistent, and damaging—the combination of psychological and physical abuse. Psychological abuse involves failure to meet the child's most basic needs during the early stages of her life—that is, failure to care for and love the infant, protect her from separations, and provide a stimulating protective environment. In addition, many children are exposed to violence, high tension environments, and physical punishment. During the early years of life, the child develops a basic concept of herself as good or bad, lovable or unlovable. She categorizes others as trustworthy and safe, or unpredictable and dangerous. She learns that her feelings and moods are valued and that others will respond to them or that they may be dangerous to her well-being. In an abusive environment, she may become tentative and afraid of neglect or punishment. A girl may be well on her way to fearing her feelings before sexual abuse begins.

Sexual abuse. Typically, sexual abuse entails the exchange of attention and the semblance of love for genital touching and, less often, intercourse. While it may occur in a nonviolent setting, the sexual abuse is often combined with psychological and physical abuse. Sometimes it is too simple to think that the girl became damaged only because of sexual victimization. For a family member to use a child as a sexual partner requires a lack of respect for her safety, health, and future. This lack may have been translated into psychological abuse long before the sexual use of the girl began. There is seemingly no end to the variety of ways children can be psychologically, physically, and sexually abused by overwhelmed, deteriorated, insensitive, or unprepared caregivers and exploitative persons. Typically, the abusing person is a male, though males certainly have no monopoly on sexual immorality with children.

Misfortune

Interruption of the bond between the little girl and her mother or other primary caregiver though death, prolonged incapacitation, or forced separation constitutes bad luck and probably increases the risk of arousal problems. These misfortunes can be eased if there is an adequate substitute caregiver, but a family disrupted by a mother's sudden death, disease, or imprisonment may have trouble locating such a person. The impact of the loss of the mother figure may lead to the little girl's chronic despair, confusion, and sense of abandonment that leaves her wary of all subsequent attachments.

One long-term consequence of such misfortune may be the avoidance of adult sexual experience. The woman treats sexual behavior as if it were a reenactment of her attachment to mother who proved undependable years ago.

> Marjorie's husband convinced her to seek help for her sexual avoidance and lack of pleasure when he was going through a work crisis. Although he never liked her attitude about sex, during the last year when he felt so needy, her unwillingness to make love enraged him. Her mother had developed a brain tumor when Marjorie was three and died when she was four-and-a-half. Child care for her and her year-old brother was shared by aunts and several housekeepers. When she was six, her father remarried. When she was eight, he divorced. At ten, she met her current stepmother from who she remained aloof. Over a six-month period, discussion about her losses enabled her to dare allow herself a little pleasure. This delighted her because she had thought that she was biologically incapable of arousal. Her husband thought a miracle had been wrought—his internal rage dissipated and he felt he could stay married and live in his home with his children.

Guilt

Women with arousal problems who spend a great deal of time in therapy often go through a phase when they feel guilty about their childhood sexual feelings. They eventually remember childhood excitements and, in particular, the Oedipal conflicts involving their triangular dilemmas with their parents. Sexual and affectionate impulses toward the father produce guilt because they feel like a forbidden betrayal of the mother. Oedipal guilt may seem like an explanation of the problem, but the larger question is, "Why could this little girl not outgrow her Oedipal dilemma like most girls do?" Did she misunderstand environmental messages about sex, overreact to her own sexual interests in her family members, or did she actually participate in abusive or incestuous sexual experiences of which her parents are unaware?

When sexual abuse is not part of the picture, a woman may be fearful of a specific aspect of subjective sexual excitement.

> During her therapy for arousal intolerance, Ruth, a very attractive middle-aged woman, had great difficulty acknowledging that she enjoyed being looked at, admired, and viewed as statuesque. These wishes kept showing up in dreams, fantasies, and in fleeting images during masturbation. One day she confessed that she was withholding a "sick" truth about herself: She often wanted to be displayed naked to an admiring gallery of men.

The source of such an embarrassing erotic image, such as Ruth's, may be ordinary childhood experience. The wish to exhibit oneself, for example, is an almost universal experience in childhood. Who has raised a three- or four-year-old who did not gleefully run naked after a bath? Who has raised a little girl who did not ever enjoy lifting her dress over her underpants? These charming childhood pleasures that precede modesty forever remain a possibility and show up in new forms throughout life. They are not sick when they arise in adulthood. Exhibitionistic imagery generally expresses the wish to be loved and admired. The woman must accept her erotic images without guilt but it helps if she knows their origins.

How Much Can a Girl Tolerate?

Abuse, misfortune, and persistent guilt about past sexual excitements do not affect everyone the same way. The inability to feel any arousal is not the usual adult response to these problems. For every physically abused girl who cannot tolerate sexual excitement, there are many who can easily be aroused. Similar traumas do not lead to the same adult difficulties. No one knows how much abuse a child can tolerate before her personality development in general, and her sexual capacities in particular, are seriously affected.

New Arousal Problems Upon Engagement or Marriage

Some women are gripped by sudden fearful sexual avoidance when they become engaged or shortly after they marry. Some of them can pinpoint its appearance to the day they decided they cared enough about their partners to get married. Their initial joy of feeling loved is spoiled by a sudden anxiety about sex.

> Rhonda used to enjoy sex with her partner and was easily aroused to orgasm. Her recent sexual avoidance is not explained by concerns about his character, background, or lifestyle. It is clear that her sexual nervousness is not a consequence of resenting him; they are getting along just fine. Her background does not include apparent neglect, abuse, misfortune, or incest. She nonetheless rejects him as a sexual partner.
>
> It makes no sense to her fiance that the reason she feels she cannot have sex with him any longer is because she loves him. But the problem seems to be that Rhonda is not able to tolerate both sexual excitement and profound love with the same partner. She affectionately loves him, but the prospect of passionate sexual behavior with him now is incongruous. Loving him has rendered him a family member in her mental world. She is unable to consider him in any other light. When she attempts to make love, she feels the wish to flee. "Suddenly I feel

> as though he were my brother! We're not lovers, we're good friends and roommates. I don't want to make love any more. I can't believe it! What's happened to me?"

This dramatic result of falling in love raises the question of how someone comes to both affectionately and passionately love the same person. Sigmund Freud thought the tendency to maintain a separateness between tender affection and sexual passion was almost a universal consequence of the Oedipal phase, when the girl found that passionate longings for the father were too guilt-provoking and too threatening to her relationship with her mother. Thereafter, tenderness was saved for family members while passion was reserved for those of lesser stature. The many private excitements, crushes, and brief relationships with partners that occur during adolescence were thought to be opportunities to practice bringing excitement and affection together.

I'm not certain this is the complete explanation, but I hold onto it for several important reasons. It reminds me that the capacity to love freely and fully may have a great deal to do with what has gone on before. It helps me remember that engagement and marriage, though everyday events in society, are major events in individual lives that require and cause profound psychological changes. With women and men alike, new arousal problems when adult love is finally found are like red flags that warn of hidden forces at work shaping desire and arousal capacities with a spouse, and that more is to be learned about female sexual development.

Toward a Problem-Free Sexual Life

A woman who has lost her capacity to be aroused should ask herself these questions:

- Have I rejected my partner? Why?
- Has my partner's new physical, mental, or sexual condition caused me to be disinterested?
- Am I too depressed in general to be interested in lovemaking?
- Am I too unhappy about one particular problem to be interested?
- Is my medication causing my arousal problem?
- Are alcohol or street drugs producing the problem?
- Is there a possibility that I am not physically well?

A woman who has never been able to be aroused with a partner needs to ask:

- Why am I not talking with my partner about what is on my mind?
- Are my childhood experiences not letting me enjoy sex?
- Why am I not seeking professional help with this serious problem?

A woman who loses the ability to feel excitement after she falls in love should consider herself in need of immediate professional help to prevent the couple's new equilibrium from becoming asexual.

14

WORKING WITH MR. AND MRS. J

Let's shift our focus to considering the sexual problems of one specific couple. Be a psychiatrist with me for awhile. We are scheduled to see a new patient referred from her gynecologist because of vaginismus.

Vaginismus is the inability to tolerate penile or finger entrance into the vagina. Its name derives from the Latin words for vagina and spasm. When the woman anticipates that vaginal entrance is about to occur, her pelvic muscles involuntarily contract. In severe cases, as far as the partner is concerned, the vagina literally closes off and disappears. In the usual, less severe cases, vaginal entrance is possible but the woman's fear and her spasm produce pain. Some women cannot insert their own fingers or tampons without triggering a mild spasm; even this feels like an entrance into an unknown, dangerous space. The woman's phobia for penetration may cause her to avoid intimate contact all her life. Some women delay intercourse for years and seek help when their partners threaten to leave or when they wish to become pregnant. This delay ends some relationships because the partner loses hope of a normal future.

On the phone, I invited Mrs. J (Joan) to bring her husband to our first meeting. Even when only one partner has a symptom, I prefer to see both partners since the sexual equilibrium is so important. I never am quite sure who is the patient—the woman, the man, or the relationship. However, Joan appeared reluctant and said that her husband had trouble leaving work. So I scheduled a one-hour visit with her alone.

Joan appeared quite comfortable during the introductory small talk, her voice lively and filled with energy. But as soon as I invited her to tell me about why she was there, her gaze shifted to her feet and she began to fidget with her wedding ring.

My game plan on first visits is to let the person talk freely. I am interested in listening closely to his or her story and in experiencing his or her style of expression. I watch the person's face for subtle signs of emotion. When I am with a woman with vaginismus, I am curious about why she would be so afraid of intercourse that her body screams, "No, don't! I'm not ready for this!" I wonder what has traumatized Joan and why she has been unable to deal with her feelings in other ways. Was it rape or sexual assault? Participation in sexual activity as a child with an older person? A painful medical procedure on her genital area? Or is it a secret sexual identity concern such as male identification, homoeroticism, or masochism?

Here is the essence of the first meeting with Joan:

Joan: My gynecologist, Dr. Brandt, sent me to you after we discussed the reasons for my infertility. Roger and I have been trying to conceive for five years but have had no success. I really want a baby, but I have this pain that makes me scared of intercourse. We don't actually have intercourse very often.

Doctor: Oh?

Joan: Dr. Brandt found it hard to imagine but I actually like sex. It's so strange, I'm actually good at it. At least Roger thinks so—he's been my only sexual partner—and I can easily have orgasms. I just can't have intercourse. I feel like such a dummy (suddenly crying). Why can't I do such a simple thing? It's like I have a line drawn through my, you know, private parts—above the line I am fine, below it I am a disaster. Dr. Brandt said she has had other patients with the problem, but I never even heard of it.

Doctor: How long did you work with her on this problem?

Joan: I saw her twice alone and once with Roger. I couldn't tell her about my problem at first, but during my examination—it was so embarrassing—I kept scooting off the table. She knew something was wrong. Dr. Brandt gave me the choice of referral or having her help me try to dilate my vagina. She was very nice and didn't seem to mind when I decided to go elsewhere. She agreed with me that this wasn't a simple thing.

Doctor: Why do you say that?

Joan: Because, I know! . . . . [very uncomfortable] . . . . I knew, oh, I knew this was going to be hard! [a few deep breaths as though she were going to swim under water] I don't mean to be immodest, but I am a very competent woman. I have a graduate degree. I'm thirty-three years old and I've been promoted three times in five years and everyone thinks I have it all together. The truth is I am ruining my marriage and I'm a sexual fraud! I don't know how long Roger can take this . . . . [crying hard] . . . . We are still technically virgins together. I am a virgin and he almost is. We'll never have a baby at this rate. I'm getting old. My sisters have children, even my baby brother's wife is expecting. There are babies everywhere. [I waited briefly until she calmed down a bit.]

Doctor: You sound like you want a child very much.

Joan: Yes, but I don't know when. I mean time is running out—the biological clock, you know—but I could be the company's first woman vice president in a couple years or so. I'd like that a lot. I'd like a baby a lot too, but right now I'd just like to be able to have intercourse.

Doctor: Tell me some more about yourself.

Joan: [nervous pause] I'm very well organized. I have a thing about time and efficiency. Catherine, my friend at the office, says I am a work machine, she never saw anyone like me before. [looking at my desk] No offense, but I couldn't stand to have my desk look like yours. It would drive me crazy. Sometimes I look at Catherine's desk and have a hard time not going over and straightening up the papers. I became that way in the convent. I entered a religious order after two years of college but I left because I knew it just wasn't for me. I couldn't give up the world that much. It was a hard decision, but it was the right one. I loved the regularity of religious life when I was younger but I needed to be in control of my own life. I am still religious, but I don't think I'm guilty about sex. I know what the problem is. I just can't say it yet.

Doctor: No rush. Perhaps you'd like to tell me about your family first.

Joan: No! I have to get it out . . . . [more deep breaths] . . . . I had a fascination with the Virgin Mary. It sounds crazy, I know, but when I was in grade school I thought I was or could be the Blessed Virgin. I used to dream about her. I don't think I ever outgrew it. Every once in a while I still see her image in my dreams. I'm not a crazy person. I used to be a dreamy teenager. At various times I just thought being the Virgin, being a nun, being a devoted, hard-working person were good things to be. No one in my family was as religious as I. When other girls turned to lipstick, makeup, and boys, I fell in love with church music. I was the school organist and pianist.

Doctor: Let me see, are you saying that your earlier ambition to be the Virgin is alive today in your problem? [Seeing her embarrassed nod of assent, I continued] And you do or you do not still aspire to be her?

Joan: I don't want to be her. I don't even want to be a virgin, but I am and I can't help it!

Doctor: You have thought a lot about this.

Joan: Yes, but it hasn't done much good. When Roger touches me near my, you know, I feel a shot of fear and my whole body gets tense. The only way we can have sex is if Roger promises not to touch me there. It's a good thing he has a sense of humor or we'd be lost. We laugh a lot.

I could see that Joan was a very determined woman. She wanted to continue to see me alone because she wasn't ready to talk about the Virgin Mary with Roger. During our subsequent meetings, she discussed her religious life, her political struggles in her job, Roger and his family, and her background. Although interesting, these discussions always seemed off the mark of our agreed-on goal of trying to figure out why she needed to have such a strong identification with the Virgin Mary. The first time we felt we were on the right track was during our seventh meeting:

Joan: When I was eleven, my nineteen-year-old sister, Mary Beth, got pregnant. I knew something was wrong—Mary Beth was crying, Mother was crying, Father was irritable, I had to go to my room a lot. No one would tell me what was go-

> ing on. Mary Beth left home. By the time my parents told me, I had long ago figured it all out. The big family secret is that my brother is really not my brother—he is my nephew.

We talked about this for a while. She was cheerful because it seemed to explain her need for chastity so as not to cause the disappointment and tragedy that Mary Beth did. Her sister's life has been very difficult. However, in spite of this discussion, Joan's vaginal spasm and painful anticipation of intercourse did not improve.

At our twelfth session, another dimension of Joan's problem appeared. She had briefly mentioned her mother in a positive light for many weeks. When I reminded her that I did not know much about her relationship with her mother, she became impatient with me and joked that I was an intrusive and pushy shrink. "Being in therapy with you is like having to be at vespers. Not only do I have to come here every Tuesday at the same time, but now you are telling me what I have to do when I'm here." Her humor was not lighthearted; it only transmitted her annoyance. So I said so. She became very angry and silent. After what seemed like an eternity, she told me how her mother used to check her underwear for stains. Once when she had the first of a series of bladder infections, her mother forced a look at her genitals "to make sure she was cleaning herself properly." We talked about this for several sessions and pieced together that this occurred after her sister's pregnancy and before her mother's "nervous breakdown" which landed her in the hospital for a short time.

The Virgin Mary seemed to arise from the mind of a little girl who wanted to be good, and was insensitively intruded upon by a mentally ill mother's fear that her preadolescent daughter was sexually active. The church and the symbol of the Virgin Mary became her mother for several years while her real mother gradually recovered. I'm sure there was more to her story—there always is. However, these discussions helped her make sense of this aspect of her past, and she began to feel optimistic about having intercourse. She reported a lessening of her fear and her pain. "It's tolerable now, Doctor, most of the time."

In tales of therapeutic triumph the story would end here, but it does not. I had my chance to meet Roger after all because, as his wife overcame her problem, he discovered he could not ejaculate. He was very upset. All this time he thought he was normal and helping her. "What's going on here?" he shouted in frustration during our first meeting. I have been through this before with couples. One person gets better and the other shows up with a problem. It's the old sexual equilibrium in action—people's sexual fates are tied together. Sometimes they have similar sexual anxieties and take turns having symptoms; sometimes the reactions of a sexually healthy partner to the other partner's problem produce new symptoms. I assumed the latter was the explanation for Roger's inability to ejaculate.

Roger was a year younger than his wife. His ambition was to be a rich man by the time he was forty. He said that this ambition allowed him to be patient with Joan because he had his business to preoccupy him. Since he was able to ejaculate during masturbation, he knew there was nothing physically wrong with him. He thought he had ejaculated on one or two occasions during intercourse with another woman when he was twenty-two. This led him to believe the problem had more to do with his relationship with Joan than with his sexual capacity. He and Joan had a long friendship prior to marriage and became intimate shortly before their wedding. They chose to wait until the wedding to have intercourse. Before and after the wedding he could ejaculate with oral or manual stimulation and occasionally by thrusting between her thighs. These were an accommodation to her vaginismus. He could not understand why he had the problem now that Joan was better.

I tried to explain it to him with a few leading questions. I asked him to tell me how he felt about his wife's vaginismus in the early days of marriage. He described her scream on their honeymoon and his response: "I never heard such a sound except in the movies! I didn't know what I did wrong. She said that she was just nervous. Two days later we tried to have intercourse again and she cried and said maybe we should wait until we got into our apartment. I didn't mind too much. We had sex anyway, it was fun, and we just put it off."

Doctor: Some husbands develop impotence under these circumstances because they are scared of hurting their wives. They inhibit their excitement—they just don't erect—so as not to repeat the frightening scene.

Roger: That never happened to me. I always get an erection.

Doctor: That's great, but maybe the same fear of hurting her produced your inability to ejaculate. [casually] I never can predict who is going to get what symptom.

Roger: I don't know, if you say so, you're the doctor. I don't think I am good at understanding such things. [His polite response made me feel I was wrong.]

I met with both Joan and Roger during the next session. Joan was delighted with her progress but muted it in deference to her husband's worry. Roger showed a flicker of sadness when he said, "I don't want to have to masturbate to come!" Our conversation drifted to how similar they were in terms of their ambition and capacity to put their noses to the grindstone to get things done. They laughed and said they were both workaholics. I wondered how a baby would fit into their lives, and suddenly realized I had no idea what they were doing about birth control. It turned out that, never having needed it before, they had not done anything about it. I commented that his sexual problem was a pretty good solution to contraception. They decided that they would try a condom for the first time in their lives.

A week passed; no condoms were purchased. He was too busy with work. They had intercourse once, and Joan had a little pain, "nothing I couldn't bear!" I was persistent on the baby issue, "What would happen if he did ejaculate and she became pregnant?" Smiling, she said maybe her vice presidency could wait, then in her characteristic way, "Maybe I could do both." We both noticed that her husband was uneasy and we looked at him as if to say "What gives?" Another piece unfolded.

Roger: Look, it's no big deal to me if we don't have kids. I only want them because you want them. You know that, Joan. Maybe I won't be such a good father. I don't want to be like my father.

Doctor: [I had previously heard from his wife that his father was imprisoned for embezzlement when Roger was thirteen.] I'm not sure I understand.

Roger: My father was a bastard. He beat my mother, beat me and my sister. He terrorized all of us! I hated him. I was relieved when he was away. By the time he got out of jail, my mother divorced him. I didn't want to have anything to do with him. I'm not even sure where he is today and I don't want to know. When my sister tries to tell me about him, I get mad all over again.

Doctor: How does this translate into not wanting kids? Do you think you will turn into a bastard, too?

Roger: I don't know, you're the doctor. [This sudden sarcasm made me feel like I was a bastard for asking!]

Doctor: You must have plenty of good reasons to be mad at your father. Does Joan know all about this?

Roger: . . . . Almost. [You could cut the tension with a knife. Joan had prided herself on their openness, even though Roger didn't really know the entire story about the Virgin Mary and its origins.] I'm sorry, Joan, it's too horrible to think about.

Joan: [reaching for his hand, lovingly] It's okay; you don't have to say. [It felt so right not to push him at this point. Joan sensed he needed his privacy and her support. It was quite a lovely moment.]

That night Roger told Joan about his disgraceful humiliations at his father's hands. Roger had at least several experiences in early grade school with his drunken father who awakened him from sleep by forcing his erection into Roger's mouth and onto his buttocks and thighs, possibly his anus. But it was difficult to know because either Roger was uncertain, could not remember, or found it mortifying to say.

I was aware all along that Roger kept a tight lid on his feelings. I thought of him as an emotionally inexpressive person. The feelings associated with these memories were, of course, intense. Telling them to Joan and later to me exhausted him. Joan said that Roger was red-faced, hard-breathing, and tearful when he initially told her about them. He was more factual when he told me, but it was evident from his posture that he was feeling very uncomfortable.

Doctor: This is why you hate him the most.
Roger: He really is a bastard!
Joan: [crying quietly] I hate him, too.
Doctor: You had to passively endure awful things. You were so young and defenseless.
Roger: [rubbing his eye as if to disguise the few tears] Let's change the subject.
Doctor: May we discuss this another time?
Roger: Please, no more today. I hate this.

I'm sorry to say that Roger did not dramatically get better that night and live happily ever after with normal ejaculatory response. We continued to work together for eight sessions. I repeatedly explained that a man must allow himself to get lost in his sensations in order to ejaculate. He tried, but this form of sensuality was foreign to him. We wondered if it felt sinful in some way; he, too, had been a fairly religious teenager. We tried to understand why he would not allow himself to become more excited in the vagina—why he would not "lose control" and have an orgasm. After the sixth session, he did have an orgasm without the use of birth control during Joan's safe time, but the next time he did not. Roger did not develop the ability to regularly attain orgasm in Joan's vagina, and the burden of discussing his feelings did not lighten for him. He became busier at work and we decided to end our regular meetings.

Joan and Roger both had a little of the Virgin Mary in them—they each had strong motives not to have intercourse. I suspect intercourse was linked in Roger's mind to the oral or anal penetration that he endured as a youngster, although I cannot be certain. Roger, who, unlike his father, never took a drink, was uncomfortable talking about most of his past. I always wondered what else he had seen or endured that made him unresponsive to intercourse. However, my curiosity was not to be gratified. Roger was a present- and future-oriented man; he was not interested in mental archaeology.

A decade has passed and they are now in their forties. She has intercourse without pain on most occasions. He ejaculates in the vagina every once in a while. Emotional intensity continues to be a struggle in every part of his life. There never was a pregnancy. Joan, who is now a first vice president, seems to have accepted this with grace; Roger does not think about it much. They are an active aunt and uncle. They have sex once or twice a month except on vacations when they have more time with each other. He is almost rich, but his definition of rich has expanded upwards. "A million dollars does not go as far as it did a decade ago!"

Toward a Problem-Free Sexual Life

A woman who has pain and spasm during intercourse needs to:

- have a gynecologic examination to be sure that an infection or some other cause of inflammation is not the reason
- clarify whether it is intercourse alone or if any other form of penetration frightens her
- correctly label the problem as vaginismus if fear and discomfort combine to produce intense pain when penetration is imminent
- seek therapy for vaginismus since it is a highly treatable condition that some gynecologists and most psychotherapists can help with
- expect that her partner may need some time to adjust sexually once she is improved

A man who is having trouble ejaculating in his partner's body or in his partner's presence but who can reach orgasm when alone needs to:

- realize that unless he is on a new medication or has an unusual neurological disease, this pattern is caused by fear of sharing excitement with another person
- seek medical evaluation to identify any physical causes of the problem
- concentrate on maximizing his sensations during intercourse by thrusting at his preferred rate without worrying about pleasing his partner, who will be delighted when he is able to ejaculate
- seek psychotherapy if the above does not help

15

NYMPHS AND SATYRS

Problems of sexual desire are not only due to lack of motivation or drive. Some people have too much sexual desire. Their lives conjure up mythological images of half-human, half-animal satyrs and seductive mermaids, woodland nymphs, and horned men with powerful beast-like bodies. These creatures are wonderful symbols representing the struggle to tame our sexual-aggressive selves. They symbolize the challenge facing all children and adults—to overcome our beast.

However, the nymphs and satyrs discussed in this chapter are not symbols, they are actual people whose lives are so dominated by relentless sexual excitement that they can pay little attention to other activities. Most people who think they are too preoccupied with sex do not qualify as nymphs and satyrs. Their sexual thoughts are mild in comparison.

Most comments such as "I think I'm becoming a nymphomaniac" or "I can't stop being horny" are made by people who are simply surprised by the intensity of their new sexual feelings. Many normal adolescents brimming with sexual drive, or adults who find an exciting new relationship after years of being alone, are surprised by their sexual exuberance.

> Cleo, a thirty-six-year-old divorced mother of an eighth-grader, "finally" met a man she liked after seven years. "I thought I was in a Biblical drought of seven lean years and my sex life had died on the vine." For several weeks since being with Russ, Cleo felt she was on fire. She thought of sex with him all the time—day and night she felt sexually excited remembering what they did to each other. During this period, having her daughter home in the evenings suddenly became a burden. "God, I hope it isn't going to be this way for seven more years. I don't think I can keep this up! I've turned into a nymphomaniac."

The boundary between those with relentless sexual desire and those surprised by their hunger for sexual experience is not difficult to define. Healthy sexual intensity is related to a person, real or imagined. Its intention is mutual pleasure, it is a positive rather than a destructive force, and it can be satisfied. Often, it is most intense early in a relationship. It promotes rather than destroys that relationship and it is experienced as fun. Once this need for sex is satisfied, it frees people to turn their attention to other activities. Cleo's "nymphomania" did not last much longer, though her sexual pleasures with Russ did.

Portraits of unbounded excitement, although found in the classical literature of ancient and modern times, most often occur in pornography. Excesses of male and female appetite are a common theme in sexually explicit movies and books. This unfortunate link with pornography makes it difficult to give any serious consideration to overwhelming excitement because the topic feels tainted—too seedy for legitimate discussion.

In a superficial sense, the study of nymphs and satyrs deals with the subject of sexual perversions. Perversions are thought to be unpleasant, not only because of their association with pornography, but because they deal with thoughts, feelings, and behaviors that most cultures and religions consider to be evil or sins. In a more profound way, however, this subject is about some of the long-term effects of childhood sexual abuse.

Upper Limits of Sexual Capacity

The lives of nymphs and satyrs demonstrate that the upper limits of sexual capacity are far greater than most people experience. Questions such as "How long can the sexual organs function before the body quits in exhaustion?" and "How many orgasms per day are possible?" have surprising answers. The following are actual examples from my practice.

> Almost every morning for two years, Mary, a fifty-year-old woman awakened with a genital excitement that was only absent for ten minutes following masturbation. When the excitement returned, she tried to distract herself with household chores, a fulltime job, and jogging. Whenever her attention was not diverted by outside matters, she was aware of a strong genital tingling sensation and the need to have an orgasm.

> Pam was astounded by her forty-year-old fiance's sexual interest in her. Two weekends prior to the marriage, he had intercourse to orgasm fourteen times. She was correct in her assumption that this level of sexual activity could not continue. After the wedding, his interest declined to the point where he only initiated sex three times a day! She began to dread his coming home. He could not be near her without having sex and considered her menstruation a minor tragedy. Pam moved out after one month, having gained a new understanding of his two other brief marriages.

Jason, a homosexual teenager, had at least four orgasms a day for two weeks in a row—with different men each time. Actually, he had more than four partners per day; sometimes he had sex without orgasm. When he was not orgasmic, he just moved on to another bath house, bar, or street pick-up.

Andrea, who estimated her number of sexual partners during her teenage years at perhaps two hundred, was faithful to her husband for a year. They usually had sexual intercourse twice a day and she supplemented this with masturbation. After several serious arguments with her husband about matters outside the bedroom, she began seducing men in her office. Sometimes she would have sex with two men during an eight-hour work day. During one summer, she walked the streets at 3:00 A.M. enticing strangers into hard-thrusting intercourse to relieve her tensions.

Emotional Illness

People with an extraordinary need for sexual experience, relentless spontaneous sexual arousal, and inability to be sexually satisfied are not fun-loving, sensuous, carefree creatures. They are emotionally ill. This fact is carefully hidden by those who benefit from this problem. The oversexed are rarely depicted in books, stories, and films within the broad context of their lives because their sexual behavior is more fascinating to the audience than their depression, poor judgment, and inability to concentrate and coherently organize their thoughts. Pornographers and others know that voyeuristic pleasure must not show too much of the person's life to be erotic.

One day my former barber was making conversation and asked me about my specialty as a psychiatrist. His demeanor changed instantly when I told him that I treat people with sexual difficulties. He immediately assumed that people came to my office and had sex in front of me so I could give them tips on what they were doing wrong and how they could improve their performance. At first, I thought he was pulling my leg. Soon I realized that he was dead serious. I explained that my work did not involve anything like that. He didn't believe me. I told him that people come to talk to me about their difficulties making love and their problems being together as a couple. The lustful leer on the barber's face showed his disbelief. "Do you ever use surrogates?" he asked. "If you ever need somebody to give a woman a good experience, call me. I can't believe this," he went on, "I have been cutting your hair for two years and all this time you have been talking to people about humping. Terrific, I'm serious, doc, I want to be one of your surrogates." I was about to disappoint him. "We really don't use surrogates. The treatment of sexual difficulties is often the same as therapy for other emotional problems. You know: talk, relationship, conflict, tears, parents—just the ordinary stuff of living." His answer indicated his shallow understanding of pornography. "Hey, doc, I'm not interested in all that heavy stuff—just give me the sex part. It'll be just like in my magazines. Don't worry, I'll take good care of your patients." By this time, he seemed to be both kidding and serious.

Sexualized People

I use the term sexualized to describe people with a relentless need for sex. Sexualized individuals describe themselves as having an excessive amount of spontaneous arousal. "I'm oversexed, that's the only trouble." They believe their lack of self-control is a natural consequence of the strength and frequency of their sexual drive. "Something so powerful is going on in me and there's no stopping it. I can't help this." These people are not easily sexually satisfied, they substitute excitement for memories and feelings, they have difficulty connecting emotionally with others, and most of them have atypical sexual identities.

Lack of Satisfaction

The orgasms of sexualized people do not take their tensions away; the relief provided may last as little as a few minutes. Orgasm, especially in nonsexualized men, normally causes physical satisfaction and an immediate lack of interest in further sex. How this is brought about within the nervous system is not known. It is possible that the neural mechanisms for satiety are biologically defective in sexualized individuals. Perhaps a brain dysfunction predisposes certain people to being sexually insatiable; however, usually the illness seems more complex.

Excitement Substitutes for Memory and Feelings

Sexualized people substitute sexual excitement for unpleasant memories and unsettling emotions. Their minds can instantly switch from sadness, anxiety, rage, or guilt to preoccupation with genital sensations. Many people are able to use sex to distract themselves briefly from their problems, but sexualized people use this mechanism to deal with almost anything unpleasant. They cannot tolerate life's painful emotions. In fact, their arousal occurs so quickly that they often do not even know they have these emotions. While some cannot bear their sexual excitement for long without masturbating, many others refuse to give in to the sensations and go through the day uncomfortably excited.

Being "oversexed" means that the substitution of excitement for other feelings has become automatic, leaving the person without a sense of self-governance. "I am out of control—gone. This thing runs me day and night!"

> Marvin, a drug-abusing lawyer in his thirties, could not stop sexual liaisons with a series of women. During periods of extreme pressure, preparing for trial or some other high-tension deadline, he would manage to have intercourse with two different women before he went home. Eventually he began spending a great deal of money on prostitutes. "It's quicker and disrupts my day less." For years he told himself he could stop the quaaludes or co-

caine and the women anytime he wanted. But when his wife threatened divorce after she discovered one instance of his infidelity, his new marital tensions actually increased his sexual arousal.

Kathy, a divorced, college-educated woman, had spent her days masturbating for several years. She lost exact account, but she estimated that in a typical eighteen-hour waking day, she brought herself to seventy-five orgasms—not because she wanted to, but because she couldn't get her clitoris to stop tingling. Her life was in shambles; she could not concentrate, she could not work. Much to her and my surprise, she was able to go through an entire week without these crippling urges while on medication in a psychiatric hospital. And then, during a session while Kathy was still on the medication, I asked her to close her eyes and imagine the worst moment of her life. Before she could even describe a painful scene with her pregnant teenage daughter and husband—when she was just remembering it—her genital excitement returned with its old fury. "Oh, my God! It's back!"

Some researchers, including psychiatrist, Fred Berlin and psychologist, Ronald Langevin, believe that at least some of these people may have excessive sex drives because of a brain abnormality. More likely, however, they have learned early in life to focus on their genital feelings rather than other emotions because they had to cope with sexual behavior far too advanced for their age.

Relentless sexual excitement may be an unusual way of remembering childhood sexual experience. Instead of being able to fully recall an event of incest, for example, just some of the feelings are remembered; their original source is forgotten. To use a nonsexual example, I know a very thin adult who could not swallow any solid food in her parents' house after her divorced parents remarried each other. This symptom turned out to be related to the frequent high-tension dinners that were caused by her abusive father when she was a child. The feelings of tension in her throat were a form of memory of bad times; the bad times themselves were only vaguely recalled.

The continual arousal of sexualized people is a way of remembering bad times. What happened to them was either too painful to recall or occurred before they could be expected to remember.

> For several months, six-year-old Lyle played a game with his two older sisters in which he ended up dressed as a little girl. They were unusually delighted with him during these games—giggling, hugging him, giving him more attention than he usually received from them or from his busy parents. Although Lyle was initially humiliated and worried about playing "baby sister" and putting on lipstick, he was swept away by their infectious excitement. During adolescence, he had no explanation for his interest in cross-dressing during masturbation. He felt driven to masturbate three or more times a day, while fantasizing about being a girl, hurting a girl, or being tied up by girls. He had no recollection of the "baby sister" games for the first three months of therapy.
>
> Gina, an eight-year-old who was unable to concentrate and learn anything in school, was removed from her home when it was learned that her father was using her as a sexual partner. In a foster home she was unable to sit quietly, listen to instructions, or relate to other children. She urinated on the floor without being self-conscious. Within a few hours at the foster home and within a few days at a new school, she was unabashedly suggesting fellatio, genital rubbing, or intercourse to older boys. School officials and the foster parents who independently described Gina as a "little nymphomaniac" did not initially know that she was raised as a sexual object for her father and his friends. Her drug-addicted mother offered no protection. Being sexually useful was Gina's means of relating to others and establishing her worth.

Premature sexualization. No child is equipped to understand and process experiences such as Gina's and Lyle's. When biologic drive normally increases during adolescence, the prematurely sexualized child may experience an intense surge of unexplained excitement. Either the memory of the inciting circumstances is completely forgotten, as was the case with Lyle, or its significance is not appreciated. The woman who had two hundred partners as a teenager knew she had been involved sexually with her father and uncle during grade school; she could not see this as a source of her being sexually driven, however. Remembered or not, the result of childhood abuse may be a teenager who seeks sexual experiences without being able to achieve relief from tension.

Most of the oversexed people I have treated were psychologically traumatized during childhood. There is nothing subtle about these experiences—for example, months of incest, physical beatings, cross-dressing as punishment, or anal penetration.

How adults deal with sexual trauma. When people are traumatized as adults, they usually remain conscious of the event and their feelings about it, and have a difficult time concentrating on other activities while the trauma is still fresh. Adults do not generally react to trauma with sexual excitement unless it involves sexual behavior.

> Thirty-year-old Matt allowed himself to be seduced by a woman at a convention. During intercourse, the husband, calm and friendly, quietly appeared. Although Matt did not know it, the seduction had been planned by the couple. After they reassured him he was in no danger, all three became intimate. They were inseparable for three days which included much intercourse and watching each other. On the last day, with the assistance of a lot of Scotch, the couple enticed Matt into letting them dress him in the wife's clothes. For months afterward, he could not stop thinking about his bizarre vacation; he remained excited, but quite anxious.

How children cope with trauma. Young children who have experienced traumatic events are not usually capable of analyzing and discussing the experience. If good coping is achieved, it is usually through fantasy, play, and the understanding of adults who are able to put the child's feelings into words for them. Young children who have been hospitalized for operations, for example, usually play doctor, nurse, surgeon, or other hospital games for months afterward. Playing these games with a doll or another child allows them to actively perform on others what had to be done to them. This behavior helps the child get rid of the feelings associated with being held down, intruded upon, physically hurt, and embarrassed by strangers having access to his or her body. The child plays these games until the situation is psychologically spent.

In the early 1900s, psychoanalysts discovered that many heterosexual adults who preferred anal erotic pleasures to intercourse had been given frequent enemas as children. This observation suggested that lifelong sexual interests could be determined by traumatic childhood experiences. Being intruded into by a parent with an enema nozzle seemed to fix the child's sexual interests to the anus for life. The anal intrusion not only stimulated the child's outrage over bodily violation, but it combined this feeling with pleasurable sensations. The child grew up to generally prefer masturbation with anal erotic images rather than turn his or her body over to a partner. As an adult, this person forgot about the enemas or did not grasp their relationship to the anal erotic interests. In other areas of life, many people with such patterns are emotionally all right. Just in terms of their sexual development, the enemas may have been too much to cope with.

There are many other childhood experiences that can leave lasting emotional scars.

> Frank, a sixteen-year-old who masturbated as often as six times a day, had been preoccupied for years with images of raping and hurting women. After walking in on his divorced mother having intercourse, he was both sexually aroused by what he witnessed and infuriated that he had to see it. He went on a rampage—within an hour he broke fifteen windows in the neighborhood. He was bitter that she chose to have intercourse when he usually got home from school. He felt that this was just another example of his parents' lack of concern for him.

Most of the time, in fact, he stayed away from home by keeping busy with his friends. After his outburst, Frank recalled that he had been exposed to a great deal of his parents' chaotic life when he was a small boy. Sex was inseparably linked with anger for Frank. He had been excited by his parents' intercourse and simultaneously enraged that they ignored him. In his fantasies, he managed to combine his excitement and rage through rape images.

Difficulty Connecting Emotionally with Others

Occasionally an inexperienced young man, who has repeated fantasies of being initiated into sex by a nymphomaniac, actually meets a sexualized woman. The outcome is usually disappointment and anger—he feels used and does not immediately understand why. The reason is that her need for relief of tension far outweighs her ability to relate to the partner.

Pam, who left her husband when she understood his insatiable lovemaking had nothing to do with her, thought during their engagement that his exuberance showed his joy in the relationship. She could not hold on to that view when she became aware that her interests and wishes were steamrolled by his need to relieve his sexual tension.

The final force that pushes many people with high sex drives into the oversexed category may be a desperate feeling of hopelessness about forming a caring relationship with another human being. Nymphs and satyrs have intense wishes for psychological and physical intimacy like the rest of us, but they often dramatically lack sufficient social skills and trust to form relationships. They are trapped in a psychological prison. They wish to have an intimate relationship, but they also have a strong motive not to be involved with another person. However, their sex drive is overwhelming. These three elements of their sexual desire—wish, motive, and drive—combine to produce people who are excited much of the time, who say that they want more from relationships, but who avoid being close.

This middle-aged man, who avoided sex with his wife for the first four years of marriage, has such a dilemma. Here is a favorite masturbation fantasy that he used at least once a day.

> I see a tall woman in a yellow rubber raincoat and spiked high heels. She is standing there like a statue on a pedestal in a museum. You can't get too close to her. I never actually see her face, it's her raincoat and shoes that excite me, that hold my interest and attention.

Studies by Nicholas Groth, Gene Abel, Judith Becker, and others in America and Europe have shown that many nymphs and satyrs have been traumatized as children by premature, intense, physical excitements generated by those they depended on for protection, affection, and instruction. These experiences are so disruptive that they interfere with their ability to learn, socialize with peers, and regulate moods. They are thrust into a vicious cycle relatively early in life: Their problems with parents make it hard for them to trust and learn how to relate to friends. This makes their love relationships during adolescence and young adulthood difficult, which in turn predisposes them to extreme loneliness that ultimately triggers the insatiable excitement. It is not surprising that many oversexed people are chronically depressed, socially isolated, or addicted to drugs.

Atypical Sexual Identity

As described in previous chapters, sexual identity has three dimensions—gender identity, orientation, and intention, and each has a psychological and a behavioral aspect. Atypical sexual identity is one common characteristic of many nymphs and satyrs. In this chapter, I have mentioned cross-dressing, anal eroticism, sadistic need to punish women, male homosexual searching, and attraction to rubber and shoes. Other unusual aspects of sexual identity such as sexual attraction to children and masochistic fantasies can be included in this list. Kathy, whose improvement was set back by remembering her most painful moment, used to fantasize during many of her hours of masturbation that an older homosexual woman was spanking and humiliating her.

Relentless sexual interest sometimes is found among those with such atypical gender identities or orientations, but most of those who see mental health professionals have atypical intentions. Marvin, the drug abusing lawyer, thought of himself as merely sexually addicted. Eventually, however, he was able to talk about the many unusual forms of his intentions that preceded his addiction to prostitutes.

> "I used to call and talk dirty to women whose names I picked from the phone book. This was very exciting. Once, when I was drunk in college I stood naked waving my penis at passersby from the dorm window. My friends howled. I was excited for months afterwards. Sometimes, I wanted to rape and sometimes I wanted to be raped. There were times I never knew what was coming next. I seemed to be interested in anything sexual."

Both men and women can use their frequent masturbation or liaisons to distract themselves from their interest in hurting or being hurt. They often seem to have an entirely conventional sexual identity—they are masculine or feminine, heterosexual, and just trying to have intercourse—but they are running from sadistic or masochistic intentions. They are traumatized children who have lost most of the memories of their pain and unconsciously cope with them through driven sexual behavior. Therapy is frightening because it asks them to remember. The drug-abusing lawyer soon fled therapy. It was easier to lie to his wife and visit prostitutes several times a week.

Most sexualized men do not victimize children and most nymphs are not on an indiscriminant prowl for men. The majority of those who experience relentless sexual arousal deal with it privately through frequent masturbation and never do fully understand why this is their fate. Even as adults they continue to be victims of a psychological pain disguised as sexual drive.

Those with relentless sexual desire and excitement can be found everywhere—from derelicts to doctors, from hookers to socialites. The majority of those who are sexually out of control with others are men as seen in psychiatric clinics and courts, but women are not spared. They more often bear their burden privately.

Many sexualized people are also drug-addicted because they have learned that alcohol or some other substance quiets their inner turmoil. Others can be found among those treated for sex offenses. Many people who have repeated sexual contact with children, make obscene phone calls, peek in windows, rape, or display their genitals to unsuspecting women fall into this category. Another group is to be found among the profoundly mentally ill who have trouble regulating their moods, thought processes, and self-esteem. Highly sexed people undergoing considerable stress can become nymphs and satyrs also. But being oversexed is not a lifetime condition. It is a product of a poorly understood balance between the brain's hidden biology and the personality's coping style, and it can be changed.

The oversexed are driven to a world of sex without commitment, closeness, and a caring, supportive relationship, not only by their excitement but by their inability to relate to others. These people are often alone for much of their lives. When they do get involved with others, their fear of closeness can prove destructive to their partners. They often privately, discreetly partake of activities that others sense as dangerous, unwholesome, or depraved. This accounts for the seediness of the entire subject of sexual perversion.

Pedophiles

Among the most dangerous of the satyrs and nymphs are the pedophiles, people who prefer children as sexual partners. Very few pedophiles are women. Over their lifetimes, pedophiles often victimize large numbers of children, keep the cycle of abuse going from one generation to another, and cause serious mental health problems. Although some pedophiles are isolated individuals, many others are fathers who initiate their own children into genital intimacies. Some of the fathers have sex with each daughter in succession; others with only the sons. Some fathers share the child with their friends and, in particular, with the persons who initiated them into adult-child sex as youngsters.

> An alcoholic man and his wife, an abuser of pain medications, rarely had sex together after the birth of their three daughters. During the girls' teenage years, one ran away from home for a year, another made two serious suicide attempts, and the third became alcoholic. By age eighteen, all were permanently gone from the home, preferring subsistence living to their well-appointed dwelling. The girls grew up to require considerable mental health care. In their late twenties, they began talking to one another about their sexual experiences with their father. When each of them was between twelve and fourteen, he often surprised them while they were undressing or after a shower. With a glazed look in his eye and alcohol on his breath, he performed various sexual acts, including touching their genitals and rubbing himself to orgasm on their buttocks or thighs; making them touch his semen, which he called "disgusting"; occasionally telling them how terrible they were for doing these things; joking that he hated their pubic hair; and threatening them into silence.
>
> The daughter who ran away from home briefly prostituted and was heavily involved with drugs until her early twenties. The daughter who almost died from an overdose of pain medication and alcohol continues to have no interest in any sexual behavior. The alcoholic daughter grew up to experience periods of relentless sexual arousal. Still struggling with their various emotional problems, the young women are good friends. They visit their parents briefly and together during the holidays.

When we hear what has happened to some boys and girls at the hands of adults, stunned disbelief is often our first reaction. But soon, outrage—often accompanied by murderous impulses—follows. "Well, if we can't shoot them, let's at least put them in jail where they can't hurt anybody else!" Although society may tolerate many people's unusual sexual intentions and even joke about their perversions, when it comes to acting these out with children, we draw the line.

Medication and the Out-of-control Man

Some men who cannot control their socially destructive sexual behavior have benefited from weekly injections of depo-Provera. This medicine works by lessening the amount of male hormone in the body and quieting the sexual drive center, thus causing a reversible form of castration. It has helped some dangerous men become better citizens and more productive individuals, and it has prevented many people, especially children, from becoming victims. After the medication takes effect, the patient no longer feels sexually out of control. Although it is encouraging that these men can be helped in this way, they are not yet well. They still are isolated, lonely, and depressed. They must find other ways to cope with their unpleasant feelings now that they no longer instantaneously convert them into sexual excitement.

Psychotherapy is provided along with the medication and the patient is led to realize that even with the drug in his body, sadness or anxiety continue to produce the tendency to behave sexually. He may have to fight this tendency for many decades, but with courage and luck may learn to feel better about himself and gain self-control.

Toward a Problem-Free Sexual Life

Children, including teenagers, need to be protected against premature sexual experiences with people much older than themselves because:

- They do not know what they are consenting to and the experiences can be highly disruptive to their personalities.
- As adults, they are likely to have limited interest in sex or periods of relentless sexual desire.
- If they are boys, they are more likely to become sex offenders.
- If they are girls, they are likely to be afraid of sex for the rest of their lives.

16

BOUNDARY CROSSERS

The most dramatic sexual identity problems are found in people who seriously consider crossing the boundary between male and female. In 1952, an unknown American soldier named George Jensen went to Denmark to have a sex-change operation and returned famous to live as Christine Jorgensen. This event startled conventional society and raised questions we are still asking today. Why would anyone want to do this? Is it proper for the medical profession to help someone do this? How can sex be changed?

In the decades since, our culture has become more familiar with terms like "transsexual," "transvestite," "sex-reassignment surgery," and "cross-dressing." Male and female boundary crossers have been featured in talk shows, magazines, and the movies. One positive result of this media exposure has been that more people now realize that sex refers to body parts and functions whereas gender refers to the psychological experience of these parts and functions. Sex-change operations redesign the genitals, but this alone will not change gender, the psychological sense of oneself as male and masculine or female and feminine. The person must feel that his or her gender is completely and hopelessly wrong before undergoing a sex-change operation.

Since the famous operation in Denmark, approximately twenty thousand sex-change surgeries have been done in Europe, the United States, Mexico, and Algeria. Fewer operations are being performed now because transsexualism is more clearly understood to be a psychiatric disorder. Despite this, very few mental health professionals work with these people for any length of time because patients and doctors are often at odds with one another. Patients are eager to change their genitals, not just talk about doing it in psychotherapy. Mental health professionals are bothered by the removal of normal body parts to change feelings and attitudes, and insist upon psychotherapy before undertaking any surgery.

Cross-Gender Worlds

> When I see an attractive woman on the street I think how lucky she is to have such a pretty wardrobe. I want to be her!
>
> Men don't know how fortunate they are. I'd like to cut my breasts off and put on a suit and tie to go to work every day.

A subculture of people with significant cross-gender identifications exists on the fringe of the much larger and varied homosexual community. Effeminate homosexual males, masculinized homosexual females, female impersonators, transvestites in drag, females who live as males, and pre- and post-operative transsexuals are among its cast of characters. Usually an urban bar is its social center.

Many men and women with strong cross-gender identifications, however, do not participate in the life of this subculture because they do not know about it, live near it, or feel comfortable with it. They live instead in social isolation nurtured by their fantasies.

> I'm forty-four years old. I have an important job, a dear wife, and three fine children. I can't stand these masculine burdens. I'm exhausted by playing the role of executive, husband, and father. I long to be done with each day so I can close the door to my room, strip down to my female garments, put on a flowery robe, and be Debra. I dream of being a woman, of having breasts and a vagina. I don't mean at night, though that happens, too. I think about it all the time during the day when I'm not busy. I know I retreat to Debra and should spend more time with my family. But I am miserable as David and I feel at peace as Debra; she is comfort. I am really Debra. David is a social role I have been trapped into playing by some biological quirk—God's little joke! I know who I am: I am Debra, a woman, and I can no longer keep her locked up in privacy.

This is the cross-gender world familiar to me because I have worked with the David/Debras, Patricia/Patricks, Thomas/Michelles, Barbara/Lances since 1973. I have seen them transform their secret fantasies into a dramatically new public self and watched those who have cross-lived for years suddenly want surgery to be complete. I have watched a number of people change their minds and back out after finally getting permission for surgery. And like other professionals, I have worked in therapy with people who just want to discuss their hard-to-share feelings about their genders without having to change their lives drastically.

Gender problems are not easy to bear. Most people who have them live painful lives. When they were children, almost all of them had cross-gender interests, and some showed cross-gender behaviors that tended to isolate them from playmates and peers. It is widely recognized that both masculinity and femininity are defined along a very broad spectrum. A boy at the feminine end of the spectrum likes to play with girls, avoids rough-and-tumble activities, and likes to dress in girl's clothing. A girl on the masculine end of the spectrum prefers to play with boys in rough-and-tumble activities, avoids feminine clothing, and scorns the interests of other little girls. Feminine boys are more conspicuous than masculine girls, as we discussed in chapter 8. To a great extent, feminine boys in grade school and, to a lesser degree, masculine girls during adolescence have particularly difficult times. Since there are only a few students with obvious cross-gender identifications in any large school, these young people often do not know others like themselves.

Cross-gender-identified people are usually a source of embarrassment for parents, siblings, and, if they marry, spouses and children. Relatives usually have a fervent wish that they outgrow their "foolishness" and exert considerable pressure for normal behavior. Sometimes a child does give up the interest and the behavior. Sometimes, however, the pressure seems to be successful, but the interests continue to be expressed more privately. Occasionally, teenagers run away from their families trying to find acceptance somewhere else.

Alienation from others is almost an inevitable part of cross-gender identity problems. Some of it derives from their weird appearance when they are poorly cross-dressed. When people with normal gender identity meet someone who passes poorly, they may be shocked, curious, amused, angry, disgusted, compassionate, and frightened. Cross-dressers are often thought to be dangerous or crazy or both, and most people avoid them.

> Cynthia, a very bright, athletic twelve-year-old, who admired her ball-playing father much more than her busy mother, developed a fantasy that she was the identical twin of a male movie star. This fantasy appeared after she was once again mortified by being mistaken for a boy. She loved this fantasy, wrote poetry about it, and in her thirteenth year began to live it out. She learned to pass herself off so well as a male that within a year, as a boy she was able to be with her girlfriends without being

recognized as Cynthia. In her fifteenth year, she "dated" some of these girls as Curt. This was very exciting to her—she was the confidant of her girlfriend during the day and was her boyfriend during the evening. When she was sixteen, Cynthia had her first physical intimacies with a girl as Curt.

Her parents remained unaware of the masquerade until the father of her girlfriend discovered it and told them. They were flabbergasted. They had simply regarded their popular daughter as a tomboy. By her sixteenth year, however, Cynthia had grown to hate her breasts and genitals. She defiantly refused their pressure to give up her "craziness" and seek professional help.

She told her parents that her popularity as a female was a sham. "The real me is Curt!" "Curt" graduated from high school as Cynthia and broke off contact with her family for several years while she perfected her male social behavior. The parents went to therapy to comprehend, to learn to accept the loss of Cynthia, and to try to love "Curt."

Not all boundary crossers change their gender roles permanently. Based on my experience with many patients and the writings of others, I believe that perhaps one out of ten thousand people live continuously in the opposite gender role for only several years. Cross-gender living is more physically, socially, and psychologically demanding than either cross-dressing in privacy or within a marriage. Most men who cross-dress spend the majority of their time in ordinary male social roles. Transvestite clubs quietly exist in large cities and occasionally hold conventions. Perhaps one in a hundred men cross-dress occasionally. The clothing styles available to women allow them to more freely indulge their masculine identifications without raising cross-gender suspicions; as a result, it is not possible to estimate the frequency of cross-dressing among women. Today it is easier for either sex to dress in ways that satisfy their most private identifications.

Transsexuals

When people first come to me with a transsexual problem, they usually want a prescription for hormones or permission to undergo sex-reassignment surgery. They describe themselves in terms that sound like a psychiatry textbook: I hate my genitals. I want to be rid of them. I am trapped in the wrong body. I'm a freak. I have no comfort ever; I cannot live this way much longer. Hormones and surgery are the only answer.

When they hear the rigorous requirements for hormones and genital or breast surgery—to see a therapist regularly for six months before hormones, and to live and work full-time in the opposite gender role for at least a year before undergoing surgery—they say they are eager to comply. But soon thereafter, many of these people just disappear, never to be heard from again by the therapist.

The few that actually fulfill these requirements can be called transsexuals. The same psychological dilemma that drives one person to surgery is dealt with by others by cross-gender living without surgery, by episodic cross-dressing, or by recurrent cross-gender daydreams. For one person, surgical transformation of the genitals is the only means of survival, while for another it is a comforting fantasy.

Transsexuals fervently hope that surgery will relieve their anxiety about having bodies that do not match their gender identities. They feel as though they are frauds and often bristle at being treated as members of their biological sex.

> Cynthia used to yell at her mother, "Don't use that name! I can't stand it. If you really loved me you would call me Curt!"

> David begged his wife to call him Debra when the door was closed to their bedroom and especially when they were being affectionate.

Their wish to be treated according to their "true" identities keeps many transsexuals from physical intimacy because their sexual organs seem to be wrong. They think their genitals are the only things preventing them from being able to have sex.

Many transsexuals dream and fantasize about transformation for years before they discover it is possible. In their fantasies, the surgical transformation is quick, complete, painless, and free of charge. The reality is much different.

Surgical Transformation of Male into Female

It is possible to surgically remove the penis, scrotum, and testes and, in their place, construct a vagina that may be deep enough to contain a partner's erection. No functioning clitoris, however, can be made. The new pelvis still contains the prostate gland and, therefore, orgasm still may produce semen, though not sperm. The creation of labia is possible, but no inner little lips are developed. In several months, pubic hair covers the scars so that no one, including their partners, sees their genitals closely.

Some transsexuals become frustrated because their vaginas may eventually shorten to the point that a normal erection no longer fits. In addition, they are disappointed that more surgery than was originally anticipated is necessary. Good surgical result or not, there is much physical pain to be endured, and the operations, not usually covered by insurance, cost thousands of dollars.

Surgical Transformation of Female into Male

The complete surgical transformation consists of the removal of the breasts, uterus, tubes, and ovaries and construction of a genital appendage that resembles a penis. It is not yet possible to create a penis that can erect, carry urine, and feel exquisite sensations. Sex-reassignment surgery requires multiple operations and is quite an ordeal.

Many females wisely choose an easier way. They have only a mastectomy, which helps them to pass confidently as a male, and they permanently rely upon male hormones to stop their periods. They keep their female genitals which allows them to use the clitoris for pleasure.

The Decision to Change

The transsexuals seen on talk shows and read about in magazines, those who can live in society without raising suspicion, are an inspiration for aspiring boundary crossers. However, not everyone who imagines changing sex possesses bodily characteristics that can be convincingly disguised with makeup, clothing, and artful gestures. When they see the person on camera, they think that they, too, will look completely feminine or masculine. This can trigger a decision in some people to follow a transsexual course that steamrolls beyond caution.

While they are learning to pass, their appearances are often so bizarre that they alienate others. They regard this as unimportant, however, because their emotional satisfaction in bringing their formerly private selves into public is exhilarating. What used to be only a comforting fantasy promises to become reality—they believe others will eventually react to them as members of the opposite sex. When they are warned that successful cross-living injures those who love them and requires a preoccupation with appearance that usually undermines friendships, family relationships, work, and education they say, "It's worth it. I could never be happy as I am—never! I'll be reborn. I'll build a new life. Nothing else matters." Several of my patients have lived alone in near starvation to accomplish cross-living. Their lives became possessed by one idea, one goal, one fervent hope that dwarfs everything else.

It is not just the media, of course, that can turn a gender-disturbed person into a boundary crosser. Most people decide this on their own after years of comparing the comfort of their fantasies with the discomfort of reality. Many of those who decide to seek a sex-change operation may need more help than surgery could possibly provide.

> Jamie, a twenty-five-year-old effeminate man, homosexually active since early adolescence, now terrified of dying of AIDS, described a lifelong sense of himself as a woman. He feels his otherwise soft features are spoiled by his bearded square chin that seems to be growing more masculine each year. In addition to hormones and

genital surgery, he wants plastic surgery on his chin. Since high school graduation, he has often been so depressed he cannot organize his thoughts and get to places on time. He has only occasionally been employed in low-level positions from which he gets fired because he fails to come to work regularly. Besides becoming a woman, he wants to be an architect, although he has not yet attended college. He feels that there is no hope for him in a gay lifestyle. His new lover recently asked him to move out because he just sat around the apartment all the time. When he was questioned about his gender identity, Jamie said, "There is no way I can live as a man; I've never been like other men. I'm not sure if I am a woman. I don't know what I am. I just like clothes, makeup, and being me, whoever that is at the moment. I'd really like female hormones to stop my chin from becoming more masculine."

Transvestites

A transvestite is a male who is able to maintain a separate male and female self. There is no female equivalent. Many transvestites seem to be masculine in their social behaviors. They typically have masturbated during adolescence while holding or wearing female undergarments. Over time, however, cross-dressing ceases to be erotic and becomes a means of relaxation. During sexual intimacy, the transvestite usually finds that female clothing stimulates sexual desire and excitement. He likes to pretend he is a female with breasts and a vagina during lovemaking. Without the help of the clothing and the fantasy, he may be impotent. During very stressful periods, a transvestite may become convinced that he requires surgery in order to be happy. Once the stress is over, he will probably again be satisfied with his old patterns.

The majority of gender-disturbed individuals do not fit into transsexual or transvestite groupings. They simply have gender problems. Regardless of their current way of living, these men and women are unable to establish a consistent, comfortable sexual sense of themselves. Their gender identities are confused, fragmented, ambiguous, or fluctuating. They either are currently male or female or have been fragmented into two, and often, four identities—male, female, neuter, and confused. The urgency to live in the opposite gender role is understandable: They wish to be internally whole, to put an end to their fluctuating sense of self. The lives of some gender-disturbed people constitute a psychological adventure.

> Richard, a thirty-seven-year-old businessman who cross-dressed for a year during adolescent masturbation, eventually married and had two children. He was quite unhappy but did not know why. His wife decided that his uncommunicativeness and sexual apathy were beyond hope, and divorced him. He then became involved sexually with a man. Almost immediately he experienced an upsurge of fantasies about being a woman. His relationship blossomed into an intense, mutually loving bond. They lived together and he began to cross-dress at night. Making him into "Sharon" was very exciting for both of them. Eventually his lover confessed that he would like to explore cross-gender behavior himself. After doing so for several months, "Sharon" returned to the male role and his lover became the woman.

Sources of Boundary Crossing

I believe that the most important causes of transsexualism and transvestism are familial and psychological, but there may be physical forces as well. Most of these people had very difficult early years of life when their core gender identity was formed. Cynthia had been in an orphanage for six months as an infant. Her adoptive mother became depressed and was unable to care for her until she was a year old. David's seventeen-year-old mother and sixteen-year-old father took turns caring for him in their respective homes for three years until finally the paternal grandmother became the designated parent. Richard insists he had a normal childhood but refuses to say more than that.

At some time during the first few years of life, all intact children notice that there are only two sexes and that their families have labeled them as one or the other. To achieve a normal gender identity, a child must accept the label, strongly identify with its biological counterparts, and practice male or female behaviors.

Parents and family members teach the child what they consider appropriate for each sex and reward him or her accordingly. The child must be valued for his or her sex, no matter how disappointed the parents may have been initially. The child's temperament, however unstereotypic, must be accepted—boys can be gentle, girls can be athletes. When a child expresses envy of the opposite sex, as many youngsters do, parents should patiently explain that he cannot grow up to be a mommy, even though his mother is his favorite parent, and she cannot grow up to be a boy, even though her brother is her most admired sibling.

Sometimes a child tries to solve an early life dilemma by imagining a separate new identity. David once told me:

> "When I felt the pain of loneliness, rejection, and disapproval—and there were many such pains—I soothed it with a reminder that if I were a girl others would find me more acceptable and provide me with the love I was not receiving."

Many factors push the child in the direction of an appropriate core gender identity: love from both parents; a secure relationship with each one; consistent, patient behavior from caregivers without threat of violence; the family's calm acceptance of the child's disappointment about his or her sex; parental pleasure in the child's sex; and the absence of painful illness. Even without all of these factors, most children grow up with conventional core gender identities. Those who develop unstable gender identities are usually coping with a great deal of chaos in their families. The child's atypical sexual identity is created in his or her mind as a response to problems in many of these factors.

> Ben's ninth year of life: An older brother was sent home from Asia in a coffin without much explanation from the military. His alcoholic, chronically depressed father com-

mitted suicide two months later, and four months after his burial, Ben's fourteen-year-old brother was arrested for robbery and assaulting a woman and spent several years in juvenile detention. Ben's mother was emotionally paralyzed for years by these events. Ben retreated into his private world and decided that it was easier to be a girl. He named her Beth after his father's mother whom he remembered fondly. A decade later, after periodic cross-dressing during adolescent masturbation, he grew his hair and his nails very long and enrolled in sewing class. He looked weird—more neuter than male or female. But Ben knew what he was doing: he was finally letting ten-year-old Beth out of the closet.

Attraction of Boundary Crossers

Not only those with obvious cross-gender identities think about being the opposite sex. Many homosexual men and women have such thoughts, fantasies, and feelings and quietly accept them. As discussed earlier, between 8 and 12 percent of the population may struggle with strong cross-gender desires during early childhood. Many people may become homosexual because of early childhood cross-gender identification wishes. These lead to an atypical orientation even though the gender wishes have been largely outgrown.

Even men and women with conventional identities may have a cross-gender dream, fantasy, or attraction occasionally. These images usually make them very uncomfortable. Despite the fact that most people cannot recall ever wanting to be a member of the opposite sex, these may represent repressed memories of their temporary childhood wishes.

Many "normal" people are fascinated with the idea of boundary crossing because they would like to know how it feels to be a member of the opposite sex. Part of this fascination has to do with the allure of bisexuality. Although gender disoriented people may not think of themselves as bisexual, others consider them to be combinations of male and female who offer bisexual gratification which can be erotic, anxiety provoking, or both.

Their Lives After Crossing

If a heterosexual man has sexual relations with a man who lives convincingly as a female, is he to think of this as a heterosexual or homosexual episode? And what if he falls in love with this person? If a woman becomes emotionally bonded to and sexually excited by a man who began life as a female, is her experience classifiable? These experiences take place, and when they do, one person must be able to love the other regardless of their sexes. It is mind-boggling to outsiders, but it may occur with ease.

> Bonnie, a widow with grown children, fell in love with a person she knew had been a female for the first thirty years of life. She had known Lance as a charming, friendly, masculine woman before the sex change and, like many others, readily perceived him as a male after the operation. Bonnie sought consultation shortly before her marriage to Lance to talk over the situation—Lance seems to her to be a normal man except for his past. He walks, talks, works, and makes love like a man. She has never been interested in females as sexual partners and is not now, but it is not difficult to stimulate Lance's clitoris. "I know this sounds strange, but the fact is that it feels perfectly natural because I think of Lance as a man."

Cross-gender people prefer to pass inconspicuously in society as members of their chosen sex; they usually do not want to make spectacles of themselves. All have found their choices and decisions painful and just want to get on with their new lives. After years of problems with family and peers, however, they may find it difficult to be intimate or trusting with others. Some find they are still conspicuous, even though they pass well physically, because they seem emotionally "different."

> "Well, we sit around and talk, but I always have to be quiet. They are talking about their boyhood experiences. What they did at twelve, their bratty sisters, the football team. What am I supposed to tell them? How I got my

period when I was twelve? How much I hated wearing a dress? How I bound my breasts with ace bandages? I'm just quiet and after a while, they notice."

"Everyone was nice and friendly to me. I was surprised that so many people were supportive. Women commented how nice my clothes looked. Men were a little less comfortable. A few comments were passed about work. But when these social gatherings are over, I am just a middle-aged woman alone. No one invites me home. I invited a few people, but the excuses were not to be believed. It has been three years now and I have not had a one-to-one relationship. You know, I didn't as a man either. Maybe there is something wrong with me! Thank goodness for work or I wouldn't talk to anyone. I think about moving to another city where no one knows about me, but I don't think I could face starting over again."

There are some wonderful exceptions, however. Some transsexuals meet others who can contact the human being behind the cross-gender role. Some cross-gender males and females can be warm, friendly, and capable of sustaining friendships and sexually intimate love relationships. Unfortunately, these do not seem to be the rule, especially for males who live as women. It is possible that females who live as men have a slightly better chance.

After years of hormones, preoccupation with appearance, and numerous operations, many transsexuals remain relatively isolated and generally unhappy, but without regret for having crossed the barrier. Even though a small percentage revert to the gender role from which they previously fled, and a few eventually commit suicide, most find that cross-gender living relieves their previous pervasive distress. It allows them to get on with their lives and just deal with the normal problems of living such as working, relating, and learning how to use time pleasurably.

Boundary crossing does not dramatically change the personality. If a male had been mean and unfriendly before, he may still seem cruel and suspicious. If a female had a great wit and was extremely well-organized in her old life, she probably is still funny and efficient. What does change is the distress of being trapped in the wrong body, and that is why the odyssey began in the first place.

Toward a Problem-Free Sexual Life

People who are distressed about their bodies and their lifestyles enough to fantasize about being members of the opposite sex should know that:

- They often can be helped in psychotherapy.
- They can change gender roles, but with such difficulty that it should be seriously considered over a long period of time with professional help.
- Their current distress, which feels as if it will never go away, can disappear.
- Many people can become comfortable by changing their gender roles without having surgery.

17

AIDS AND SAFER SEX

There have been other sexual epidemics. The most famous was syphilis, The Great Pox, which plagued Europe for centuries. Epidemics of gonorrhea have produced genital pain and infertility in both sexes since biblical times. In the early twentieth century, medical science lessened the impact of these epidemics, but it was only when penicillin began to be routinely used in the 1940s that their devastating complications began to disappear.

In the last four decades, troublesome but not usually life-threatening viral diseases such as genital herpes, hepatitis, and venereal warts caused small epidemics. Medications have modified their effects, but up to this time no wonder drug has been developed for these diseases.

Sexually transmitted diseases are an ever-present danger for people who casually have sex with relative strangers, but many do not take this danger seriously because of the effectiveness of antibiotics. However, even today, the quality of people's lives is limited by infertility from repeated gonorrheal infections of the fallopian tubes and by recurring painful genital blisters from herpes. Some people stop having casual sex once they catch any venereal disease, but the risk of these illnesses has not been enough to stop casual sex from flourishing in many cultures. Until now.

A devastating new disease, AIDS, an acronym for Acquired Immune Deficiency Syndrome, was recognized in 1981. Fear of AIDS, at times bordering on panic, is changing sexual practices throughout the world. Initially, the American public believed that AIDS was an illness limited to homosexuals because 70 to 75 percent of people contracting the disease in the United States were homosexual or bisexual men. Several years later, the significance of two other facts began to be appreciated: (1) Intravenous drug abusers, bisexuals, and hemophiliacs develop AIDS and transmit it to their heterosexual partners and newborn children; and (2) most people with AIDS in Central Africa are heterosexual. Public attitudes have shifted—AIDS is now considered the worst epidemic of this century and has the potential to kill many thousands of people, regardless of their sexual orientation.

AIDS is a Viral Illness

AIDS respects neither color nor gender, economic status, age, or sexual lifestyle. It is caused by a virus, the Human Immunodeficiency Virus or HIV, that grows and reproduces itself in certain blood cells when conditions are right. This virus can infect heterosexuals, homosexuals, intravenous drug abusers, male and female prostitutes, newborns, teenagers, and adults of all ages.

The HIV infects and multiplies within lymphocytes, blood cells that usually protect the body from abnormally growing cells that can produce cancer and from invading bacteria, viruses, protozoa, and fungi. When lymphocytes function normally, they destroy abnormally growing cells and respond to these invaders by producing antibodies which, in turn, fight off infection by neutralizing the disease-causing potential of the invaders. The HIV interferes with this immune mechanism.

The presence of HIV antibodies in the blood signifies that the virus was once in the blood stream. When people think they are getting tested for AIDS, they usually are having their blood examined for antibodies to HIV. If these are present, the person is said to test positive.

Once inside the lymphocyte, the HIV may reproduce itself and spread to other cells of the immune system and increase the person's susceptibility to many forms of infection. For reasons that are not yet clear, the time required for this to occur varies from person to person, and may never occur for some people. When HIV infection does lead to AIDS, the person suffers with most of the following symptoms: prolonged fevers, night sweats, diarrhea, weight loss, rashes, weakness, coughing, and shortness of breath. Death generally occurs from unusual infections of the lungs and brain within several years of the time of the diagnosis. Pending a scientific breakthrough, AIDS is always fatal.

How AIDS is Spread

The blood, semen, vaginal secretions, breast milk, urine, and saliva of men and women, teenagers, and children who carry the HIV are dangerous to those who have not previously had contact with the virus. Behaviors that lead to the contact with HIV-containing blood or semen are dangerous; casual contact such as living together, sharing of utensils, or shaking hands, is not dangerous. In people with AIDS, the virus exists in highest concentration in the blood, in high concentration in semen, and in much lower concentration in other fluids. Semen is the usual means of passing the virus to a sexual partner. The AIDS virus is quickly absorbed into the body through the tissues that line the vagina, mouth, anus, and rectum. In the United States, men most commonly give the virus to other males, but they can also give it to women.

Women can pass the virus to men from their vaginal secretions into the opening of the male urethra. Nursing babies can take the virus into their bodies through breast milk. The virus is not absorbed through intact skin, but it can be taken into the body through open sores and recent cuts.

Those at greatest risk for AIDS are homosexual men who have had large numbers of partners, often have been penetrated anally, and have had sex with someone who eventually came down with AIDS. The HIV lives in semen and is readily absorbed through the rectum or through small tears in the skin of the anus.

Intravenous drug users pass the HIV to each other by sharing unsterile needles. The invisible virus is contained in the tiny amount of blood that passes between them on their shared needle. Using the same unsterilized needle is a very common practice in "shooting galleries" and other places where illegal drugs are sold and used by addicts. Transmission of the HIV can be prevented by sterilizing needles with heat, alcohol, or household bleach, and of course, by not sharing needles.

Pregnant intravenous drug users who are infected with the AIDS virus pass the virus through the placenta or through vaginal secretions during delivery to their unborn children. The newborn may very likely die of AIDS. Women who carry the virus but are not ill increase their risk of developing AIDS if they become pregnant. Babies who develop AIDS almost always are the offspring of mothers who either have HIV antibodies or who have AIDS, and who are often intravenous drug abusers or prostitutes.

Many people with hemophilia acquired the AIDS virus during the late 1970s and early 1980s when the national blood supply became contaminated by blood donors who eventually came down with AIDS. Most hemophiliacs require multiple injections of a blood product called Factor VIII or Factor IX that allows their blood to clot. These blood products are collected by pooling plasma from at least several thousand donors. When only a few of the donors whose plasma was used to make this blood product had the HIV, everyone who used the blood product was exposed. As many as 80 percent of hemophiliacs in some areas were exposed to the HIV before anyone knew that AIDS was spread by blood transfusions. With the passage of years, the number of new cases of AIDS among hemophiliacs has increased at an alarming rate. Some cases of AIDS have appeared among the sexual partners of men with hemophilia, and a few of their babies as well.

About 2 percent of the people with AIDS have developed the disease from blood transfusions while in the hospital for some other problem. Some of these patients who received multiple transfusions already had weakened immune systems from medications used to treat their cancer or kidney disease.

The national blood supply became safer in 1983 because people in high risk groups for carrying the virus were no longer permitted by blood banks to give blood. In 1984, it was discovered that the AIDS virus was killed by heat. Simply heating the blood product made Factor VIII safe once again for those with hemophilia. In 1985, tests to detect HIV antibodies in blood of donors substantially reduced the risk of passing the virus during transfusion. Therefore, receiving a blood transfusion is a great deal less risky than it was in the early 1980s.

Sexually active people whose lifestyles since the late 1970s consisted of frequent sex with relative strangers or prostitutes are very frightened. The fear is greatest among male homosexuals, but many heterosexuals are terrified as well. They know they may come down with one or another form of the illness. There are several reasons why no one can completely reassure them:

1. The lapse between the time a person is first infected and when he or she shows evidence of impaired immunity to infection is not known with certainty. It may be four and one-half or more years. Without this information, people who have had past risky sexual encounters do not know when they can feel safe.

2. Between one and two million Americans have HIV antibodies in their blood. The presence of this antibody does not predict whether the person will develop a mild illness, a fatal one, or no illness at all. With each passing year, it is apparent that more previously well people who have the antibody are

becoming sick. It remains uncertain how long a person has to be well before he or she is forever safe from an AIDS-related illness. Even though the immune system does its usual protective job for some individuals and they remain well, *they can still pass the HIV on.* Since there is no way yet to identify the ones who will become ill, everyone is concerned.

3. At least one-fourth of those infected with the HIV may develop a mild flu-like illness with swollen lymph nodes that is not AIDS. However, this illness—AIDS-related-complex or ARC—may be followed by AIDS within five years in a large percentage of people.

4. We have less than one decade of medical experience with AIDS. No one is certain what the HIV can do to individuals after ten, fifteen, or twenty years.

Since no medication to prevent the development of AIDS is yet available, people who have had sex during the previous decade with those who might have been carriers of the virus must simply wait and see. This is terrifying, of course, especially since new cases keep appearing.

Practicing Safer Sex

Although there is currently nothing we can do about past exposures, we can do a great deal to avoid future ones. The male homosexual community was the first to develop a public information campaign to teach how to minimize exposure to the virus during sexual behavior. They coined the term "safe sex" (subsequently modified to "safer sex") and have shown that unsafe sexual activities have declined. The educational efforts of the gay community will save the lives of thousands of homosexual and heterosexual people in the Western world.

Safer sex begins with the knowledge of how the virus is spread. It should be emphasized that AIDS is usually a sexually transmitted disease. It is not spread by merely being in a classroom or apartment or by just touching, by hugging or kissing on the cheek. It is reassuring to know that people who live closely with AIDS victims sharing kitchen utensils and bathroom facilities do not become infected with the virus unless they practice unsafe sexual behaviors and share needles with them. Health care professionals who are in contact with the body fluids of AIDS patients have added risks. However, for most others, unsafe sex and shared needles are the major sources of transmission. Unfortunately, both are very common.

Safer sex prevents virus-containing fluids from making contact with the mouth, vagina, rectum, or anus. If vaginal or anal intercourse is to occur, the semen must not make contact with any body cavity of the partner. Those who receive or insert objects into their rectum, or who urinate on or are urinated on during sex, must realize that these activities are life-threatening until a cure is discovered.

Safer sex also prevents the female's virus-containing vaginal fluid or saliva from making contact with the penis or mouth. This means that the mouth or the penis of the man must not come into direct contact with the vagina and saliva of a virus-infected woman.

Safer sex is brought about by several adjustments of sexual techniques such as the use of condoms, limited oral sex, mutual genital stimulation, masturbation, lip kissing, and the avoidance of other dangerous behaviors.

Using Condoms

While some couples have happily used condoms, sometimes called rubbers or prophylactics, for many fulfilling years, there is a widespread belief that condoms interfere with sexual pleasure by dulling the sensations of intercourse for both partners and by decreasing spontaneity. Condoms may dull sensations somewhat, but not enough to stop the pleasure, and they need not keep sex from being impulsive and exciting. Putting on a condom correctly can take an experienced person four to six seconds—leaving ample time for spontaneity.

Occasionally condoms may break while being used, but there are several ways to prevent this: (1) Use only lubricated rubbers; (2) do not carry a condom in a wallet for a long time—body heat dries it out and increases the likelihood of its cracking; (3) use rubbers with tips—these serve as reservoirs for the semen and prevent too much pressure after ejaculation; and (4) if the rubber does not have a tip, pinch the last inch when putting it on to create a reservoir.

Condoms are now on public display in drugstores so people can buy them more easily. It is a good idea to buy in quantity to avoid running out of them and risking unprotected intercourse. "Oh, what the hell, just this once!" carries more risks than it did in the past. Also in the past, it was the males who bought and carried condoms. Now both sexes wisely take this responsibility.

Increasing numbers of women are making sure they are protected from disease as well as pregnancy by carrying condoms themselves. They ask their partners to use condoms while they use other contraceptive methods to prevent both getting and giving AIDS. They are also using spermicidal or contraceptive jellies that contain a chemical called nonoxynol-9 that has been shown in the laboratory to inactivate the AIDS virus. Many common brands of these spermicidal jellies contain nonoxynol; labels should be carefully examined. Spermicidal jellies should be used *along with* a condom—never as a substitute for one.

The most important danger in the use of condoms comes from the tendency of the man to fall asleep after his orgasm while his erect penis is still inside his partner. This very lovely moment is dangerous when a rubber is being used. If the man falls asleep for two to four minutes, enough time passes to allow his penis to shrink back to its unexcited size. The condom is no longer filled out by an erection and the semen leaks around the rubber, exposing the virus-containing sperm to the lining of the vagina.

After orgasm, the man should remove his penis from his partner's body, remove the condom, flush it in the toilet, and wipe his penis dry. Then he can go to sleep. Many of us were conceived by parents using condoms who fell asleep after orgasm. The stakes are higher now.

Limited Oral Sex

Lip, tongue, or mouth stimulation of the male or female genitals is dangerous because of the AIDS virus. The semen *must not* make contact with the partner's mouth. Receiving the semen into the mouth is *not safe.* The few drops of semen that are secreted from the urethra before the man's orgasm may contain the virus. Thus, stopping oral stimulation of the penis short of ejaculation is not completely safe either. Mouth stimulation of a penis sheathed with a condom is safe but unappealing to many people. Mouth stimulation of the penis before the man gets excited enough to secrete any semen is safer, but the partners need to have sex enough to know when the secretion takes place. The sensations produced by oral-genital contact may be more safely simulated by caressing the penis with a wet hand, or applying a body lotion to the penis and scrotum. The use of a silky or satiny material to caress the penis may also be a sensual substitute for oral stimulation.

A woman at high risk for having the AIDS virus should not permit her partner to orally stimulate her genitals. Even if she does not already have the virus in her vaginal secretions, there is the possibility that her partner may introduce the virus into her body through contact of virus-containing saliva with her genitals. Until the woman is certain that she and her partner are not in a high-risk group, mouth stimulation of her genitals should be avoided. She and her partner can use the same sensual substitutes as described above for men.

Mutual Genital Stimulation

The AIDS virus does not pass through unbroken skin. Even those who test positive may safely use their hands to provide sensual pleasures as long as they do not have open sores or recent cuts. These pleasures can also be provided by vibrators or other sex toys. Orgasm can be readily induced by attentive stimulation of the penis, vagina, or clitoris. Such behavior is safer.

Masturbation

Many people have discovered that in a trusting relationship self-stimulation to, or short of, orgasm can be highly exciting for the partner. In either sex, this practice is entirely safe; it will not pass the virus.

Lip Kissing

Long, deep, "soul" or "French" kissing for people who test positive is not recommended. Although the virus exists in low concentration in the saliva, it can be there. Brief lip kissing seems safer than tongue kissing.

Other Dangerous Behaviors

For safer sex, individuals must change other behaviors in order to reduce their risk of contracting the AIDS virus.

Drugs and sex. Some people use street drugs such as marijuana, cocaine, "uppers," and "downers," as well as alcohol to make them less anxious, to enhance their sensations, or to delay their ejaculation. While there is no evidence that these substances increase the susceptibility to infection, they are dangerous if they make the couple less careful about practicing safer sex.

And, of course, if people inject intravenous drugs and share needles, the purpose of safer sex is defeated. Needles must be sterilized or considered to be a very private possession.

Prostitutes. Female and male prostitutes are far more dangerous sources of sexually transmitted diseases than ever before. Male prostitutes may be less safe than female prostitutes because there is much more HIV infection among gay men than among heterosexual men. Not only may prostitutes of either sex be intravenous drug users who share needles, but they never know the medical history and health status of their customers. They may have recently done business with someone who harbors the virus and have become infected without knowing it. The most reassuring response by male or female prostitutes is to be able to prove that they were negative on their last AIDS antibody test. The safest procedure is to ask to see written evidence of the prostitute's negative test for HIV antibody. Prostitutes should practice safer sex for their own and their customers' protection.

Pregnancy. It is not wise for women who test positive to conceive a child because of the risks to themselves and the fetus. Pregnant antibody-positive women are thought to increase their chances of rapidly developing AIDS. Delaying pregnancy is recommended, in fact, whether the woman or the man is antibody positive. Such painful decisions should be made using the latest medical information about risk to the infant and mother.

Health care providers recognize that this is a particularly troubling problem for young husbands who have hemophilia, for married bisexual men who have not told their wives about their homosexual behavior, and for drug-addicted unmarried women. However, few people want to go through the even greater anguish of an ultimately fatal illness of the mother or the baby.

Who Should Worry?

Everyone, not just homosexual men, intravenous drug abusers, and the sexually promiscuous, needs to be vigilant in the conduct of his or her sexual life. Relationships that have been monogamous for over a decade are safe if fidelity can be guaranteed and neither person has had a blood transfusion. People in these relationships need not worry or use a condom. Others should conduct their sexual lives more defensively.

Heterosexuals who are not part of long-standing monogamous relationships and people who are just starting to behave sexually with others must be mindful of the risks. The risks are not yet high among most heterosexuals in the United States. However, those neighborhoods where drug addiction is common are at great risk. And there is a distinct danger to women from bisexual men who keep their homosexual behavior a secret.

Homosexually active men are at risk wherever they live. The more active they are, the greater the risk. If they live in New York City or nearby New Jersey, San Francisco, or Miami, the risks are even greater because these areas have the highest rates of AIDS.

Regardless of a person's sexual orientation, casual sex with a relative stranger is more medically risky than ever before. Many people have declined sexual opportunities or have tailored them so that either intercourse does not occur, is always protected by a condom, or is delayed until the partners get to know each other much better.

The single most important factor for a person to consider in weighing the risks of acquiring the virus is choice of partner. Partners who have AIDS or are known to have the HIV antibody are dangerous to health, even for those who practice safer sex. If a partner's antibody status is unknown and he or she falls into one of the high risk groups—homosexual, bisexual, hemophiliac, intravenous drug user, prostitute, former resident of Central Africa—it's a signal to practice safer sex.

What to Say

Some people will pressure their partners to engage in unsafe sexual behavior because they are uninformed, believe the risks do not apply to them, or lack concern for the partner's safety. Until medical advances are made, intercourse without a condom can be life-threatening for the uninfected partner. And it should be equally clear that even though the following conversations are depicted as taking place between a man and a woman, they can and do apply to two men.

New sex partner:	But it doesn't feel as good when I wear a rubber!
Woman:	It's going to feel a whole lot better than no sex at all!
New sex partner:	You wouldn't take a shower with your clothes on, would you?
Woman:	Of course not. So?
New sex partner:	Let's start and I'll pull out before I come—you don't have to worry, I can control it.
Woman:	No thanks. That's what my father said to my mother!

New sex partner:	Listen, you don't have to worry about me. I'm clean and I've never slept with anyone who wasn't.
Woman:	That's probably true, but nobody can really be sure about things anymore.
New sex partner:	If you really loved me, you wouldn't insist I put on this stupid rubber!
Woman:	Really? I should prove my love by risking my life, the life of any possible child, and our future together for you to have a tiny bit more feeling while we're doing it? Do you hear what you're saying?
New sex partner:	If you really loved me, you wouldn't insist I put on this silly rubber!
Woman:	Asking you to use a rubber doesn't mean I don't love you. It only means we're both being sensible.
New sex partner:	If you really loved me, you wouldn't make me wear this damned rubber!
Woman:	If you really loved me, you would.
New sex partner:	You're overreacting—the AIDS risk is exaggerated.
Woman:	Maybe you're right, but I'm still scared and I can't have fun in bed when I feel this way.
New sex partner:	That won't happen to us—we're young and healthy and we'll live forever.
Woman:	I love your optimism, but I don't want to have to worry about this AIDS thing. Kiss me and put on the condom.
New sex partner:	No rubber or I'm leaving!
Woman:	Goodbye!

Rules for Safest Sex

Here is a list of ways to prevent exposure to the AIDS virus. Not all of them can be used by every person, but some people may find one or more of these comforting.

- total abstention from sexual behavior with partners
- no infidelity
- penis-vagina intercourse only with a condom
- no intercourse until monogamy is well-established either through exclusive dating for a long period, living together, or marriage
- no intercourse until the partner's background is well known
- no intercourse until the partner's body has been carefully examined for needle tracks
- no contacts with male or female prostitutes
- no sexual contacts when high or drunk
- no contact with body fluids until one or two recent AIDS tests have been negative
- masturbation in front of the partner
- mutual genital stimulation (sometimes called mutual masturbation) with ejaculation into kleenex or on the partner's body
- use of a vibrator to attain orgasm

Silver Linings

Despite the obvious grimness of this epidemic, AIDS may actually lead to some social improvements. It is providing couples with an opportunity to increase the range of their sexual behaviors. Instead of relying on quick intercourse, some people are learning other means of giving and receiving sexual pleasure. Many people may become better lovers. And because survival is the issue, people who would not or could not talk about sex realize that they must be able to frankly and clearly discuss current and past sexual behavior. AIDS, condoms, and safe sex have become frequent topics of conversation on first or second dates. Women are asking men whether they are bisexual, and asking them sooner with the clear expectation of a truthful answer. Truthfulness and morality is no longer an issue of fidelity; it is a matter of life itself.

Couples are discovering that their basic relationship is not as dependent on sexual intercourse as they previously thought. They are discovering that it is possible to grow attached and to trustingly love someone without immediately sharing physical intimacies. Some people who felt pressured into physical intimacies before psychological intimacy was established are actually helped by the AIDS scare. They now have a socially acceptable reason for slowing down the pace of physical intimacy and talking more about their feelings. They can get to know each other better before sex.

By exposing societal problems, AIDS may actually improve some of our national patterns. Parents feel more responsibility for sons' and daughters' sex education now that the issue is not just pregnancy. Sex education in the schools may develop a new national purpose—to save the lives of children by teaching them how to protect themselves from AIDS when they are older. In addition, more government funding may be allocated to provide free sterile needles and to treat intravenous heroin addicts with methadone. Currently, there are long waiting lists for such treatment.

Finally, AIDS seems to be signaling the end of the much-discussed sexual revolution. Fear of this disease may slow the spread of other, less dramatic, sexually transmitted illnesses, decrease teenage pregnancies, and prevent some infidelity and its complications.

Stay Tuned

There is an enormous research effort underway to discover how to prevent and cure the diseases caused by HIV. One serious obstacle to prevention is that the AIDS virus is really a series of ever-changing virus particles; an antibody to one AIDS virus will not work against another AIDS virus particle. While other viral illnesses have been subdued by the development of vaccines, finding an effective AIDS vaccine is a more complicated medical challenge. AZT, a drug that has shown promise in slowing the devastating course of AIDS, is currently undergoing extensive testing with patients. Other drugs are being tested in laboratories in the United States and Europe.

Millions of dollars are being spent on this effort, but, unfortunately, money does not guarantee prevention or cure. Medical progress typically jumps ahead after some important technical fact is discovered. At this writing, the medical community, indeed the world, is anxiously awaiting the breakthrough that will signal greater hope for people with impaired immunity and those at risk to develop it.

The media are doing a good job of accurately and responsibly providing the latest news about AIDS, its treatment, and its social implications. Current information in newspapers, radio, and television are more useful than articles written just a few months ago. Stay tuned.

In the meantime, there is safer sex, thorough public discussion of emerging facts, and the challenge to lead our lives in a way that is responsible to ourselves, our current and future sexual partners, and our families.

Toward a Problem-Free Sexual Life

People must practice safer sex to minimize their risk of AIDS, ARC, and spreading HIV to others. That means:

- No male homosexual behavior should result in semen entering any body cavity or making contacts with the anus.
- All male homosexuals, IV drug abusers, female and male prostitutes, and hemophiliacs should be considered high-risk groups because they are likely to transmit the HIV during unsafe sex.
- Condoms should be correctly used with any sexual partner whose status is unknown or who is a member of a high-risk group.
- A sexually active woman, unless she is in a long-term relationship, should have condoms for her own protection.
- A teenager should understand the dangers of AIDS before she or he begins to have sex.
- All people must know about the developments of AIDS research to be sure that their sexual lives are conducted in the safest manner possible.

18

SEXUAL COMPLEXITIES

In the first chapter, four questions were raised about our sexual selves: What exactly is our sexuality? What are the sources of our private, specific sexual interests, behaviors, and capacities? What role does sexuality play in our lives? And what determines our sexual fate over a lifetime? Although answers have been discussed in many ways throughout this book, I want to emphasize some key thoughts about each of them in this last chapter.

What is Sexuality?

As we have seen, this "simple" question has many related answers:

- Sexuality is a vehicle within each of us for pleasure, self-discovery, and attachment to others.
- Sexuality is a personal, multidimensional experience consisting of gender identity, orientation, intention, desire, arousal, and orgasm.
- Sexuality is a resource requiring thoughtful management. Its challenge is to realize physical and emotional pleasure as well as self- and partner-love. Its major dangers are personal and partner despair, premature or unvalued pregnancy, and venereal disease.
- Sexuality is the intimate physical interaction with partners and the complex meanings that we, our partners, and society give to this behavior.
- Sexuality is a type of voice, a running dialogue in our privacy that sheds light on our psychological selves at every stage of life. This voice speaks to us of our needs for attachment to others and our comfort in being intimate. The voice blurts out unsociable and unkind truths that, when occurring with persistent repetition, motivate us to make changes in ourselves and our relationships.
- Sexuality is a repair mechanism with the power to cut loose our painful pasts and allow us to experience our bodies and our psychological selves (they are ultimately inseparable) as good and loved, even though as children we might have been uncertain about ourselves. This repair mechanism does not work for everybody—many peoples' adult sexual lives are constricted by severe problems.
- Sexuality is an ever-changing natural force like the wind, a force whose basic nature and origins are mysterious. We still do not know many of the biological foundations of sexuality. Although there has been an explosion of information about sex during the last two decades, there is much to be learned about the basic anatomy and physiology of sexuality.
- Sexuality is another vantage point from which to study

how our minds work. It is an introduction to the psychology of intimacy. Intimacy is often held up as a goal for long-term relationships without sufficient appreciation for what it is and how difficult it is to achieve and maintain.

Roy and Tanya have had an asexual equilibrium for five of their twenty years together. During most of the first fifteen years, his potency was never dependable. Despite her sexual frustration, Tanya continued to be a very active, positive, hard-working person who appreciated her faithful, nonalcoholic, employed husband, for neither of her parents possessed these traits. She was, however, distressed by their lack of lovemaking and by Roy's occasional descriptions of her as a "nag."

"Am I really?" she tearfully asked. From her viewpoint, the nagging was only because he did not otherwise listen to her. When it came to sex, it was worse—he refused to talk even if she yelled or cried. He offered no intimate sharing of himself on this aspect of his inner life.

Roy understood that sex was supposed to be pleasurable, but he privately believed that he was "undersexed," his penis was too small, and he was never good at performing the act. Whenever Tanya requested that they try sex more often or in a different way, his internal dialogue said "fear." Although he often promised to surprise her in the kitchen one day, he had not even kissed her there in recent years. When Roy's sexual drive mysteriously appeared, he often developed a fascination for something he was reading and the horniness passed. Tanya privately wondered how long she could stay faithful to her inexpressive husband. She knew she could not share these thoughts with him. It had been at least a decade since Roy and Tanya were able to regularly use sex as a vehicle for reaffirming their affection for each other. They knew, but did not like to acknowledge that they were drifting apart.

During our fourth therapy session, Tanya told me

about Roy's mother, widowed at thirty-three when Roy was seven. She was so pessimistic, long-suffering, and clinging, and they agreed that it was uncomfortable to be with her. Roy had been very nervous around his mother during his teenage and young adult years without knowing why. On their fourth wedding anniversary, after another unenjoyable family party, Tanya explained to him how his mother made him feel tense: "Your mother sighs, complains about something trivial, passes a what-can-you-expect-life-is-so-rotten comment, tells us she loves us so much, and then asks when you will call her." So Roy watched closely and to his amazement, with only occasional exceptions, these sequences kept recurring. It was a little victory for Tanya when one day Roy confessed that he used to get annoyed at her for being irritated with his "poor" mother. They had a good laugh, and Roy decided to limit his visits to his mother.

After sixteen weekly therapy sessions, Roy and Tanya were able to resume intercourse. By that time, he had heard me often describe his attitudes about his ever-supportive wife as "prejudiced." I deliberately used this word when I heard him accuse her of "*always* wanting something," "*never* caring about what he felt," and "*irrationally* resenting his need to be by himself." I also used this adjective when, pretending to be exasperated, he sighed, "Women!" This was my way of convincing him that Tanya did not have a chance because he assumed that she was turning into his manipulative, chronically depressed mother. This was made easier when I learned that her family and teenage friends had called Tanya "Sunny." "No way that this positive, life-embracing woman is like your mother, Roy. It's your fear of reencountering your mother that keeps you away from Tanya and has created your 'undersexed' condition."

I was trying to enable his potency to be cut loose from his nervous responses to his mother. I was hoping lovemaking could repair his painful past which caused him to be wary about being too close to a woman. Roy needed to relax and trust Tanya to be the substantial person that she clearly was. Although he often said he understood, I was not certain because he kept remarking how relieved he was to be performing in his bedroom again without "disgracing" himself. At our last session when I used the word "intimacy" yet another time, Roy said, "Doctor, if I want intimacy I'll come to see you. I just want to be able to make love to Tanya normally!"

What are the Sources of Sexual Interests, Behaviors, and Capacities?

The psychology of sexuality is far less mysterious than it used to be. For decades, mental health professionals have been preoccupied only with the effects of childhood experience on adult sexual problems. They know now that the present also has a great deal to do with sexual experience. Actually, sexuality is right-angled—it exists at the intersection of the past and the present. The current relationship selects either the painful past for recall or stimulates memories of the pleasant past. What is on our minds determines our sexual abilities.

Claire became nervous about sex after enjoying it for thirty-five years when, in response to her husband's lessening potency, she began to use her mouth to bring him to orgasm. She had avoided mouth-stimulation of Liam's penis throughout their marriage, but never told him exactly why. Prior to meeting her husband, she was forced at knife point to perform oral sex. The rapist taunted her "This is good practice for you because you are going to have to do this to your husband." Now, forty years later, when Claire wanted to continue their mutually orgasmic behavior, she became disabled by memories of her trauma and trapped by her previous decision not to share this painful experience with him. With the therapist's encouragement, she found the courage to tell her Liam about the experience. He responded kindly and images of their pleasant sexual past overcame memories of Claire's sexual attack.

The answer to the question about the sources of our specific sexual selves is never easy. The four factors of biology, personal psychology, person-to-person interactions, and culture always interact to produce sexual thoughts, feelings, behaviors, and capacities. The best that usually can be said about any sexual trait—for instance, the capacity to be multiply orgasmic or ease of arousal—is to describe what each of these four factors may be contributing. Although many of us may believe we know the answers to this question, it is safer to consider these answers as tentative.

Howard: Alice is a sexual person. She loves sex, always has. She'll have sex almost anytime I want to. I don't think her parents and her upbringing have much to do with it—they never even talked about sex in her home. It's probably genetic. Her sister is so uptight, ungiving, more like my first wife. Some people have it, and others don't. I have it, she has it, and we're happy together.

Doctor: But, didn't Alice tell you that she didn't like sex with her first husband and avoided it most of the time?

Howard: Don't you see, that's just it. She's naturally quite a sexual person. Her first husband was a jerk, he turned her off. Now Alice can be her genuine self—sexual.

There is another way to look at how biology, individual psychology, person-to-person interactions, and culture come together to produce our sexual selves. An individual's sexuality is also unique because his or her character is unique. Character organizes the personality and creates a specific style for each woman and man. Even though this style continues to develop throughout a person's life, its essential features are permanent. Character creates a person who is friendly, well-organized, reliable, religious, or irresponsible, violent, competitive, argumentative, for example. Character consists of what is usually true about a person, not what is true under special circumstances.

Doctor: Are you saying that Alice, unlike many human beings, is a sexual person and that it simply took the right partner to allow her to share her bodily pleasures in this way?

Howard: Is that what I said?

Doctor: I'm not sure. You said it was genetic, having nothing much to do with her upbringing. I thought you were implying that her ability to use her body for pleasure had nothing to do with her values, her ambitions for herself, or her sister's unhappy self-centeredness. Howard, I think even her sensuousness has something to do with her development as a person and is not just genetic. It's now part of her character.

Howard: You're making this very complicated!

Doctor: I worry about that sometimes. Perhaps I'm just missing the obvious.

Howard: Perhaps I'm making it too simple.

Doctor: Anyway, it's clear you're delighted with Alice's willingness to share her sexual self with you, and that's wonderful.

The stylistic constraints that shape our general behavior also shape our sexual behavior, which usually does not depart very far from these constraints. A quiet, unexpressive man preoccupied with efficiency probably will not make love for hours interspersed with conversation and vocalizations of his pleasure; it is just not his style. A passive, indecisive, compliant person often reflects these same features even during lovemaking. Often, but not always.

The concept of character, however, is not comfortable. It implies that humans become defined with time into more or less predictable, knowable, limited beings. This makes it difficult to hang on to the idea that we are a bundle of possibilities. One of the luxuries of the young is their right to consider themselves as potential—as having their development ahead of them. Somewhere during adulthood, however, this notion becomes an illusion. We become. We are. This is how we stay.

Most well-organized, loyal, judicious young adults will still demonstrate these character traits when they are older. Most indecisive, argumentative, untrusting people, though tamer, will still be difficult in twenty years. This does not mean that people do not psychologically evolve and enrich their lives. However, the continued evolution of personality occurs within the boundaries of the character traits already established by young adulthood. These traits create the quality of our lives, and in many instances lay the groundwork for premature loss of health or death or a long, healthy life. They, of course, determine our sexual lives as well.

Howard: Do you think I can count on Alice remaining sensuous all of her life?

Doctor: That depends most, I believe, on the quality of your relationship. If that remains mutually respectful and loving and you both are fortunate enough to be physically and mentally well, yes.

Howard: Even when she gets old?

Doctor: I know people who are "old" who have wonderful sex lives.

Howard: I want to be one of them.

Doctor: Me, too.

What Role Does Sexuality Play in our Lives?

In the past, sexuality was considered to be the driving force of life, the very center of it, the energy behind all psychological development. The consequences of this notion were enormous in the first half of the twentieth century. Sexual gratification was understood as the motive lurking behind all behavior. Art history, literature, sociology, anthropology, religion, and psychiatry took turns reinterpreting their fields in the light of the importance of sexuality. Words such as "repressed," "ego," "suppression," "defensive," and "sublimate," which began as a theory of psychoanalysis, became part of everyday language within a few decades.

In psychotherapies conducted during the early and mid-twentieth century, emotional problems were assumed to be the result of the failure to resolve childhood sexual conflicts. The specific location of this failure was thought to be within the mind of the child, rather than in the relationship between the child and his or her environment. Even a child with a good enough environment was thought capable of becoming neurotic because bodily and mental excitements were considered to be inherently difficult to master.

Today, such explanations seem too simple. This concept of neurosis has become more complicated than an adult still struggling over childhood mental and bodily pleasures. The child's unique temperament and abilities and the adequacy of the caretakers for the specific child are as important as the intensity of the child's natural conflicts about bodily pleasures.

Sexuality no longer seems to be the basis of personality development–it is more the end product. Consider this sequence of how a person's sexual experience evolves over a lifetime:

- discovering the sexual self
- becoming comfortable with the sexual self
- beginning partner sexual behavior
- forming an intense relationship bond
- exploring the capacity to be constant, loving, and committed
- managing disappointment and hostility to preserve the attachment
- parenting
- being alone again due to death or divorce
- reattaching to another
- loving apart from genital sex
- giving up genital sexual behavior.

Even when a person keeps the same partner, life experiences change the relationship, and these experiences cause sex to have different meanings. The clumsy initial intimacies of teenagers may have an excitement that will never again be matched throughout life. An estranged couple who decides to end their miserable separation may have their best sex because of the personal meanings in their reunion. When two retired people establish an intimate bond, the quality of their new sexual experience is determined by the value of the relationship to each of them—not by the fact that they are less sexually vigorous than they used to be.

> "We just placed my dad in the nursing home. It was very hard for my wife and me, and for Dad. He knew we couldn't manage him at home any more. He wandered away from us during the day and couldn't find his way back again, and he began to wet himself more often.
>
> "In his day, Dad was a great socializer, very popular with everyone. He was a terrific dancer, the life of the party. When my mother died, he got around with the ladies quite a bit for about ten years. I didn't like it at first, of course, but I grew to admire him even more. Well, wouldn't you just know it! Within two days in the home, he had a girlfriend. They would hold hands and go off together in her room. All the staff thought it was so cute. I sure hope they're having sex."

What Determines Our Sexual Fate?

This question is easier to answer when each major age group is considered separately. The determinants of the sexual fate of children, although not simple, are as uncomplicated as they will ever be throughout life. A boy or a girl's sexual fate is determined by the child's biological characteristics, the quality of the relationship with each parent, and protection from psychological, physical, and sexual abuse.

The sexual fate of teenagers, while still involving the quality of emotional bonds within the family, is also heavily influenced by their self-esteem, their understanding of sexual behavior's potentials for harm and enhancement, their moral values and personal ambitions, the values of their peer group, and the degree of psychological intimacy they establish during their early forays into sexual behavior with partners.

The sexual fate of young adults is subtly influenced by the extent of the emotional separation from their parents and comfort with their emerging adult selves. This, in turn, has much to do with the characteristics of the partner they select. Soon new complex forces are added—the ease of their nonsexual relationship and the degree of mutual pleasure within their sexual equilibrium. Some young adults seem to know how to cooperate with their partner's use of sexual behavior for self-regulation; others find that it is a struggle to lend themselves to the partner. Young adult sexual life is also heavily influenced by the ever-changing needs of their children as well as economic strains.

All these forces continue to exert their influence in middle-life. While some stresses lighten over time, others, such as diseases and medications, often appear and limit sexual capacity and pleasure. The regard each partner maintains for the other never ceases to be a major determinant of sexual fate.

Among the older age groups, sex is heavily influenced by the decline of the male's sexual drive and erection capacity, both partners' health, and the quality of their previous relationship during middle-life. At every stage of adulthood, including well into frail old age, comfort with our sensual selves and the regard of our partners enable us to love fully with our bodies or cause us to miss sexuality's richness.

Perhaps Howard is correct. If not everyone, at least some people, have a great sexual potential and need only the correct conditions to bring their bodily pleasures into being. Perhaps all the ingredients that make up our characters are not as relevant as those special conditions that allow our sexual selves to come out of hiding—the ability to relax, to temporarily give up worldly concerns, and to narrow our attention to our mental and bodily selves.

When we permit ourselves to live comfortably with what goes on in our heads, when we can calmly allow our minds to drift without fear of where we are going, when we are courageous enough to set free our basic, lonely-for-connection selves, we have a better chance of realizing our sexual potential and ensuring that our sexual fate is a positive one.

But Howard may be making it too simple. So many of us are unable to deeply relax, unwilling to even briefly separate from our usual worldly concerns, and unable to focus our attention on our sensations. The sources of this alienation from our inner, sensual selves have to do with relationships, past and present, with notions of sin and danger, with meanings both apparent and hidden. No, Howard, I think our characters have a great deal to do with whether we can easily let our sexuality out of its usual hiding place. Some people, like you and Alice, have reached a wonderful resolution to your dimly recalled struggles and are in a position to love yourselves and each other through your sexual bodies. This is quite an accomplishment. Guard it vigilantly.

Limitations of Experts

The main subject of this book has been sexuality and its complexities, not therapy for sexual problems. Many people with persistent sexual concerns and difficulties, however, will eventually find their way to a psychotherapist for assistance in achieving or regaining sexual comfort. I hope it is no surprise that I am very supportive of individuals and couples seeking a therapeutic environment in which to consider their personal difficulties. In doing so, please keep in mind that professionals like myself, who appear to be experts, face a dilemma as therapists: We must choose between basing our therapeutic strategy on a strong belief in current knowledge or basing our help on an awareness of the limitations of this knowledge. There are advantages and disadvantages to each approach.

When we emphasize current knowledge, we sometimes can efficiently evaluate problems and attempt to solve them. However, today's facts and cures may be wrong tomorrow. And even when the facts are correct, the emotional forces that shape sexual problems are often far more lasting and powerful than initially appreciated. There have been many instances in which experts have been mistaken or too narrow in their perspective.

When therapists emphasize the limitations of knowledge and the tentativeness of facts, we are more likely to prefer wait-and-see solutions to problem-solving techniques. The disadvantage of this approach is pessimism and hesitance to help patients in new ways.

It is reassuring to realize whichever approach is taken, qualified professionals in human sexuality try to avoid both of these traps. In addition, despite professional knowledge, extensive therapeutic experience, and proven ability to help, we have limitations. We cannot completely penetrate anyone's privacy or fully understand why a particular person has a specific problem. Often it is a mystery how to best approach a patient's sexual difficulty. Therefore, people should be wary of therapists who smoothly promise a cure, who arrogantly suggest that therapy is simple, or who confidently predict that treatment will only take a certain number of sessions. Such individuals may be dangerous pretenders or, at the very least, they may be inexperienced though sincere.

Those looking for simple, clear answers about sexuality are bound to be frustrated by the fact that it is part of so many other contexts, and that any information about sexuality must be modified for each individual. The knowledge that there are no clear answers should protect patients from dangerous or naive therapists. Sex was never simple. Its problems are rarely one-sided.

Sexual health and illness both deserve respect. Sexual health commands respect for the basic developmental steps that have made it possible. Sexual illness requires respect for the physical problems and psychological dilemmas that produce its symptoms. Despite our best attempts to unravel them, both sexual health and illness maintain some mysteries. I suspect they always will.

Toward a Problem-Free Sexual Life

Sexual behavior has wonderful potential for people who are psychologically ready for it, but sex has never been simple.

- Sexuality can be understood in many ways.
- Knowledge of ourselves and psychological intimacy with another are probably the best aphrodisiacs in the universe.
- Many forces keep us from intimacy with our partners including character—our habitual style of dealing with our feelings and resolving our conflicts.
- Sex is not the driving force of personality development—it is the product of our development.
- Those seeking advice about sexual problems should understand the limitations of experts.

REFERENCES

Abel G.G.; Blanchard E.B.; Becker J.V. 1978. An integrated treatment program for rapists. In Rada, RT (ed), *Clinical Aspects of the Rapist.* New York, Grune and Stratton.

Althof S.E.; Turner L.A.; Risen C.B.; Levine S.B.; Bodner D.; Kursh E.D.; Resnick M.I. Why do men drop out from intracavernosal treatment for impotence? Presented March 1988 at the *Society for Sex Therapy and Research* meeting, New York.

Barbach L.G. 1976. *For Yourself: The Fulfillment of female sexuality.* New York, Anchor/Doubleday.

Bayer, R. 1981. *Homosexuality and American Psychiatry: Politics of Diagnosis*, New York, Basic Books.

Becker J.V.; Skinner L.J.; Abel G.G.; Treacy E.C. 1982. Incidence and types of sexual dysfunctions in rape and incest victims. *Journal of Sex and Marital Therapy,* 8:65–74.

Bell A.P.; Weinberg M.S.; Hammersmith S.K. 1981. *Sexual Preference,* Bloomington, Indiana University Press.

Bergler E. 1951. *Neurotic Counterfeit-Sex.* New York, Grune and Stratton.

Berlin F.S.; Meinecke C.F. 1981. Treatment of Sex Offenders with antiandrogenic medication: Conceptualization, review of treatment modalities, and preliminary findings, *American Journal of Psychiatry,* 138:601–607.

Bradford J.M.W. 1983. Research on sex offenders: recent trends. *Psychiatric Clinics of North America.* 6(4):715–731.

Brindley G.S. 1986. Maintenance treatment of erectile impotence by cavernosal unstriated muscle relaxant injection. *British Journal of Psychiatry.* 149:210–215.

Clement U.; Schmidt G.; Kruse M. 1984. Changes in sex differences in sexual behavior: a replication of a study on West German students (1966–1981). *Archives of Sexual Behavior.* 13:99–120.

Clifford R. 1978. Development of masturbation in college women. *Archives of Sexual Behavior.* 7:559–574.

Cole H.M.; Lundberg G.D. (eds.), *AIDS From The Beginning,* Chicago, AMA, 1986.

Comfort A. 1972. *The Joy of Sex,* New York, Crown Publishing.

Ellis L.; Burke D.; Ames M.A. 1987. Sexual Orientation as a continuous variable: A comparison between the sexes, *Archives of Sexual Behavior,* 16:523–530.

Finkle A.L. 1980. Sexual Impotency: Current knowledge and treatment in urology/sexuality clinic. *Urology.* 16:449–452.

Frank E.; Anderson C.; Rubinstein D. 1978. Frequency of sexual dysfunction in "normal" couples, *New England Journal of Medicine.* 299:111–115.

Freud S. 1905. Three essays on the theory of sexuality, *Standard Edition of the Complete Works of Sigmund Freud.* Vol. 7, pp 135–243.

Freud S. 1926. The question of lay analysis, *Standard Edition of Complete Works of Sigmund Freud,* Vol. 20, pp 179–250.

Green R. 1987. *"The Sissy Boy Syndrome" and the Development of Homosexuality.* New Haven, Yale University Press.

Groth A.N.; Burgess A.W.; Holmstrom L.L. 1977. Rape: power, anger, and sexuality. *American Journal of Psychiatry.* 134:1239–1243.

Gong V.; Rudnick N. (eds.), *AIDS: Facts and Issues,* New Brunswick, Rutgers University Press, 1986.

Harry J. 1985. Defeminization and social class. *Archives of Sexual Behavior,* 14:1–12.

Hunt M. 1974. *Sexual Behavior in the 1970s.* Dell Publishing Company, New York.

Kaplan H.S. 1974. *The New Sex Therapy.* New York, Brunner/Mazel.

Kinsey A.C.; Pomeroy W.P.; Martin C.E. 1948. *Sexual Behavior in the Human Male,* Philadelphia, W.B. Saunders.

Langevin R. 1985. *Erotic Preference, Gender Identity, and Aggression in Men: New Research Studies,* Hillsdale, New Jersey, L. Erlbaum Assoc.

Levine S.B. 1987. More on the nature of sexual desire, *Journal of Sex and Marital Therapy,* 13(1):35–44.

Levine S.B.; Yost M.A. 1976. Frequency of female dysfunction in a general gynecologic clinic: an epidemiologic approach, *Archives of Sexual Behavior,* 5:229–238.

Marcus I.M.; Frances J.J. 1975. *Masturbation: From Infancy to Senescence.* International Universities Press, New York.

Masters W.; Johnson V. 1970. *Human Sexual Inadequacy,* Little Brown, Boston.

Masters W.; Johnson V. 1966. *Human Sexual Response,* Little Brown, Boston.

Rubin A.; Babbitt D. 1958. Impotence and Diabetes *Journal of American Medical Association.* 168:498–500.

Saghir M.; Robins E. 1973. *Male and Female Homosexuality.* Baltimore, Williams and Wilkins.

Sarrel P.; Sarrel L. 1984. *Sexual Turning Points: Seven Stages of Adult Sexuality.* New York, MacMillan.

Schein M.; Zyzanski S.; Levine S.B.; and others. 1988. The frequency of sexual problems among family practice patients. *Family Practice Research Journal.* 7(3) 122–134.

Shainess N. 1975. *Authentic feminine orgasmic response, in Sexuality and Psychoanalysis.* (E. Adelson, ed.) New York: Brunner/Mazel.

Singer J, Singer I, Types of female orgasm, *Journal Sex Research.* 8:255–267, 1972.

Steege J.F.; Stout A.L.; Carson C.C. 1986. Patient satisfaction in Scott and Small-Carrion penile implant recipients: a study of 52 patients, *Archives of Sexual Behavior.* 15(5):393–400.

Tiefer L.; Mellman A. Follow-up of patients implanted with penile protheses since 1981 Paper presented at *International Academy of Sex Research Annual Meeting,* September, 1986. Amsterdam, Netherlands.

Index

T